بسم الله الرحمن الرحيم

www.shaykhabdalqadir.com

First edition: Madinah Press 2012
All rights reserved

Madinah Press
Postnet Suite 402
Constantia 7848
Cape Town
Republic of South Africa

madinahpress@gmail.com

ISBN: 978-0-620-52382-0
Printed by Lightning Source

COMMENTARIES

Shaykh Dr. Abdalqadir as-Sufi

TEXTS PREPARED AND EDITED BY
AISHA WRIGHT

MADINAH PRESS

CONTENTS

Text of Qur'an: taken from
the Algerian State Edition of Imam Warsh.

English meanings: from the Emirates-approved
text of the Hajjis Abdalhaqq and Aisha Bewley.

1

COMMENTARY

ON

THE MIRACLES
OF THE TARIQ

– from the Diwan of
Shaykh Muhammad ibn al-Habib

Four commentaries
given between May 14th
and June 6th 2005
at the Masjid al-Mahmoud,
Constantia, Cape Town

I

MAY 14ᵀᴴ 2005

I would like to look at a Qasida from the Diwan of
Shaykh Muhammad ibn al-Habib, rahimahullah. It is
called The Miracles of the Tariq. The Shaykh says in it:

> **Praise belongs to Allah, may Allah bless
> the Prophet Muhammad, the Shelter.**
>
> **Abu Hamid at-Tusi, the Sufi**
> **(– referring to Imam al-Ghazali –)**
> **and proof of Islam said:**

First of all he is taking these points from Imam al-
Ghazali. It is very significant that he not only gives him
the intimate name by which he is known among the

Sufis, but he also calls him 'the Sufi' and the Hujat – 'the proof of Islam'. In other words, he gives him this title as a great 'alim, because he wrote this at a time when the wahhabis were very powerful and made terrible attacks on Al-Ghazali. Shaykh Muhammad ibn al-Habib pointed out that he was a highly renowned 'alim and qadi before he took the path of Tasawwuf, so he calls him by his name as a doctor of Shari'at.

Abu Hamid at-Tusi, the Sufi, and proof of Islam said:

The marks of honour for the one who enters the Tariq are twenty in number:

The first of them is that Allah remembers him as is fitting. Oh what good news that is!

So, the first of the marks of honour is that Allah remembers him as is fitting, and this comes from Surat al-Baqara (2:152):

$$\text{فَاذْكُرُونِ أَذْكُرْكُمْ}$$

Remember Me – I will remember you.

Thus in that line of the Qasida he is referring to this Ayat of Qur'an, and the first of the marks of honour is that he becomes one of this elect group of human beings who have this contract with Allah, made by Allah, subhanahu wa ta'ala. Allah remembers him as is fitting, and "as is fitting," means, "according to this Ayat." And he says, "What good news that is!"

The second sign is that he is exalted among people.

This means that once he has taken this Path, Allah raises him up from whatever condition he was in until people recognise him. The best example I can give you, which I have mentioned many times before, is of Hajj 'Arafa in Casablanca. He was a great Sufi and he had a very humble position in life. He had a tiny little stall in the souk where he sold ribbons for the piping of the jellabas. He lived very simply. I saw him in the souk, and he was one among hundreds of people selling things. But then I went with him in Fes to where Mawlay Idris is buried and when he entered, people almost fell at his feet – he had to pull them up and stop them kissing his feet! Among the Sufis he was like a great prince entering their company, and one saw that among the people of knowledge he had this high, high esteem.

The Fuqara of Meknes complained to Shaykh Muhammad ibn al-Habib saying, "Why is it that when Hajj 'Arafa comes, you shut the door and sit with him, and we never get to sit with you!" He said, "It is because he has a pocket with no holes in it." In other words, when he took knowledge from the Shaykh he did not lose it or forget it, it was something he kept for all his life. He got wisdom and held on to it, which is part of knowledge – to hold on to what you know and to keep it, not disperse it or throw it about.

**And the third is a love
which finds no reproach.**

That is that Allah gives to the one who is on the path a capacity to love people in the way of Allah. They do not love for their nafs, they do not love because they desire someone, they do not love because they want their wealth, they do not love because they want their influence, they do not love because they are flattered – their love is without reproach because they love them in the way of Allah. It is **a love which finds no reproach**, which is that the Sufi on the Path discovers this other dimension of his own existence – that he can love people for the sake of Allah. This love which he refers to is embodied in the verse of Abu Madyan in his famous Qasida of the Fuqara, when he says:

The pleasure of life
is only in the company of the Fuqara.
They are the Sultans, the masters, the princes.

When will I see them, where will I see them?
When will my ear hear some news of them?

Shaykh Muhammad ibn al-Habib continues:

**And everyone Allah loves,
is loved by the creation
– what good fortune he gains!**

This is another thing which reverses how everyone else understands existence. The world is before you like a mirror, so what you look on is the reflection of yourself. So whomever Allah loves, creation loves him. They think they are loving Him but it is because of Him that they are loving Allah. The mirror of the Salih reflects the Divine Light and people recognise the Divine Light through that person. This is the alchemical change that takes place among the Sufis and it is known and recognised by its people, and those who are not of its people do not recognise it.

The example of this is Mawlana Jalaluddin Rumi who speaks of the enemies of Rasul, sallallahu 'alayhi wa sallam, saying of Abu Lahab: "When he looked on Rasul, sallallahu 'alayhi wa sallam, he saw the son of his father," so in fact he did not know whom he was looking at. Even this terrible man, Abu Lahab, it is like the wasp that falls into the honey and becomes pure honey because his name, even though there is a curse on it – "Perish Abu Lahab!" – by Allah's miracle Abu Lahab is made forever part of the Qur'an and we recite that Surat and get blessing and Baraka from it. Millions and millions of Muslims say his name, "Perish Abu Lahab!" but at the same time he has been exalted by the love of Allah, subhanahu wa ta'ala.

The fourth is that Allah directs all his affairs, and so he remains constantly full of joy.

This is another very interesting reversal of how people think things are. **Allah directs all his affairs.** This is a theme which one is never finished with explaining or, even as one explains it, with understanding it oneself because it is the very secret of how existence is. **Allah directs all his affairs.**

The simple people – good people, but simple people who do not understand, who have not been taught, because in this age people are not teaching Tawhid properly and you see it in the terrible things you have to listen to on the Jumu'as – the simple people make a du'a and say, "O Allah, give me this," or "Give me that," or "Save me from this," or "Save me from that" – they ask for something and of all 'Ibada, Allah loves best the du'a, but there are degrees of making du'a. The degree of the common people is to say, "Take me out of this," "Help me," "Give me," "Let me have it," "Save me from it" – this is pleasing to Allah, but this is the du'a of the common people.

The next level of du'a is where people make du'a not for themselves but for others. They ask Allah to give someone the good, to give someone their health, to restore someone. The du'a is not for the self but for others and that is rahma so it is a higher level of du'a. This is the du'a of the elite. The du'a of the elect of the elite follows the way of Rasul, sallallahu 'alayhi wa sallam, who said: "O Allah, give me the good of the day that is coming and protect me from the evil of the day that is coming." In other words, let me be like a ship that misses the rocks by Your decreeing it. Let me do what is pleasing to You and let me be preserved from what is not pleasing to You. So the affair is returned to Allah.

Allah directs all his affairs. This does not mean that you cease from action, but that you move in the Way of Allah, and this makes you different. It makes you have wisdom. It makes you sometimes hesitate, and it makes you sometimes move forward without a reason. It makes you hold back without a reason and it makes you move forward without a reason. Moving by reason is a good thing because Allah has given you reason in order to estimate things. Nevertheless, the one who moves without having calculated or holds back without having calculated is the one who is moving fisabilillah. His action will be higher than the one who has calculated.

**The fifth is that Allah
makes his food easy to get,
and he does not have to struggle to get it.**

This, again, is an enormously important aspect of
Tawhid which has not been taught, and is not taught
today and this undermines the Muslims and makes
them feel weak. Anxiety about provision is a withdrawal
from an understanding of Tawhid. It is a withdrawal
from acknowledging the Majesty and Power of Allah,
subhanahu wa ta'ala.

**Allah makes his food easy to get, and he does not
have to struggle to get it.** Why does he not have to
struggle to get it? Because it has already been decreed
for him. I will give you an example: I was with a Faqir
in Tangier, and we had been at the Siddiqi Zawiyya up
in the Kasbah. The evening went on very late and when
we left it was pitch dark, and the Kasbah in Tangiers
is very complicated. We could not find our way back
and we got lost through these little lanes. Suddenly a
door opened and there was a room with a blazing light
shining out from it. We thought that we would ask them
the way back down to the town so we approached it. In
the room there was a low Moroccan table with a giant
plate of couscous and lamb and there were four men
sitting around it. One of the men called out, "There
you are at last, come in! We have been waiting for you,
we could not start until you came! Sit down!" So we sat

down and the man said, "This meal has been written for you since before the creation of the world. We could not start until you came. Bismillah!"

This was Allah giving us a proof of His power and of the truth of every meal because the Sufi teaches in the Sahara in the desert to the people, but when the meal comes onto the plate, it is not said, "Ah, there is our guest and there is the food." He says, "This meal has been coming to you from the shop where the goods were, and which were then bought. And the meat was from the farmer who sold it to the butcher, and before that it was a sheep in the field, and the man who had the sheep sold that sheep. The lambing time was three years ago which produced this sheep so the birth of this sheep was already a meal being prepared for you these three years later through its path of going to the butcher and being sold to the one who bought it, who took it to the people in the kitchen who prepared the meal, and now the meal has come to you. But in this way, it has been coming to you from before you even knew you were hungry!"

So the fifth mark of honour is that Allah makes your food easy to get. In other words, He removes from you any idea that you will not be fed. Allah is the Provider. Once you have understood that, you have understood one third of Tawhid. **He does not have to struggle to get it.** Why? Because it is a gift from Allah, and you do not have to struggle to get it, just as you do not have to struggle to eat it. It is not difficult to eat.

I remember walking with Sayyidi Hammud, the great Sufi of Blida, in Algeria. We sat down, it was a hot day, and someone brought Shaykh Muhammad ibn al-Habib a glass of water. Sayyidi Hammud turned to me and said, "You know, life is not difficult. Look at the Shaykh – it is not difficult to drink a glass of water." I thought, "What is he talking about?" I did not understand what he was talking about but he continued, "Look, the Shaykh is drinking a glass of water. It is not difficult."

The whole process of life is the same as that – it is not difficult. It is not difficult to eat the food and it is not difficult to get the food. Allah has set it all up for us to be fed. It is a promise. Rabi'a al-'Adawiya said, "O Allah, my job is to worship You and Your job is to feed me." This is what is called the Maqam al-Uns, the Station of Intimacy. She spoke to Allah as though she were speaking to her neighbour. She spoke like that to Allah by love.

The sixth is that he is helped against his enemies by miracles, with constant protection.

This is another warning to the one who begins on the Path. Allah helps you against your enemies so you must not have enemies. They may be enemies of you but you yourself cannot have enemies, you cannot afford to have someone as your enemy. Allah will deal with the matter. If you try to deal with them or even to keep them out or even to reject them, even to announce that they should be rejected, then you are putting yourself in a prison. That is not necessary. If you step away, then the sixth is that he is helped against his enemies by miracles, with constant protection. So it does not just happen in an ordinary way, but it happens by miracle. It happens that Allah turns things over from where that person is not looking, and thus people are saved from the enemy.

**The seventh is intimacy with Allah,
so he is never lonely whatever happens.**

The seventh gift which is a miracle of the Tariq is intimacy with Allah. Intimacy with Allah is allowing yourself that time alone with Allah. In the night-time – a few Rak'ats, and just sitting and calling on Allah by His Name, ALLAH. That removes from the nafs the idea of being alone. Loneliness is not that you are not in company, the loneliness of man is that when all activity stops, he realises that he is going to die. Rather than look at that, he withdraws away from it and says, "I am alone, I have no-one to help me, I am on my own." Loneliness is not remembering the Presence of Allah, subhanahu wa ta'ala. The Presence of Allah, subhanahu wa ta'ala, is the healing for this.

One of the great Sufis of Andalusia said a thing which, when I read it, shocked me very much and at first I rejected it because I thought it was not correct: "What is it," meaning life, "but five prayers a day and waiting for death?" I was very shocked and thought it very depressing news! But I did not understand that it is like saying that the reality of your body is that you are already a skeleton. You are already that thing which will be in the grave. Onto this skeleton, which is your death certificate, Allah has put all the organs of senses, of appetites that give you desire for food, for intercourse, for intellectual discovery, for seeing all the things of the world. Into this skeleton Allah has put this whole system which allows you to experience the whole universe.

The reality is that all the world is yours, but five times a day you glorify your Creator because you have a contract of the moment, where Allah gives you everything. You see everything, you hear everything, you do everything, but at the same time the end of the matter is your death. Then your death walks with you and you are not afraid of it. You are not scared of it because you have this feeling of intimacy with Allah so that you do not have this loneliness which is not being able to confront the nature of death. It is something you live with in the instant. That is what the prayer is at the five points of the day – to remind you of this.

I was in a tiny little Mosque in the Sahara, and as you

went out from it there was what looked like a stretcher, it was four planks of wood with handles at the end. As we walked out of the Jumu'a of this tiny little Mosque I looked at it, and the Sufi I was with turned to me and said, "That is what we go out in," and it was the stretcher with which to take the dead bodies to the cemetery. It was left at the door of the Mosque so that at every Jumu'a you would walk past what you will go out in. It was incorporated into his life, yet it was something as delightful as saying, "Now we are going to have lunch." It was part of existence.

The eighth is his power over the self, so that creation serves him without confusion.

This is a tremendous thing! The eighth miracle is his power over the self. This means that the one who is a person of dhikr can order himself. You are not the victim of what has happened to you and what you make happen. You can master yourself. You can make you obey you. A conscience is that thing that all human beings have to remind them that they are not doing what Allah wants, but the Sufi can change how he is. He can turn on himself and say, "It is no good, I do not like it! It has got to go," and it happens. He can do it.

This is another level of capacity of the human being, and our Shaykh links this to saying that **creation serves**

him without confusion. If you have got yourself under your orders, the whole creation will obey you. If you are struggling with yourself, whatever it is, it is like the fish's mouth, the hook will come from creation, and gulp! – it will get you, and pull you this way and pull you that way because you are not the master of yourself. But this is the eighth miracle of the way: you are given power over yourself. This is enormously important news.

> **The ninth is the elevation of his himma**
> **above every temptation**
> **that might obsess him.**

This, again, links to the previous matter. The ninth miracle is that it raises up his ruhani expectation. It raises up what he expects will be the gifts from Allah. He then thinks and expects, 'Allah will give me illumination. Allah will give me insight. Allah will make me among the elect. Allah will make me someone who has illumination and knowledge directly from Him.'

> **The tenth sign is the heart's wealth**
> **and lack of need,**
> **so every matter that calls for struggle**
> **is made easy.**

The tenth sign is the heart's wealth, so richness, the Ghaniy, is in the heart. The heart's wealth is lack of need, because the heart is already so wealthy that the needs fall away. The Sufis are not zahid in the sense of ascetic, they do not deny themselves anything – they simply do not want it any more. Not wanting it any more is higher than zuhud or, if you like, it is the true zuhud because it falls away. So the heart is wealthy and the need disappears. Every matter that calls for struggle is made easy. This is an astonishing business, the business of the Sufis is very practical.

You might say, "I am having a struggle!" Well, why are you having a struggle? Is it the right thing you are struggling for? Is it pleasing to Allah? Then the question is: Am I pleasing to Allah? Mawlana Jalaluddin Rumi says in the Mathnawi, "All these 'ulama tell you: 'This is haram, that is not halal' but stop all this! Ask yourself, 'Am I halal? Am I acceptable to Allah?'"

Shaykh Muhammad ibn al-Habib then goes on to the marks of honour which, inshallah, we will continue with next week.

DHIKR and HADRA

We ask Allah, subhanahu wa ta'ala, to give Baraka and light to all the Fuqara present in this dhikr. We ask Allah, subhanahu wa ta'ala, to move the hearts of the Fuqara and to give them illumination in the dhikr and in the Hadra. We ask Allah, subhanahu wa ta'ala, to give protection and support to the Fuqara in their travels fisabilillah.

II

MAY 21ST 2005

We reached the first ten signs of the blessings of the Tariqa, as taught by Imam al-Ghazali, whom the Sufis refer to as Abu Hamid at-Tusi. Shaykh Muhammad ibn al-Habib continues his commentary thus:

> Here briefly follow the rest of them,
> stressing only some of them,
> so pay attention, O reader!
>
> Enlightenment of the heart
> which is guided by His light
> to an understanding of the secrets
> through the gift of their Lord.

He is saying that the Faqir is given this inward illumination but that it is in itself a gift from Allah, subhanahu wa ta'ala. It is not something he achieves or something he arrives at but it is something that, from the beginning of his being on the Path, is coming to him, it is arriving at him. You might say that this enlightenment of the heart becomes his property.

And the expansion of his breast so that he is undisturbed by whatever trouble comes to him.

Thus the genuine condition of the people of the Path of Ma'rifa is not one of contraction. Contraction is a very passing thing. To the people who are seeking Allah in their lives, of its nature this Path is one that gives expansion of the breast so that well-being begins to settle in the breast. Remember that as well as trouble, and people becoming dark and negative about their lives which ordinary people who are not Muminun have all the time, there is something in the middle between that and having a good state about your life, which is like a kind of marshland and which is doubt and scepticism. These are almost worse than having a bad feeling. They are worse than contraction because from contraction you have to come out, you cannot stay in it. There is a kind of marshland between contraction and expansion which is a kind of freezing and paralysis of the self which is nothing to do with doubt and nothing to do with scepticism. Beware of being sceptical! Being sceptical is like saying that you are not sure, astaghfirullah, that Allah will take you out of your difficulty.

And the expansion of his breast so that he is undisturbed by whatever trouble comes to him.

Allah, subhanahu wa ta'ala, says in Surat al-'Ankabut (29:2):

$$ اَحَسِبَ ٱلنَّاسُ أَن يُتْرَكُوٓاْ أَن يَقُولُوٓاْ ءَامَنَّا وَهُمْ لَا يُفْتَنُونَ ۝ $$

Do people imagine that they will be left to say, "We have Iman," and will not be tested?

We are all tested by difficulties, and these difficulties are not between us and the world – the world obeys the Command of Allah in order to see whether we come out of it well or not. That test is what creates us. It is like the forging of the sword where the sword is put into the fire until it is red hot, and then is plunged into cold water. It is between these two things that the steel is tempered to be of value and of worth. In all of these experiences, the basic condition of being one of the people of the Path is your certainty of expansion.

He possesses dignity as well as unquestioned good standing in the hearts of people.

Once a person has undertaken for himself dhikr of Allah between himself and Allah, subhanahu wa ta'ala, a chemical change takes place. You could almost say an electrolytic exchange takes place in how he is with other people. That is that the hearts of people begin to recognise something in him that causes him to be treated with a respect that is not a social respect, but which is a ruhani recognition. Even the one who recognises one of the Salihun is in turn ennobled. This light that comes on the hearts of all of you people here, becomes something that in itself has an effect on other people. One of the terms for this that the Sufis use is 'Baraka'. This is something that begins to emerge from the people whose lives are founded on dhikr of Allah, subhanahu wa ta'ala.

And love towards every single
human creature
through the undoubted promise
he has from his Lord.

It is very interesting that Imam al-Ghazali and our Shaykh echo this "Love towards every single human creature." This is because of a view that the Mumin begins to get. Remember the beginning of Qur'an:

أَلَمَّ ۝ ذَٰلِكَ ٱلۡكِتَٰبُ لَا رَيۡبَ فِيهِ هُدًى
لِّلۡمُتَّقِينَ ۝ ٱلَّذِينَ يُؤۡمِنُونَ بِٱلۡغَيۡبِ

Alif Lam Mim
That is the Book, without any doubt.
It contains guidance for those who have Taqwa:
those who have Iman in the Unseen.

The Book of Allah is for the Muminun who believe
in the Unseen. This is a dimension of human existence
whereby, if you do not have it, you are sub-human. We
are living in an age where the mass of people are in a
sub-human state because they have been cut off from
belief in the Unseen.

He says, "Love towards every single human creature,"
because the one who has knowledge of Allah, subhanahu
wa ta'ala, recognises that we are Bani Adam. We are all
the children of Bani Adam, but this is not humanism.
This is recognising that we are all in the same boat, and
that boat is one of mortality. That mortality is that each
one has to answer to Allah on the Yawm al-Qiyama and
present what he has done. All the creatures are the same
in the sense that they are all carrying with them their
account. They are all carrying with them, not a bank
statement, but a destiny statement of their lives.

In that sense, you sometimes find that, in the words

of a Moroccan Sufi of the past, "The Sufi has more compassion for the murderer than for the murdered, and more compassion for the judge than for the one he condemns," because he sees the other side of things. He realises that each one has a story, each one has an account that he takes to Allah. We do not know what that account is, only Allah knows. In that sense, the beginning of a true, real knowledge of Allah, subhanahu wa ta'ala, is recognising that all creatures are creatures of the Divine Contract they made with Allah before the creation of the world: "Alastu bi-Rabbikum?" – Am I not your Lord? And all of creation answered, "Yes."

This changes how we look at everything. It is like the materialist who can see in front of him and who looks to the future, and he tries to work out from how things were, how they are going to be. This is the materialist philosophy. It is the philosophy of the twentieth century to try to analyse things from the point of view that everything is wrong and must be put right. "How do we put it right?" But it is as though the Mumin has glasses of several lenses. He has a lens for the immediate present, and in the immediate present it is his life that is at issue. In other words, in the ordinary daily affair, he has got anchor points to help him not lose sight of the fact that there is a long-term reality. So his Shahada is the confirmation of the instant, of the moment.

One of the Sahaba said to the Rasul, sallallahu 'alayhi

wa sallam, "O Rasul, I want to strengthen my Deen, how can I make it stronger?" He said, "Repeat the Shahada. Say it again," like it is a new beginning for you. Shahada is the truth of the moment for you. Then, in the day, the five points of the prayer are the points of remembering in the immediacy that the whole business in fact has nothing to do with your ideas, it has nothing to do with what is going on in the world – with all the media giving you news of floods in Asia – YOU have to account for YOU, and the Deen is designed for that.

In the day you have the Five Prayers, and in the year you have the fast of Ramadan to tax your body and remind you, and the Zakat to tax your wealth and remind you that you do not take your wealth to the grave, it does not belong to you. All your wealth is borrowed from the Creator Who created the wealth in the first place.

With these glasses which have, as it were, all the lenses, the Mumin then begins to see what is Unseen. Rasul, sallallahu 'alayhi wa sallam, said, "Fear the basira of the Mumin because he sees by the Light of Allah," subhanahu wa ta'ala. So you begin to have inklings, flashes, moments where the unseen things open up to you. We will come in a moment to the landscape, as it were, that will become a reality for you as you continue on this journey.

> He possesses Baraka –
> as we have indicated –
> and proper adab,
> even after he has turned to dust.

Again this is the wisdom of the Sufis. The one on this Path possesses Baraka and proper adab, and proper adab is that when he addresses himself in 'Ibada to Allah, subhanahu wa ta'ala, he does it with gravity and dignity. The example of this is that Sayyiduna 'Ali, karramullah wajhahu, when he heard the 'Adhan he began physically to shake, and he said, "O Allah, the time has come to present myself to You and I am not ready." The moment of Salat was so terrible for him. This is the proper adab – fear of Allah, subhanahu wa ta'ala. That is why, for all of us, from the moment the 'Adhan is given in the Mosque to when the 'Iqama is declared, nobody should speak.

He says, **Even after he has turned to dust.** In other words, once the Salihun have become dust, still from that spot where they are there is the dynamic of Baraka, and your coming towards them in their grave awakens in you those same good manners that you would have had with them living. This is the recognition of the spiritual truth of the one in the grave.

> The earth is subjected to him
> so that he may go
> with speed and without fear
> wherever he wishes.

This is the absolute guarantee. This is a very important thing because in this age we live in, everyone thinks that this is a place of accident, but it is not a place of accident. The world is a place of determined events. If you think about it, even what is called a crash is understood as an accident. "He was in an accident." But what exposes more to you the destined nature of events than what you call an accident? "It is because he did not see the corner," "It is because he did not turn the wheel," "It is because the car he was in had not been fixed, and he could have fixed it but he was saving the money for something else," "It is because he was in a bad temper," and so on – but nothing is more determined than every detail of that moment that is 'accident'. There is nothing more determined than an accident!

It is like the people abolishing the House of Lords who say, "Why should we be governed by people who are governing us because of the accident of birth?" But it is not an accident, it is absolutely determined. What is more determined than a birth? It is absolutely the most determined act of all existence! That is not the reason to supplant them. Everyone is where they are because of what is called the 'accident of birth'.

Everything is determined. Remember, in every event there are different elements. There is the element of the given, of the one who is in the event – he is there because he has that liver and those kidneys, and that heart and that intellect – and all of these things have determined that he should be in point A and not point B. Thus the first dimension of event is his actual pre-determined nature of his total being, including his intellect and his ruh and his aspiration, because his aspiration might take him out of something and make him go to something else.

Then there is the web of what we call the Rububiyya, the inter-connectedness of things. All events, all people, all living creatures from the smallest insect to the great animals – all of these are connected in the web of Rububiyya, Allah's Lordship and knowledge of every single leaf when it falls. That is another dimension of event.

Then there is the third element which is of the Unseen. Allah has a purpose. His purpose is not your purpose. Rasul, sallallahu 'alayhi wa sallam, said, "Allah wants something and you want something. What you want will not happen, and what Allah wants is certainly going to happen." So want what Allah wants. Be the one who wants what Allah wants. If you look at the du'as of Rasul, sallallahu 'alayhi wa sallam, he is saying, "O Allah, give me the good of the day and what is in it, and protect me from the evil of the day and what is in it." He wanted to be in harmony with how Allah determined the things.

You then have to realise that the Muminun see differently all these things like wars and disasters because, for them, those things have a different meaning. They understand that, as He, subhanahu wa ta'ala, said in a Hadith Qudsi: "Allah sends people to the Fire and He does not care. He sends people to the Garden and He does not care." Allah does what He wants. He only has to say to a thing: "Kun!" Fa yakun. "Be!" It is. He is not to be measured in the result of the event. Mawlana Jalaluddin Rumi, in his extreme, high Ma'rifa says, "Thousands of children were put to death by the Pharaoh in order that Sayyiduna Musa should be put in the basket and pushed into the river, and found and brought there so that he could in the end confront Pharaoh face to face." But to do it, thousands had to be killed.

Remember, Allah puts people in the world to help with these enormous destructions. He puts into a man one dimension of manhood that is so intense that he becomes the catalyst for the death of millions. Great generals and great leaders – these men in history are suddenly the focus of the death and genocide of millions of people. Yet this is part of Allah's moving in events that we cannot understand, and it is not our business to see it. What we recognise in these terrible events is that, with a close part of the lens of the spectacles, we see the Rahma of Allah on the individual, on the one who escapes – as Sayyiduna Yusuf, 'alayhi salam, escaped from the well. Where there is disaster, there is one that Allah takes out and protects. This is a knowledge that comes with being on this Path.

> **The land, the sea and the air**
> **are his servants without doubt.**

This is a categoric promise from Allah, subhanahu wa ta'ala. One of the messages for the people who take this Path is that they are safe. Part of security, part of Yaqin which reaches this high condition is the underlying certainty that the land, the sea and the air will serve you.

> **The wild animals, the beasts of prey**
> **and the reptiles**
> **have all been subjugated to him**
> **by the Lord forever.**

> **And the keys of the treasures and the mines**
> **offer themselves to him, but he has no need.**

> **In every thing that happens, people petition**
> **Allah through him because of his rank.**

In the age we live in, this has offended the so-called modernists because they have really adopted the religion of the enemies of Islam who have to deny this, so they deny it also. That is that in every thing that happens, people petition Allah through the one of Ma'rifa because of his rank – they recognise that it is a quick access. The kuffar have that relationship with people in political power in order to get their material request granted, whereas they object when we do it at the threshold of the Unseen, at the grave of the Wali, at the grave of the Sahaba, at the grave of Rasul, sallallahu 'alayhi wa sallam.

> So the Lord provides for him
> from His gifts, with ease.
> There is no hardship experienced, or rather,
>
> That has been left to the choice of his Lord
> in His previously ordained decrees.

In other words, what does happen to the Mumin on the path of terrible things, are those things which Allah has decreed for the benefit of that Mumin. That in itself is part of his security and his certainty.

> So do not say, "I called on Him
> and He did not respond."
> That is the condition of the doubters
> and the heedless.

Then he goes on to the next stage, that of the marks of honour which he has in the Akhira, which, inshallah, we will look at in the next stage of our commentary.

Therefore, what we are presented with is that the people

of the Path are living an enormously rich life because they are living in the immediate present, and they can look way beyond events. Today, everybody takes their news from the media of what has happened in the instant but we have been taught, by the Surat which describes the story of Sayyiduna Yusuf, 'alayhi salam, to look past the crisis of the moment to its outcome. We know that everything has an outcome, and we look for us to have a good outcome. That is why the du'a of the Mumin is: "O Allah, give us an Iman that is lasting." In other words, "That at the moment of death I will have the certainty of Shahada."

The way the people of the Path live is different, you take on a different quality. In doing so you must realise that you cannot take on this Path without becoming, despite yourselves, or later, because of yourselves, instruments of Da'wa. Let me give you an example of how this is: I have three Fuqara whom I had sent to the Sahara in Morocco. They were travelling late at night and had to get to a particular place. They thought they knew the path but it was in the desert which was very rocky and stony, and they lost their way. In fact, if you lose your way at night in the desert you can die of extreme cold.

So these Fuqara were completely lost, but in the distance they saw a cloud of dust and a motorbike went by. Then it came back again and headed towards them. The man riding the motorbike said, "What are you doing out at this time? Where are you going?" They said that they were going to such and such a place, to which he said, "You are completely off the way! I will take you to my father's house." So on his motorbike he took the three Fuqara to his father's house. The father said, "You are Fuqara of Shaykh Muhammad ibn al-Habib are you not?" They said, "Yes, we are!" He said, "I knew it." They were fed, and then they asked, "How did you know?" He said, "Well, about ten years ago I was in a city in the desert. In the open square where the people buy their camels and sell their goods, there was a very big foreign car, and sitting inside of it was this gentleman in a white jellaba. He got out, and his presence had an effect on me. This man called me over and I went to him, and he said, 'As-Salamu 'alaykum' and I said, 'Wa 'alaykum salam' and my heart became very disturbed and excited. I said to someone, 'Who is that man?' and they said, 'He is a Sufi Darqawi Shaykh from the north visiting Fuqara here. He is Shaykh Muhammad ibn al-Habib.' So I knew at that moment that I had a task to do – I had to serve this man but I did not know what it was. I waited for ten years and tonight I saw that my job was to save you in the desert and bring you home and feed you."

This is the nature of this adab and this light that the Muminun have that affects them and all around them.

DHIKR and HADRA

We ask Allah, subhanahu wa ta'ala, to make us a company of Salihun and 'Arifin. We ask Allah, subhanahu wa ta'ala, to raise up among us the Awliya that will strengthen the Deen and spread it throughout the whole world. We ask Allah, subhanahu wa ta'ala, to give a great power of light to awaken the Salihun and the strong people of the Deen in Iraq and Afghanistan. We ask Allah, subhanahu wa ta'ala, to give an unprecedented, majestic and magnificent illumination of the Deen of Islam and its power to survive by the will of Allah. We ask it to be manifest in these lands that the people should begin to feel their freedom and their nobility and their dignity as Muslims.

III

MAY 28TH 2005

We have been looking through the Qasida, The Miracles of the Tariqa, and the commentary of Shaykh Muhammad ibn al-Habib on the teaching of Abu Hamid of Tus, that is to say, Imam al-Ghazali. We come to the next part of it which says:

> **As for the marks of honour**
> **which he has in the Akhira,**
> **they are also twenty in number**
> **and they follow here:**

Then he gives these twenty marks of honour that come to the people in their relationship to the Akhira. Because of the age we live in, we have lost touch in many important aspects with our true nature, with what in Islam is called 'Fitra'. It is as though we have been anaesthetised from Fitra. So things which were easy to understand in the past have become difficult to understand.

I want to introduce you to a word which, in the technical language of Tasawwuf, is specific to Muhiyuddin ibn al-'Arabi who, as you know, was called the Imam of the men of this science. He was the Shaykh of the Shuyukh. It is a term which is called Al-Khayal. In brackets, I would just like to warn you against reading ANY books on Ibn al-'Arabi written by kuffar, because they are so profoundly wrong at such a basic level, that if it were a medical treatise they would all be arrested for inciting malpractice. They are so wrong on such a basic level of understanding the terminology and the science of Tasawwuf.

This term Al-Khayal is very interesting. You would say that it means 'to make things appear', but the root of the word Khayal as a collective noun means 'horses' or 'cavalry'. The meaning of this is that when cavalry charge, you do not see the horses. First there is a cloud of dust, then emerging from this cloud of dust come galloping horses. It is important that you hold that as a very valuable metaphor in understanding where we will go with this word Khayal.

Without this word Khayal, we cannot even look at the

things listed by Abu Hamid because we are cut off from seeing it in the proper way. In other words, the aspects of the Akhira must, in the intellect of the Sufi and in the intellect of the Man of Allah, have the same reality and the same weight, and the same importance as the dunya. In other words, the dunya is this world and the Akhira is the Next World. Or, even more correctly, the dunya is a disappearing world and the Akhira is an approaching world. So the reality is that you are living in two realms, always.

The realm of all the physical, tangible things that are dunya is passing you by. It is all leaving you. The immediate recognition of that is the food we eat – it is coming towards us from before we sit at the table. We sit at the table and the body assimilates it, and the waste comes out from the other end of our bodies, so it is leaving us – everything in the dunya is coming to you and leaving you. Nothing is permanent, nothing is held and nothing is constant. The Akhira is something which is far yet is coming nearer to you and approaching you, because in the process of living through the dunya events, you are approaching your death. Every day you are opening nearer to complete, vivid experience of the Next World in the same way that you have vivid experience of this world.

Another aspect of Khayal, about the actual word itself, is that it can also mean pride and even arrogance. This is also very important because although Khayal is a kind of pride – not in a negative way or a bad way, even though it does means arrogance – in this science of Tasawwuf it is not arrogance of the ignorant man, but it is like an aristocratic arrogance. It is an arrogance that we might say of the people of Ma'rifa: they know, and the ignorant do not know. It is not something he shows, but it is something he has in his bearing because he knows the secret of existence.

Al-Khayal. Before I come to explain it, I would just like to simplify it for you. If we look at how we understand a mad person and a sane person, medically speaking, we see that the distinction between the mad and the sane is not one of stupidity and cleverness, it is that the person who is genuinely mad cannot distinguish the forms. To the doctors, the indication of complete madness is when they sit in their own waste matter and they sit with food, but they play with either in the same way. They cannot distinguish between the clean and the unclean, which is why the foundational aspect of the behaviour of Deen is to do with cleanliness. It is as though a prior necessity to take on the Deen is that before you make Salat you have to make the Wudu. It is that distinction – the washing before the Jumu'a, the washing of the dead body – everything in Islam is about purification because it is grounded in sanity.

It is because Islam is grounded in sanity that the man of

knowledge of Allah can have experience of ecstasy and intoxication. In a sense, the Sufic Path is an organised, structured kind of going-mad in which the foundation is safe. In other words, with dhikr and with the Hadra, and with Khalwa – all this reaching for intoxication and drunkenness and drowning is like what the madman has, but without losing the limits.

We even make the distinction that the people on the Path who lose the grounding yet still they are not dirty – they have cleanliness and they love Allah but they have lost, as it were, their way – they are called Majdhub. They are not called Majnun because Majnun is the one who has lost discrimination. The Majdhub is the one whose intoxication ceases to be grounded. This is why the real path of Tasawwuf is a path of Suluk – the path of Imam al-Junayd, radiyallahu 'anhu, is the way of a training of the intellect, of the behaviour, and of how you understand existence. This is called Suluk.

Now we are going to look at this word – Khayal. The science of Khayal is the knowledge of the Barzakh. You must know this word 'Barzakh' from Qur'an. It is the division between the two seas. Allah, subhanahu wa ta'ala, says in Surat al-Furqan (25:53):

$$\text{وَهُوَ ٱلَّذِى مَرَجَ ٱلْبَحْرَيْنِ هَٰذَا عَذْبٌ فُرَاتٌ}$$

$$\text{وَهَٰذَا مِلْحٌ أُجَاجٌ وَجَعَلَ بَيْنَهُمَا بَرْزَخًا وَحِجْرًا مَّحْجُورًا ۝}$$

It is He Who has unloosed both seas –
the one sweet and refreshing,
the other salty and bitter –
and put a dividing line between them,
an uncrossable barrier.

When Allah, subhanahu wa ta'ala, speaks of putting a barrier, it is between two different things which distinguishes them so that one does not pass into the other.

The science of Khayal is the knowledge of the Barzakh. It is the knowledge of that which distinguishes and separates the forms. What separates the forms does not exist and yet it does exist. As Muhiyuddin Ibn al-'Arabi, rahimahullah, would say, "If you say it exists, it exists, and if you say it does not exist, it does not exist, but there is that which distinguishes the forms," and that is the foundation of how your brain works. The madman does not recognise the Barzakh, so he does not see where something ends and where something begins. Ibn al-'Arabi also says:

**It is the science and knowledge
of the physical world
in which Ruhaniyya appears.**

In other words, that is the realm of the Bani Adam, of human beings. Thus when Bani Adam appear,

Ruhaniyya appears, so the body appears and with the body is ruh. Just as between the two seas there is a Barzakh where one is sweet and the other is bitter, between the body and the ruh there is Barzakh, there is division. You do not see the ruh but you see the body. The recognition of this is already a change in the understanding of the knowledge of the Muslim.

When Sallallahu 'alayhi wa sallam was sitting with his Sahaba in Madinah, and the funeral procession of a jew went by he stood up out of courtesy to the dead body of the jew. His Sahaba said, "O Rasul, why do you stand? He was a jew." Rasul, sallallahu 'alayhi wa sallam, said, "Was he not one of Bani Adam?" In other words, what he was honouring was that here was a body of a son of Sayyiduna Adam, 'alayhi salam, from which the ruh had separated. Because he saw the separation, he stood in an acknowledgment of this principle, of this knowledge.

This is why Shaykh Muhammad ibn al-Habib, rahimahullah, warns us to beware of despising even the lowest atom for it is compounded of the Hayy and the Qayyum. You must never lose sight of this reality of how things are. This is also why the Sufis cannot afford to have personal enemies. There can be enemies in Shari'at but that is corporate with the body of the Muslims and has another set of rules. The Sufi has to clean his heart out of any bad feelings he bears, even if they are justified – especially if they are justified –

because by them he can lose his way.

It is the science and knowledge of the physical world in which the Ruhaniyya appears. We could take weeks on this because it opens the door on everything. It is the science of the "Souk al-Janna." This is one of the most beautiful of the Hadith of the Rasul, sallallahu 'alayhi wa sallam. We must find it, because it is in Muslim and it is in al-Bukhari is it not? It is certainly in al-Bukhari. Rasul, sallallahu 'alayhi wa sallam, in telling people about the Janna, explained that in the Janna there is a souk into which the Mumin could go, just as he would go into the souk in the dunya, and buy those things which he desired. In the Janna there is a souk where all the forms of creation are there and he can take whatever form he desires. In other words, the whole realm of forms become available to him. So the Khayal is also the science of the Souk al-Janna, of how it is possible, and how it is.

This is how we are coming to the commentary of Abu Hamid. Ibn al-'Arabi says:

> **It is the science of Divine Manifestations –** of the appearances, Tajaliyyat – **of the Yawm al-Qiyama in changing pictures.**

In other words, just as in this dunya and in this Ard on which the process of dunya takes place, there manifests whole kingdoms of forms: mineral kingdoms, the kingdoms of the earth, then all the stages of the animal kingdoms from the lowest forms and from the microscopic forms right up to the great, gigantic creatures like the whale and the elephant. All these forms are in the dunya and they have reality for us because we have experience of them. Equally, the people who, for example, dwelled in Europe – forgetting about books and television and so on – when they first saw an elephant they ran away in terror. When they first saw the tiger they were terrified.

The proof of this is that on the Indian subcontinent, we know that the people who now call themselves hindu and say that they were the first people on that land and that the Muslims came in later – as if we were invaders and not the people who have the right to be in India – are telling a lie. We know that when the Muslims came in, the people who were already there had also come from somewhere else. How do we know this? Because in the Sanskrit, there is no word for elephant! In other words, when they came and they saw the elephant, they did not know what it was. They did not have a name for it.

Allah, subhanahu wa ta'ala, has said in the Qur'an that He taught Adam all the names. So where there was the thing there was the name. That is the proof that the people who lived there were another earlier people and not the Dravidians who came in, because they had a word for elephant – because Allah taught all the names to Sayyiduna Adam, 'alayhi salam.

It is the science of Divine Manifestations of the Yawm al-Qiyama in changing pictures. The Day of Reckoning has a reality that will unfold and one could say that you cannot define it, but just as the meaning of the Hajj is our obedience to its orders, we could also say that there is a meaning of the Hajj which is that it is an evidence of the Yawm al-Qiyama. It is to let you know that it will to be something like this. You have two million people in their shrouds on a plain in the middle of the desert and they are all obliged, in order to make the Hajj, to stand for a moment on 'Arafat, and 'Arafat is the place of recognition. So that picture of the Hajj is the education of the Muslim for his lifetime of what he is going to encounter on the Yawm al-Qiyama. Its reality is the way the picture of mountains and valleys are realities for us now.

It is the science of the appearance of meanings which cannot physicalise themselves by themselves, like death in the vision of Sayyiduna Ibrahim, 'alayhi salam. Ibrahim had an order and that was a reality for him because he was going to fulfil that order. Then when he was obedient, Allah lifted it from him and in fact, looking at that event, we can now see that up until that moment, worship was sacrifice. After that moment, worship was

the 'Ibada we know which is the prostration. It was
retained symbolically by the institution of the sacrifice
of the sheep – a recognition of this evolution, as it were,
of this development of man which Allah, subhanahu wa
ta'ala, granted to Sayyiduna Ibrahim, 'alayhi salam.

**It is the science of what people see
in their dreams.**

What you have to recognise is that existence itself is
made up of images. In sleep, you do not just go into
limbo, you can also, in your sleep, enter into the seeing
of forms. These forms are in the Unseen but you are
seeing them by this faculty of the Khayal which makes
sense of the forms. When you see the form you cannot
see it without a meaning. Otherwise you would be like
the madman who would not know that this is filth and
that is food. But you do. So you attach a meaning to the
form. Thus we have a faculty which gives meaning to
the form.

In the dunya we live in a sensory world, and to these
sensory things we attach meanings. In the Next World,
we live in a realm of meanings because it is not spatial.
The time-space is part of this illusion of the dunya, but
in the Akhira there is non-spatiality because the world is
gone, it is over, finished. Time-space has gone. But the
meanings are there, and in the Next World the Muslim
experiences the meanings as sensory. It is the opposite.

The kuffar do not understand this. They think in some ghastly way, "Oh, these ignorant Muslims. They think that the Next World is going to be a kind of Hollywood party." They do not understand that all these beautiful visions of the Janna are meanings, but they will be experienced as sensory. So the fruit of the Janna and the drink of the Janna will have a sensory experience, whereas our sensory drinking and our sensory pleasures in this world are experienced by having meaning. If they did not have meaning we would not benefit from them and understand them. So the world is not the way the kuffar think it is, they have got it wrong!

It is the science of the abode people are in after death, and before the Rising.

Again, from death to the rising on the Yawm al-Qiyama is a stage of a journey and it also has events in it. Things happen in the grave and these have a reality the way this world has a reality. So for the Mumin whom Allah is pleased with the grave is made like a beautiful, verdant expanse, like a beautiful lawn with flowers. Our brother, Shaykh 'Aziz, was shown his state in the grave while he was dying which was that just everywhere was covered in flowers. It was Allah, subhanahu wa ta'ala, showing him that He was pleased with him and that He was going to make death easy for him in giving him a glimpse of what was waiting for him.

Equally, when I was travelling with Shaykh Muhammad ibn al-Habib in Algeria, we stopped in a particular village. There was a very famous Majdhub there whom the Shaykh had gone to see. He told us later that evening that before he knew Shaykh Muhammad ibn al-Habib, he used to be in terror because if he went past the graveyard he could see this Khayal of what was happening to the person in the grave. So if someone had just been buried, if they had been bad he would see them in torment and being questioned by the Angels and he would fall down in agony. Then, if it were a very blessed Mumin, he would become ecstatic because what he was seeing was so beautiful. He said that it was unbearable, he could not bear it, because it was a little village and the cemetery was there, and he could not avoid it. Then he said, "Shaykh Muhammad ibn al-Habib came and he took this away from me." The Shaykh insulated his intellect – he took this vision from him so that he did not have it, as it was too much for him to bear.

It is the science through which the visible pictures appear in the polished bodies like a mirror.

In other words, it is that science by which we see the sensory world and make sense of it. As I have been saying, we attach meanings to it. This means that you have to see that your true identity, character, is not to do with your being mean or generous, good or bad. You are already, as a son of Adam, a creature who possesses the faculty to evaluate everything – not with the brain but by seeing. That is why Rasul, sallallahu 'alayhi wa sallam, said: "Beware the basira of the Mumin because he sees by the Light of Allah."

Thus, not only do you see things as they are, but you begin to see past how they are, to how they might really be despite the appearance. You will begin to decode the forms and not take the meaning that might appear to be the case. Rasul, sallallahu 'alayhi wa sallam, said, "Do not tell me things against your brothers, I would like to come out to them with a good feeling, a good view of them." What he meant was that he did not want a picture put onto the picture which is what he was seeing anyway. He wanted to see, with his Fitra nature, everything as it was.

The other dimension of that – and this is the humility of Rasul, sallallahu 'alayhi wa sallam – is that when he had insights, which he did have, he hid these knowledges. For example, when he spoke to the representative of the Iranian ruler, he gave him a message to take back to the ruler, which was to embrace Islam and to become Muslim. The man left the presence of Rasul, sallallahu 'alayhi wa sallam, then the Rasul stood up and said, "Bring him back, bring him back!" He went out to him and put his hand on his stirrup and said, "Look, don't give the message to the king. It does not matter. When you go back, the king will have been assassinated. The next king is going to embrace Islam anyway so it does not matter. As-Salamu 'alaykum." Suddenly his heart was open and he saw, but he also saw far away things.

'Umar ibn al-Khattab on the battlefield, in the famous example, called out to someone, "Look to the mountain!" because he was under attack from where he could not see, and 'Umar ibn al-Khattab saw. This is by the same process by which you deal with all the ordinary matters of life. It is the same faculty but extended, yet it is this fundamental faculty which makes you human. We have examples with Mawlay Hasan al-Majdhub, who knew from his house that people were making trouble about Hajj 'Abdalhaqq's car in the town, and he got up and ran out of the house putting on his turban to go to the aid of Hajj 'Abdalhaqq – and we were sitting in ignorance and knew nothing! He arrived on the scene and was able to help. He was a Salik Majdhub who had this capacity to see.

I do not think we should do more. This goes deeper and I would like to continue with it and in the light of that we will look at what our Shaykh says about the Akhira, and you will have a completely different understanding of it. It will be as real for you as what we are doing here in sitting together.

We ask Allah, subhanahu wa ta'ala, to give us the light of knowledge in these matters, and to expand our breasts to recognition of the high task Allah has set us to. We ask Allah, subhanahu wa ta'ala, to put before us our duty to Him to dazzle from our eyes anything that would distract us from it. We ask Allah to make us people who have knowledge of the Akhira as they have knowledge of the dunya. We ask Allah, subhanahu wa ta'ala, to make us people who have wisdom and who have insight.

BURDA

O Allah, make this circle a circle of people of knowledge. Raise up among us an elite for the community of all the Muslims of Africa. Allah, from among that elite give us the elect of the elite from among us. Make us a circle of Asrar and a circle of Anwar. We ask Allah, subhanahu wa ta'ala, to illuminate the hearts of this circle of dhikr. We ask Allah to place secretly among us Awliya that will take the Deen to all of Africa. We ask Allah, subhanahu wa ta'ala, to open our hearts to secrets of knowledge. We ask Allah, subhanahu wa ta'ala, to give us desire for knowledge of Allah, subhanahu wa ta'ala. We ask Allah, subhanahu wa ta'ala, to awaken in us love of the Rasul, sallallahu 'alayhi wa sallam. We ask Allah, subhanahu wa ta'ala, to protect us and strengthen us and give us a tongue of truth. We ask Allah, subhanahu wa ta'ala, to make all the people here become those people who will teach the Deen to those around them.

HADRA

I just want to confirm for you the importance of the Hadra, of the Imara, in the development of your being on the Tariqa of the People of Tasawwuf. It is so important in this age because the whole centre of the Muslim Community has collapsed, and our whole Community has been most horribly betrayed with the fall of the Khalifate. Since the fall of the Khalifate, Makkah and Madinah have been in the hands of the people who have basically occupied the whole of the Middle East, the drama of which is still unfolding in front of our eyes in this civil war in Iraq.

You must understand that we can approach the matter of the Hadra from the point of view of the Shari'at and the law, and you can approach it also from the way it is being looked upon in an age where the Muslim ethos has been utterly destroyed. I mean by that, that Islamic governance has basically been wiped off the earth, and it has been wiped off the face of the earth not by the enemies of Islam, but by Munafiqun – by people inside Islam collaborating with, and totally financially dependent on, the technology and wealth of the kuffar and who have guaranteed to them that Islam will not rise again as a political force.

We find in looking at the history of Islam that where the Sufis were strong, where Tasawwuf was strong, there were people whose love for Allah and for the Rasul, sallallahu 'alayhi wa sallam, was so powerful that it spilled out over and beyond not only the Fard but the Nawafil, and they wanted more. They gathered in these special places to do dhikr of Allah – places which are mentioned in the Qur'an in Surat an-Nur and in other places, in order to strengthen themselves and to be a kind of core to the Muslim Community by the strength of their Iman. From them also came great 'ulama.

It is significant that a very great Sufi who has strong connections with South Africa, Shaykh 'Alawi al-Maliki, rahimahullah, when he was slandered most viciously by the dogs of the Arabian Peninsula, the people who came to his defence were great Sufis: two of the most important 'ulama in Morocco, one of whom is the director of the Qarawiyyin Mosque in Fes, a man of impeccable knowledge and courtesy. They came to his defence and pointed out not only that these people had slandered him but had attacked him without courtesy – they were crude and brutal, uneducated people.

You must know that they approach things with a kind

of dialectical method which ends up always with you in the wrong and it is a false process because they play at being Fuqaha but they are not Fuqaha. They do not know the Fiqh. They will say to you for example, "Where is it in the Qur'an?" In fact, ironically, we can find a reference in Qur'an which all the Sufis have through the ages taken to refer to the Hadra, but this is not the point. There are many things that are essential to our Deen yet which are not in Qur'an. Where is the text of the 'Adhan in the Qur'an? The whole Deen is derived from the Qur'an AND the Sunna.

From that we recognise the 'Ijma of the Community. We recognise the Jama'at. The great Imams have always functioned within a living framework of the Jama'at. It is unthinkable that this practice could have continued through the centuries if these very strict and very elevated and exalted people had looked on it with disfavour. There has been a debate through the centuries about the celebration of the dhikr of the Sufis, but it has been about the limits of the dhikr, not the dhikr as such. It has never been questioned because there is massive evidence in the Hadith literature, and there is massive evidence in the Qur'an that dhikr kathiran is what Allah is asking of his people.

What has happened is that in our day, there came into power in the Middle East, men who were the servants of the kuffar and they had to guarantee the kuffar that Islam was finished. Not only that, but they had to guarantee them that there would not be Khalifate. When their leader was in fact offered the Khalifate by the British government he refused it, because doctrinally he was put there precisely to deny the reality of Khalifate. He denied what had been before, and he was denying that it should have continuity since he had already denied its previous existence. This was a man who had given his personal Bay'a to the Khalif in Istanbul. So already you are dealing with traitors, you are dealing with dogs, and it was these people who went on to destroy the Deen of Islam – and not only in the matter of the Hadra.

To us, at the end of the day, at the beginning of the day, the Hadra does not matter. It is not an issue for us. But we know that the people of dhikr are true and sound, and they are our license. These people who have attacked the Sufis are now known to the whole Muslim world as being the enemies of Islam. There are no two ways about it.

If you want to know about Hadra, you have to approach it with some sort of adab, with courtesy, if you want to learn. Someone said to me the other day, "I have to understand it if I am going to appreciate the beauty of it," but I said, "No. If you appreciate the beauty of it, you will understand it." It is the other way around.

Sa'id Ramadan, who is the son-in-law of Hasan al-

Banna, the founder of the Ikhwan al-Muslimun, was a good friend of mine. Sa'id Ramadan said that he broke with Maududi and these modernists, and he related that one day he had said to Maududi, "Everything you say about politics and all these attacks on the Sufis makes complete sense, but there is one thing that troubles me." Maududi said, "What is it?" He said, "Where are the tears? Where are the tears that fall on your cheeks for love of Allah and mention of Rasul, sallallahu 'alayhi wa sallam? If you had that I could be with you, but because you do not have it, I cannot be with you." That was the son-in-law of Hasan al-Banna.

So this is a matter for people in an age where Islam is not being taught. If anyone comes to you and says, "Go and ask these people 'What is this Hadra? Where do you get it? What is this part of Islam?'" Say: "Has the one who has asked this question established Zakat as a taken Fard, that is TAKEN by Zakat collectors? Show me his writings! Show me what he is standing for! Does he stand for Zakat? If he does not stand for Zakat he is worse than a Munafiq, he is a kafir."

The truth of the matter is that the ones who attack the Sufis abolished Zakat. They abolished it in Riyadh for the whole Arab world and that is why the Arab world is in a gutter of hell at this moment. They have lost their fear of Allah, and they only have fear of their dunya and their wealth which is taken out of their hands on a daily basis. They have lost love and respect of Rasul, sallallahu 'alayhi wa sallam. One of them said to me, astaghfirullah, "The Prophet was like a statesman and a governor." I said, "No, no, no! He was Rasul, sallallahu 'alayhi wa sallam. He was Mustafa, and this is the difference between us."

Shaykh Muhammad ibn al-Habib tells in his Diwan about those who do not understand the singing and the dancing of the Sufis, that if they were not ignorant they would say, "Please teach us this knowledge that we might have it, that we might be elevated to this condition of love of Rasul, sallallahu 'alayhi wa sallam, and love of Allah, subhanahu wa ta'ala":

> So submit to them for what you see
> of their ardent love,
> and the Raqs and the singing
> in the dhikr of the Beloved.
>
> If you had but tasted
> something of the meaning of our words,
> you would already be experiencing
> every Hal.
>
> And, my brother,
> you would have borne your troubles patiently,
> you would have rent the robes of shame
> and self-importance,

You would have said to the leader of the people,
"Make us love His name!
There is no shame in that song,
nor in that love!"

This is your inheritance. This city is blessed by its
Awliya. From what we know, the Unseen is with us and
surrounds us in everything, and it has been protected
and it is protected. Islam in this city will be safe, and
from this city Islam will spread to the whole of Africa.
All the problems by which the political class have failed
so disastrously – to give to the poor and the needy
and the suffering, and the people devoid of doctors in
desperate need of help – all of that has been denied them
by the political class.

However, it will be given to them at the hands of the
Muslims of South Africa who will arise and who have
the Tariqa so that you may travel from Cape Town to
Tangier, and stay every night in a different Zawiyya of
the Fuqara all the way, and do dhikr with the people.
We will unify the people of Africa, and we will unify
and strengthen the Muslim cause which is in need of
intellect and 'Aql. But that cannot survive without adab,
and adab cannot come out of a heart that is not clean,
because out of it will come hypocrisy.

We seek protection from the hypocrites and we seek
protection from their frivolity and their laughter at the

dhikr of Allah, subhanahu wa ta'ala. O Allah, give us strength, and, Allah, make us among the people who love Rasul, sallallahu 'alayhi wa sallam. Allah, make us among the exalted company that have always been in this Community of Islam who have not only love of Allah, subhanahu wa ta'ala, but have 'Ilm Laduni – direct knowledge of Allah, subhanahu wa ta'ala.

IV

JUNE 4TH 2005

We will continue with what we were looking at in the last gathering, as we have not finished with this explanation, or commentary, on this term of Muhiyuddin Ibn al-'Arabi: Al-Khayal.

We observed at the very beginning that for a Muslim to look at commentaries on these matters made by people who are not Muslim is very dangerous because those people simply have not understood the fundamental elements of it. They simply dismiss this term, which is the key term of all Ibn al-'Arabi's Futuhat al-Makkiyya, as meaning 'imagination' which of course immediately reduces its status, and also fails to understand that it has a meaning, which is not a mental meaning, about the very nature of creation itself.

We will continue to look at the term. Muhiyuddin Ibn al-'Arabi says:

> Allah has not brought about as great a station as Khayal, nor a more dominating control. Through it His judgments, Hukum, flow into all creation and non-creation.

In other words, it is through the Khayal that Allah, subhanahu wa ta'ala, in His bringing the creation into its series of forms, allows the element of discrimination. There is no creation without discrimination because the discrimination distinguishes this form from that form.

It is important to understand this as it is fundamental to the reality that there are the myriad things. There is not one kind of plasmic unity of things but, as you remember, we referred to this matter of Khayal as being determined from the created creatures' point of view that they are able, as it were, to access this energy of Khayal by the element of sanity. We noted that the insane person cannot distinguish between the objects. He plays with his faecal matter as he plays with his food, and puts it in his mouth which should be disgusting to him, as he has not got this fundamental discrimination which is what makes a complete and whole intellect. This is not to say that this IS the intellect, but it is the faculty by which the intellect functions. The intellect is like the lens in the self that is able to perceive the different objects.

The Khayal is something which goes right into the very matter of existence. Ibn al-'Arabi talks about the Sifat al-Khayal adh-Dhatiyya – the essential characteristics of the Khayal. He says:

The truth of Khayal is change in every state.

In other words, the change in every state is the truth of how things are. So the fact that you experience everything differently and in change is the evidence of the true nature of existence. You are participating in this experience of what the Khayal is.

The truth of Khayal is change in every state. Sayyidi 'Ali al-Jamal, radiyallahu 'anhu, the great Wali of Fes, his constant du'a throughout the whole of his famous book, The Meaning of Man, is, "O Allah, keep me in change." The word for 'change' in Arabic is Taghyir. In other words, he meant: 'Let me be aware of the ever-changingness of every thing because by that I am able to have a perception of the Divine, of Allah, subhanahu wa ta'ala.' It is direct perception of Allah, subhanahu wa ta'ala, because He has made everything in creation in change.

Once you recognise the change in every state, then you realise that it is not only true of the self's perception of the world, but it is true of all those things in the world that you are perceiving. Everything is in change. This also means that the 'Arif's recognition of this is that which forbids him, as it were, to have a project. At that moment, his project must be for that which is beyond change. Because whatever a thing is, it is something that is going to disappear, it is something that is going to be turned over – and it goes much further than the realm of events as we are going to see. It goes right into the business of the actual stuff of the creation.

The truth of Khayal is change in every state and appearance in every picture.

Your seeing what you see, your ability to recognise the appearance of what appears – what is happening is the Khayal. This is how everything is. Everything is appearing, and everything is in change. So the appearance is in every picture because:

There is no real existence that does not accept change, except Allah. For in final certainty there is only the existence of Allah, and regarding other than that, it only exists in Khayal.

It only exists in appearance, which is constantly changing.

Then he refers to a key term which we will come back to, but his first statement of it refers to the 'Ama. The 'Ama is a term which was used by the Rasul, sallallahu 'alayhi wa sallam, and it is found in the Hadith literature. A man asked the Rasul, sallallahu 'alayhi wa sallam, a question and, as we shall see, to the 'Arifin it is not a correct question because Allah does not have whereness, but it was this man's simple wanting to understand that, knowing that creation was in-time, he asked, "Where was Allah before the creation of the universe?" Rasul, sallallahu 'alayhi wa sallam, said, "He was in the Great 'Ama." The 'Ama is a word which means a kind of impenetrable mist. It is like a cloud that has no form. It is like going into that weather where you cannot see anything, and yet what stops you seeing is not anything you can see. It is like an absence of vision. In other words, Allah, subhanahu wa ta'ala, was in this energy of the 'Ama which is that by which He was about to create the universe.

He says that the Great 'Ama is the Jewel Essence. It is the most fundamental element of the whole world because:

The world will not appear except in Khayal,

and he quite openly continues:

For the universe imagines itself and that is why it is what it is – Huwa, Huwa.

It is, it is. The appearance of the forms IS the Khayal, so the form of itself is a seeing of itself. Thus the perception of the creation of the world is not based on your perception, because the Perceiver is Allah, subhanahu wa ta'ala. Thus in the landscape, as it were, where there is no human being, that landscape does not cease to exist because there is no perceiver, because Allah is the Perceiver. That is why Allah explains that He knows every leaf that falls. Surat al-An'am (6:59):

وَعِندَهُۥ مَفَاتِحُ ٱلْغَيْبِ لَا يَعْلَمُهَآ إِلَّا هُوَ وَيَعْلَمُ مَا فِ
ٱلْبَرِّ وَٱلْبَحْرِ وَمَا تَسْقُطُ مِن وَرَقَةٍ إِلَّا يَعْلَمُهَا

The keys of the Unseen are in His possession.
No one knows them but Him.
He knows everything in the land and sea.
No leaf falls without His knowing it.

This is the Presence of Allah. Allah is present throughout the whole of the creation but it is His Presence that is the reality of the Khayal. **The world will not appear except in Khayal**, meaning that it will not appear in Khayal except to itself, for it imagines itself. The world imagines itself and that is why it is what it is. This means that you are living in a dynamic created universe of Allah, subhanahu wa ta'ala, which in itself in every aspect has a self-seeing.

Rasul, sallallahu ʿalayhi wa sallam, spoke to things in
nature, and things in nature spoke to him. This is in
the Sira of Rasul, sallallahu ʿalayhi wa sallam. Trees
acknowledged him and spoke to him. He was aware
that the Hayy and the Qayyum are always put together
by the ʿArifin because they are put together in Qurʾan.
The Hayy and the Qayyum are opposite attributes,
contradictory attributes or, if you like, they are those
two attributes which are necessary for this dynamic
reality of existence which is in the Khayal. In this, man
is a locus of this seeing. He is a locus, if he has ʿAql, of
this ability to recognise this process.

This path of Maʾrifa of the Sufi, in his retreat, in his
turning to Allah, is the collapse of the illusion of the self
which is the barrier to seeing how it is. The barrier to
seeing how it is is the outward capacity to discriminate.
If he does not have the outward capacity to discriminate,
he could not lose it and know that he is not the observer
but he is the observed.

الله معي الله ناظر إلي الله شاهد علي

This is the Wird of Sahl at-Tustari. 'Allah is with me,
Allah sees me, Allah is the Witness over me.' The Khayal
is active. The Khayal itself is the dimension of Maʾrifa.
Now he expands it further. He says:

The nature of Khayal is to physicalise and

bring out in pictures that which has no picture or body. For it is an inner sense between the conceptual and the physical. It is a sense between what the intellect can recognise and the thing it is recognising.

There are four aspects of Khayal. The first is the Khayal al-Mutlaq. This is the Total Khayal.

This is, as it were, Khayal itself, which is the Great 'Ama, which is that from which the whole universe emerges. Remember that in our understanding of these things, Allah has built this into the Qur'anic language. Allah has built this into what we might call the cosmogony of the Muminun in teaching us how things are in this world and how things are after death. This whole process we are going to look at is in the Qasida of Shaykh Muhammad ibn al-Habib, rahimahullah, which says that in the Unseen world, all these forms have meanings:

$$ إِنَّمــا الكَــوْنُ مَعانٍ $$

$$ قائِمـــاتٌ بِــالصُّوَرْ $$

Truly created beings are meanings
projected in images.

IV

The Khayal al-Mutlaq is Total Khayal. It is that out of which everything comes.

Then there is the Khayal al-Muhaqaq which is the Khayal of the Form.

In other words, the Khayal is that discriminating factor which comes between the perceiver and the perceived. That process is also what is happening with the seeker of knowledge of Allah, because he goes from perceiving with separate distinction, and begins to understand how there are two ways of understanding existence. There is the Shari'at, and there is the Haqiqat. Where there is discrimination the separate forms have rules that must be obeyed, and if they are not obeyed there is a punishment attached to them. Among the Fuqaha, if a man is brought to the courts, by a method which you will find in all the books of the Fuqaha, of Abu Hanifa or Malik, they identify quite specifically whether he has this discrimination on which 'Aql is based. If he does not have that discrimination he is not judged under the Shari'at but is put away into the asylum. But if he can distinguish, he has to answer by the Shari'at.

The Shari'at is that which rules over all the realm of discrimination. Haqiqat is the opposite of that. Haqiqat cannot be confirmed by observation. The other cannot deny it. The ignorant wahhabi dogs say, "The Sufis are

75

wrong!" But how can they say that? How do they know what has happened in my heart? How do they know what has happened in the heart of the Sufi? To deny Tasawwuf is to deny the spiritual reality of the other person. They are saying, "I am a blind dog therefore all dogs are blind, and all are dogs."

This other knowledge of Haqiqat is known to the Sufis who say, "It is a knowledge which is like the taste of the strawberry. It is known to the one who tastes it, but it cannot be known to the one who has not tasted it." It is recognised by the one who has recognised it, among those who have put their foot into that experience. The ones who are further on the Path, who have a greater spiritual knowledge, know that this one has a foot on the Path of knowledge. That is why the Sufis always seek the company of each other so that they take the benefit in the presence of people of more ruhani strength than themselves. It is transmitted inwardly and invisibly, and by keeping company this change takes place.

Rasul, sallallahu 'alayhi wa sallam, gave the example of the man who keeps the company of the blacksmith: the smell of the dust and the dirt of the fire rubs off on him, and the one who keeps the company of the merchant of the perfumes finds that he is impregnated with the sweet scents of perfumes. He is indicating by this that the one who moves in the world of dunya gets dirty and the one who looks for spiritual meanings is elevated. Again, it is by something unidentifiable which is this invisible perfume.

IV

He then says:

**The next Khayal is the Khayal al-Mumfasal.
This is the Separating Khayal.**

This is the foundation of intellect. It is also the separating
element of all the physical creation. Even if you go down
into the mineral realm there is a separating Khayal –
gold is gold and lead is lead. Before we evaluate, it itself
has a different form, a different image, but our seeing of
that image is what makes us put lead low and put gold
high. It is an evaluation which is put into our 'Aql to
recognise the importance of gold because it has beauty,
because it has relative permanence and because it is an
adornment, it adorns. It has jamali characteristics.

**Then there is the Khayal al-Mutasal. This is
the Imagining Khayal.**

Remember that the faculty of the humans is that we
can imagine. You can imagine something happening
which is not here but somewhere else. Equally in dream
or daydream you can create the forms in the mind, and
in that sense it is a seeing of what is not there. This is a
faculty by which you can imagine as well as recognise.
The modern materialist politicians of today – often
people want to say about them, "They are evil!" but
someone else will say about them, "No, they are not
evil, they lack imagination. When they order the ship

to be sunk, they do not think of the young men being drowned uselessly when the ship goes down. It is not evil, they simply do not realise what the outcome of their acts represents." They think they are doing it for their aggrandisement, meanwhile thousands of people die in Iraq because of a decision of a weak and unbalanced identity. But the one who can envisage what may come of an act would be the one who would stop it.

So we go back to these four terms: al-Khayal al-Mutlaq – the Total Khayal, the 'Ama. Al-Khayal al-Muhaqaq – the recognising of the form. Al-Khayal al-Mumfasal – the Separating Khayal which allows us to recognise separate things, and that creation is built up of separate elements and characteristics of shape. And al-Khayal al-Mutasal – the Imagining Khayal of this faculty to also envisage what is not physically there. It is the capacity of perceiving a reality of how things are connected to how things may be.

The first one is the Khayal al-Mutlaq and it is the 'Ama. The second is Khayal al-Muhaqaq – the Khayal of the Form, and about it he says:

After accepting a picture it becomes Khayal al-Muhaqaq. It has taken on a form.

The Khayal, as it were, enrobes the object in its form. In other words, in all of the appearance of the universe in its detail and in its generality, is this process. The Khayal is what lets the thing have a form. This is the Divine Power of Allah in all creation.

The third is the Separating Khayal – al-Khayal al-Mumtasal. About this he says:

> It is a world that has its inner presence appearing in the senses being experienced as separate to the person who watches Khayal. The Separating Khayal is like Sallallahu 'alayhi wa sallam recognising Jibril in the form of the youth. The youth appeared, and Rasul, sallallahu 'alayhi wa sallam, in recognising the youth did not say, "That is a youth," he said, "That is a manifestation of the Angel Jibril who has come to teach us our Deen."

So it is the seeing and interpreting faculty, and this is at its highest among the people who are cognisant of the fact that Allah is the Ruler, Allah is the Decreer, Allah is the One Who Directs Everything. So these people see the meaning – they go from the sensory to the meaning. In this world, everything sensory must be interpreted with a meaning and recognised for its meaning. In the Next World all the meanings will be tasted as sensory things as is described in Qur'an as the gifts and benefits of the Janna.

The fourth is the Khayal al-Mutasal which is the Imagining Khayal. He says:

> **It is the power to create pictures in the mind.**

What comes from this is that when we look at the description of the Next World, there are forms which embody realities that are as real as our recognition of forms embodying realities in this world: other people, friends and enemies, objects that are desired, objects that are repellent. All this is the use of the faculty of Khayal but it simply springs into action in this other-way-round reality of the life in the Akhira.

To return to his definition of the 'Ama, Ibn al-'Arabi says:

> **The 'Ama contains all the pictures of creation. It is the first being and the first effulgence of divinity. From it appears what is other-than-Allah. From it appears the created universe. It is on the same level as Rabb.**

It is on the same level as Rabb, because when we talk about Allah as Ar-Rabb – Rabbul-'alamin – Rabb is Lordship. It is command over everything in general and in particular. Rabb is Lordship, it is the Lord. In this understanding of Tawhid we talk about Rububiyya, which is where the Lordship covers all the interrelated things, the relatedness of all the universe.

The people who study ecology see this harmony between the creatures of the forest. They see total harmony between levels from the top of the trees to the middle of the trees, to the ground – three kingdoms with very little interrelationship, but all existing, all harmonised and connected together. In the same way, Rububiyya is manifest in this gathering. The people who love Allah come together. The metaphor among the Sufis of such a gathering as this is like the bees who are attracted to the nectar. The flowers are many but they are all attracted to the nectar, and when they get the nectar they take it to the hive to make it into the honey. This is the metaphor of the Sufis for the process they go through that they themselves should arrive at a clear vision and a clear Ma'rifa of the nature of Divine Reality. So he says: **It is on the same level as Rabb.**

'Ama is the name of the Self of the Rahman. The 'Ama is that which gives the Rahma of Allah ta'ala that specificness that goes from this absolute, as it were, abstract, unthinkable Power which we cannot imagine or conceive, to the Mercy and Compassion which goes to these fine details of existence and what the Angels record of all the details of all the actions of all the people. Rasul, sallallahu 'alayhi wa sallam, not once,

but again and again in the Hadith records tells us that
one act of compassion, one act of rahma is that which
has saved someone whose whole life has been dreadful
and which, on the level of the Shari'at, would be
condemned and punished. But one act of compassion,
unseen maybe by others but seen by Allah, subhanahu
wa ta'ala, guarantees them the Janna. So the 'Ama is the
name of the Self of The Rahman.

In the light of this, look what we have. You will
remember we were looking at The Miracles of the Way,
the Qasida from the Diwan of Shaykh Muhammad ibn
al-Habib, rahimahullah. We got to where he says:

As for the marks of honour
which he has in the Akhira,
They are also twenty in number
and they follow here:

Ease of death when the seal is set with Iman
so that he will get what he wants.

You remember that ease of death is guaranteed because
Rasul, sallallahu 'alayhi wa sallam, said, "A man dies on
what he has lived, and he is raised up on what he died."
Again, this ease of death is something that has been
coming throughout the whole life of the lover of Allah,
subhanahu wa ta'ala.

**The good news of cool refreshments,
sweet basil, acceptance, and safety from fear.**

In other words, as he is dying, this other world, the
Akhira, which is right next to him begins to open up
so that already he is leaving this world as he is getting
ready to enter the Next World. In the time of the Mahdi
of Sudan, a British officer wrote that after the battle,
one of the Mahdi's men was dying in great, great pain
from his wounds, and this officer said to him, "Take
this, it will help you with the pain," and he offered him
brandy. The officer never forgot that this dying man
said, "What are you doing? The gates of the Janna are
opening in front of me and you want to shut them in
my face!"

**Such is life in the Gardens forever,
Near to the All-Merciful,
perpetually without end.**

Why perpetually without end? Because time has gone,
it has finished. Time is inside the continuum of the
existence of the world, the world of space-time. Eternity
is not "Oh my goodness, this is going on forever and
ever." It is not like that because the time dimension is
over, just as it is in a dream. The Khayal is not dependent
on time. When you dream you suddenly jump from one
place to another, and indeed all kinds of play which we
think is fixed happens in a dream.

His ruh enjoys ascent and honour,
and tribute from the Angels and bliss.

People will gather to bless him
if he is among those worthy of trust,

Who gave correct instruction when asked.
He need have no fear in the place of terrors.

The expanse of this grave is a meadow,
where he will be safe from every trial.

When the good news
comes to him from his Lord
Both his ruh and his body
will enjoy intimacy.

The birds will carry him in their beaks
Wherever he wishes to roam in the Garden.

Remember that this realm of the Akhira is a realm of meanings. It is a non-spatial, non-time event, but it is experienced as sensory. Here, to experience anything, you have to invest it with meaning. You are to recognise the meaning. You have to give value to things to experience them and to take benefit from them. In the Next World it is the opposite.

On the Day of Gathering, he will be
glorified with honour, a crown, robes of
honour and intercession.

His face will be radiantly white
and its light will be manifest
to all those gathered at the place.

He will not see the terror
of the place where they stand,
And he will receive his book
in his right hand.

Again, what the Mumin is learning in this world is
how and what is going to happen as he moves from the
world of the sensory into the world of the meaning. He
will know what its physicality is, what its sensory is, so
he is being prepared for it by his study of Qur'an and
recognition of its meanings for they are as true as the
things concerned with this world.

It will not be with severity
that he is called to account
but rather it will be with kindness
and gentleness.

His deeds will weigh heavily in the Balance
and he will drink from the Basin
of a Prophet who satisfies every thirst.

He will cross the Sirat
swiftly without struggle
to reach a Garden of timelessness.

He will not be called to account
for his actions or rebuked
and in the place of weighing them
he will not be harmed.

He will intercede for his family
and the brothers,
and he will be clothed
in the robes of honour.

Then he will meet Allah with actual vision
and without qualification or resemblance.

That will be more glorious
than entering the Garden,
as it says in the Book and the Sunna.

Take care not to forget that Allah's granting
of these robes of honour is conditional –

On knowledge, actions of Ikhlas
and the dhikr which indicates
his special place.

The dhikr which indicates his special place is the Ism

IV

al-'Adham. The recitation of the Name of Allah that is over all other names.

> The end of the Path
> consists of total absorption
> in the direct witnessing of the Creator,
> the King.

> Beware of listening to someone
> who might deny it
> through his ignorance
> of its knowledge and excellence.

> O Lord! May Your ceaseless generosity
> make its journey easy for the brotherhood.

The brotherhood is the Fuqara, these are Shaykh Muhammad ibn al-Habib's du'as for all of us, to make this journey easy for us.

> This ends The Miracles of the Way
> for the one who walks it truly.

> So have mercy on the one who related it,
> who collected it
> – that is Abu Hamid at-Tusi, Imam al-Ghazali –
> and whomever helps us to spread them.

> Its author, Muhammad ibn
> al-Habib, radiyallahu 'anhu,

asks Allah for an opening
for the community soon,

And for a victory for our beloved Shelter
through whom the poet
may overcome all desires.

May the blessing of Allah fall eternally
on Muhammad and whomever copies him.

And also on his family,
Companions, and Salikin –
those who trod the paths of right action.

This is a tremendous statement of the benefits of the
Path in this world and in the Next World. What you
have to bear in mind is that these spiritual realities are
present with us. Discrimination is present with us, so
that the men of knowledge see the meaning of every
event. They do not look to the event, they look to the
meaning of the event. The indication of this is that
when the Faqir becomes excited and passionate and
'hot', he is not seeing. When the man is lying shot and
covered in blood and the women are hysterical – all this
is the passion of the world, but the doctor comes in
and he has to deal with it. So the doctor comes in and
is 'cold', and what looks to the world like indifference
is in fact compassion because he is looking and he will
assess him thus: "That is his condition, that is how much

strength he has got left, this is what I can do, this is what I cannot do, and now I will proceed to do it." That is a seeing of a different kind to the people involved in it.

In this life you must beware not to be passionate about the dunya. It happens to all of us but you must pull out of it as fast as you can. You cannot afford it because it is in change, it is passing, it is gone. You look back and think, "What was it all about?" The strangest thing of the dunya is that you cannot remember your pain. You cannot bring it back. You can remember pleasure with sweet sentiment but you cannot remember pain. It is gone and finished.

It is important in this world to be able to interpret the event. The first Shaykh of Sayyidi Muhammad bil-Qurshi in the Sahara was a great zahid, Sayyidi bin Wali. He only possessed a Muraqqa'a, a patched robe. That is all he had and it was like a tent but with no original bits because it was all patches. There was also the Pasha of Marrakesh who was enormously rich and wealthy, yet who loved the Awliya and would send presents to them. One day, Sayyidi bin Wali was sitting in the Mosque and someone came from the Pasha and gave him a gold coin. Because it is Sunna to accept a gift he did not reject it but accepted it, and he put it in a little pouch around his neck so that it was hanging down the back of his neck.

After Maghrib the time came to recite the Hizb and he started the Hizb: "A'udhu billahi min ash-shaytanir-Rajim. Bismillahir-Rahimanir-Rahim…" – and he could not remember any further. He was Hafidh of Qur'an but he could not remember anything, it was gone. He stopped everyone and said, "Start again!" and they started again but still it was gone. This happened three times after which he thought, "What is the meaning of this?" – because he knew that you do not forget the Qur'an, the Qur'an leaves you. The Qur'an is a Divine Reality, it is a form. If you read the Hadith literature you will see that the Qur'an has a shape and a form in the Unseen – and it had left him. He thought, "What have I done?" Then he realised. He put his hand around his neck and pulled out the gift of the Pasha which was gold, and from what source he did not even know, and threw it out into the desert sands outside the Mosque. He went back into the Mosque, sat down and began again: "A'udhu billahi min ash-shaytanir-Rajim. Bismillahir-Rahimanir-Rahim. Alif Lam Mim. Dhalikal-Kitabu la rayb" – and away he went and recited Qur'an.

He looked to the meaning, and by finding the meaning he was able to make the right discrimination. When crisis comes to you, when trouble comes to you, when enemies come to you, when deprivation of any sort comes to you, you must look to the issue. The Sufi has to look to the meaning of it and take benefit from it. Remember that Allah, subhanahu wa ta'ala, says in Surat al-'Ankabut (29:1-2):

$$
\text{أَلَمَّ ۝ اَحَسِبَ ٱلنَّاسُ أَن يُتْرَكُوٓا۟ أَن يَقُولُوٓا۟ ءَامَنَّا وَهُمْ لَا يُفْتَنُونَ ۝}
$$

Alif Lam Mim
Do people imagine that they will be left to say,
"We have Iman," and will not be tested?

So you have to look to the meaning of the test. Sometimes Allah breaks you, and the test is how you deal with it. That is why Ibn Ata'illah says in his Hikam: "Days of trial are 'Eids for the Sufi," because it is Allah's test on them. So when trial comes it is an 'Eid, it is a festival. The Sufis say: "You are plunged in the fire and you are plunged in the water, and that is how the steel is tempered." Allah is tempering the steel in order that it can cut and be a sword of Allah, subhanahu wa ta'ala.

May Allah give you success in everything. May Allah give you increase in everything. We ask Allah, subhanahu wa ta'ala, to give us a yearning and a thirst for knowledge. We ask Allah, subhanahu wa ta'ala, to give us the taste of sitting with the people of knowledge. May Allah put you among the people of knowledge because you are then the people of knowledge.

2

COMMENTARY

ON

WITHDRAWAL FROM ALL THAT IS OTHER-THAN-ALLAH

– from the Diwan of
Shaykh Muhammad ibn al-Habib

given on June 11th 2005
at the Masjid al-Mahmoud,
Constantia, Cape Town

JUNE 11TH 2005

We are going to look at two commentaries on one of the songs from the Diwan of Shaykh Muhammad ibn al-Habib, rahimahullah. Before we do it however, I would like that we do some of the Ism al-'Adham. Join in when you have got your breath, do not feel that it is one time the Name then another time the Name – do it as though you were alone. So each person does it not trying to keep in harmony with everybody else. Start when you are able and continue as much as you can.

The recitation of the Ism al-'Adham is the means of the Shadhiliya's dhikr in Khalwa and which all of you can practise when you are alone any time after Isha and before the Fajr. That is the Alif-Lam-Lam-Ha – but the double 'L' is pronounced very clearly. The 'L' is held on to, then the final 'aaah' is extended as much as you are able. When you come to the end of the breath you have to expel the last of the breath for the pronunciation of the 'Ha'. So make it as long as you are able, extending the last syllable as much as you can. All join in and, for a short time, this is just to give you a sense of the impact of the dhikr.

ISM AL-'ADHAM

In the Qadiriya Tariqa this dhikr was refined. Our Shaykh, Shaykh Muhammad ibn al-Habib, rahimahullah, said, "As the time became more difficult, and the capacity of man to withdraw from the dunya and sit on what Muhiyuddin Ibn al-'Arabi called the Carpet of Adab, calling on Allah, became diminished, these great Awliya helped people and made it easy for them," because the path is not difficult.

At the time of Shaykh Shadhili, along with this recitation of the Ism al-'Adham, he introduced a practice, like an exercise, to visualise the Name of Allah, subhanahu wa ta'ala. Thus, at the same time you are reciting the Name, you visualise the letters Alif, Lam, Lam and Ha with sukun, the closed Ha. The beginning of the serious dhikr is repetition of the Ism al-'Adham. The first stage

I

is just simply visualising the Name until you have got it
fixed – when it slides down you put it back again.

Therefore, in the setting of that dhikr, let us look at two
commentaries on the same song – Withdrawal from all
that is other-than-Allah. One is by Sayyidi Fudul al-
Huwari, a very great Sufi whom we had the privilege
of knowing in Fes. The other is by Sayyidi Hammud
ibn al-Bashir who was my first teacher when I was with
Shaykh Muhammad ibn al-Habib, radiyallahu 'anhu.
He was a Waliallah who lived in Blida, in Algeria.

**My ruh speaks to me and says, "My Haqiqat
is the Light of Allah, so look to no-one
except Him."**

Sayyidi Fudul says:

O you who see beings
as the manifestation of multiplicity,
rend the cloaks of illusion
and you will swiftly find that
there are only manifestations of unity
in mankind.

Sayyidi Hammud says:

All existence comes
from the ranks of wisdom.

In other words, all existence is set up by the Khayal. This is what we spent the last three weeks examining the meaning of. Thus, all the many things are in fact things brought into being by this power of Allah, subhanahu wa ta'ala, to make the individual things which also contain within them the capacity to be seen, and creatures who will see them and be able to recognise that they are the multitudinous things.

Remember we said that at the beginning of the affair, Allah, subhanahu wa ta'ala, has created man so that he is able to distinguish all the things. He does not see everything as a kind of soup – he sees that person here, that person there, he sees that specific plant as opposed to another plant. Sayyiduna Adam, 'alayhi salam, was raised to the station of manhood when Allah, subhanahu wa ta'ala, as He explains in the Qur'an, "taught Adam the names of all things." This meant that Sayyiduna Adam could distinguish the various things.

Here Sayyidi Hammud is saying: "All existence comes from the ranks of wisdom," from this process by which Allah, as it were, emerges existence from what Rasul, sallallahu 'alayhi wa sallam, called the Great 'Ama, the Great Mist, the undifferentiated reality, bringing into being existence by the Divine "Kun". "He only has to say to a thing: 'Be!' and it is."

Sayyidi Fudul says:

> Rend the cloaks of illusion
> and you will swiftly find that
> there are only manifestations of unity
> in mankind.

In other words, wherever you look into the many things, you will find manifestations of the Divine One.

Sayyidi Hammud says:

> All existence comes
> from the ranks of wisdom.
> The tablet of the Murid
> is witnessing Him alone.

The tablet of the Murid is like the record of the Murid, the destiny of the Murid, and the destiny of the Murid is 'witnessing Him alone'. In other words, this affair of knowledge, of gnosis, is something Allah, subhanahu wa ta'ala, has chosen in advance to give to the Murid. Therefore it is not something you achieve or attain, but rather it is a gift from Allah.

> The tablet of the Murid
> is witnessing Him alone.

This means that the one who sits is witnessing Him

alone because Allah has determined that he should be the one who has knowledge. The difference in the human creature is between the one who is Mumin – the one who trusts in this reality until it becomes a reality, and the kafir who covers up and denies that he is actually that one who could have this knowledge. He denies this reality. This is kufr, the covering up of the true state of affairs, that every human creature has made a pre-time contract with Allah, subhanahu wa ta'ala: Allah gathered all mankind together before the creation of the world and said: "Alastu bi-Rabbikum?" Am I not your Lord? And all creation answered: "Yes." So the kafir is the one who, having said "Yes," lives the troubled existence of one who is covering up and has decided "I do not want to face up to this contract." That is why the plots and intrigues of the kuffar cannot succeed because they are already deceiving themselves, they are in self-deception as Allah repeats all the way through the Qur'an about how the kuffar are deceiving themselves.

Sayyidi Hammud goes on:

> So look at what the one
> who is firm in nearness clearly states.

In other words, look at what Shaykh Muhammad ibn al-Habib clearly states, because he is firm in nearness. He is one of the Muqarrabun. He has nearness to Allah. Nearness in the language of the Sufis means that they have entered a zone of non-existence and of obliteration before the Presence of Allah because where He is, there cannot be another. The reality of Tawhid is the reality of Oneness.

Shaykh Muhammad ibn al-Habib says in the first line of his Qasida:

My ruh speaks to me –

Thus he is in dialogue with his innermost being. 'He' is telling him. Remember that at the very beginning, as we saw last week, Muhiyuddin ibn al-'Arabi said that all creation looks at itself. Everything is self-reflective, from the mineral to the living creature with a hot liver. All contain the capacity of looking at themselves. It is in the nature of existence, as he says: "Huwa, Huwa." It is what it is. It exists by its being existent. Everything in that sense is alive. As we have said, Rasul, sallallahu 'alayhi wa sallam, showed this to people by his addressing trees, and stones answering him. These things were an indication of his knowledge of this fundamental reality of material existence.

My ruh speaks to me and says, "My Haqiqat is the Light of Allah, so look to no-one except Him."

So from inside himself he is telling his self by his ruh,

by his highest element: **My Haqiqat is the Light of Allah, so look to no-one except Him.** In other words, this worship of the Divine is not worship of a distant god. Our refusal to identify any form with Allah, our refusal to identify any duality to Allah, any connection of Allah to the creation is marked by this secret: **My Haqiqat is the Light of Allah, so look to no-one except Him.** So his ruh is telling him that his Haqiqat is the Light of Allah.

We go to the picture of Abu Yazid al-Bistami, radiyallahu 'anhu, in his cave calling on Allah, and a voice said, "Who is in the cave?" He said, "Yazid from Bistam!" The voice then said, "Know then, that I cannot enter. Because where I am there is no other." On that Abu Yazid went into Fana'. His whole experiencing self was obliterated because it was that Allah, subhanahu wa ta'ala, was going to unveil Himself, but for Him to be unveiled he had to vanish – consciousness had to disappear. There is a detailed description in the Qur'an of the meeting of Sayyiduna Musa, 'alayhi salam, when he asked to look on Allah, subhanahu wa ta'ala. It is exactly the same spiritual reality.

Sayyidi Fudul goes on to say:

> Being is in the darkness of annihilation.
> When the light of Allah illuminates it,
> do not look at its secondary effects.

I saw myself as His light and radiance.

These commentaries are going very far into the nature of Tawhid. The nature of understanding Tawhid is something by which you understand the nature of consciousness. As I have said, the division of men is into the ignorant and the knowledgeable. The ignorant are the people of darkness and the people of knowledge are the people who have understood this reality about themselves and about what the human creature is. The human creature has been appointed to something. Allah, subhanahu wa ta'ala, explains in Surat al-Ahzab (33:72):

$$\text{اِنَّا عَرَضْنَا ٱلْاَمَانَةَ عَلَى ٱلسَّمٰوٰتِ وَالْاَرْضِ وَالْجِبَالِ}$$
$$\text{فَاَبَيْنَ اَنْ يَّحْمِلْنَهَا وَاَشْفَقْنَ مِنْهَا}$$
$$\text{وَحَمَلَهَا ٱلْاِنْسَنُ}$$

We offered the Trust to the heavens,
the earth and the mountains,
but they refused to take it on and shrank from it.
But man took it on.

So this highest knowledge was offered and all creation could not bear it, but man, who also cannot bear it, was given this knowledge and had to take this on.

Sayyidi Fudul says:

Being is in the darkness of annihilation.

In other words, this light is hidden in the darkness of annihilation. When I was with Sayyidi Hammud in Algeria, we were walking by the Mediterranean Sea just north of Algiers and he said, "Just look at the sea! When you dive into the sea, you go from everything being light and all the creatures being distinct, and as you go down deeper the ocean gets darker because the light of the created existence begins to disappear. You go down into the depths of the ocean until everything is black and in total darkness. You swim in that darkness, and you keep swimming. Then, as you get used to it, there appear creatures of the depths of the sea which have luminous markings. So you begin to see creatures, not by their differential light of above, but by the luminosity they have, this phosphorescent light of the fish of the depths. It is like the man in Khalwa, the man who is calling upon Allah. Everything is dark, and then a whole new world like that at the bottom of the ocean begins to emerge from the Unseen, including at first the human forms and so on."

You must visit the Awliya in every place but that is why Shaykh Muhammad ibn al-Habib says in his Diwan: if your intention is strong you will see them without leaving home. In other words, they will come to you. It is part of what you might call the spiritual journey, and he made the metaphor of it like someone going into the depths of the ocean.

Sayyidi Fudul says:

> When the light of Allah illuminates it,
> do not look at its secondary effects.

So even when this darkness begins to light up, do not look at its secondary effects, do not see it as otherness. He goes on, you could say, revealing the secret of the Tariqa for its people:

> I saw myself as His light and radiance.

But this is a seeing based on his non-existence. Even the obliteration that allows these lights to emerge only comes once the hearing and the seeing and all the physical attributes have slipped away. One by one they slip away and the last one is the consciousness of the self. In that I remember saying to Shaykh al-Fayturi: "I was not able to say the dhikr but I was hearing the dhikr." He said, "What a wonderful thing is this! There were you looking for the dhikr, and there was the dhikr looking for you!"

Sayyidi Hammud says:

> When the attribute of the secret of the Secret
> spreads out,
> The sick one is annihilated
> by His description and sublimity,
> And the non-existent remains shouting.
> His words are:

Here he takes the next line of the song:

> **"If I were not a light
> I would be other-than Him.
> Indeed otherness is nothingness,
> so do not be content with it."**

So the reality of this great, vast, myriad world of creation is a nothingness on which is sustained this tremendous event of creation. However, it has no essence, it has no fundamental reality. It is this appearance which exists by this faculty which we call the Khayal whose existence is based on its seeing itself, and the human creatures seeing the whole thing in all its enormous multiplicity.

If I were not a light I would be other-than Him. Indeed otherness is nothingness. There is nothing other-than-Allah. The reality is that there is nothing other-than-Allah, but Allah, subhanahu wa ta'ala, has made this whole reality. It is not a reality in itself, it exists bil-Haqq. It is built with the Truth, with the Haqq itself. It is therefore not what it seems.

Sayyidi Fudul goes on:

Purify you heart with the water of dhikr and
strive not to witness other than the Truth alone.
Other is illusion which cuts you off
from what you desire.

Sayyidi Hammud says:

Whoever aims for Allah in what he witnesses,
and leaves stage after stage will be unified.
That is why you see him generous with words,
so learn!

We will now have a break and then we will come back to it.

BURDA

Sayyidi Hammud was saying:

Whoever aims for Allah in what he witnesses,
and leaves stage after stage will be unified.

I do not know of any other path that spells out so simply and so plainly the innermost secrets. They cannot be divulged by words, but they indicate secrets with the greatest of clarity.

'Whoever aims for Allah in what he witnesses' – in other words, in his calling on Allah, it is Allah he wants to reach. He wants to reach this knowledge of Allah. 'And leaves stage after stage' – in other words, what happens then is like an inward journey. The Tariqa is not the Tariqa across Africa or Asia, but it is across the deserts of the Unseen and in that process there are stages and meetings which take you on the way to this annihilation of the annihilation, this Fana' of the Fana'.

Sayyidi Hammud says:

That is why you see him generous with words,

meaning Shaykh Muhammad ibn al-Habib.

"If you look with the eye of your Secret you will not find a trace of other-than-Allah in either earth or heaven."

Sayyidi Fudul says:

Other is illusion which cuts you off from what you desire.

Any form is other-than-Allah, and there is no other-than-Allah so whatever forms, however beloved they are, however precious they are to you, you have to go past them, go beyond them.

Sayyidi Hammud continues:

One pours forth his affairs in his Witr.

The Witr is the prayer with one Rak'at. So it is one worship of Allah, it is unique.

So travel the paths of the people
and you will win arrival to Him.

In other words, it is by keeping the company of the Fuqara that your self, this troublesome thing that is the everyday self becomes less and less solid and more and more opaque, and less opaque to clearer and clearer until the light begins to come into the very faces of the Fuqara.

So travel the paths of the people
and you will win arrival to Him.
Annihilate nature and human nature
in His Attribute.

In other words, all of the created forms of existence and the created form of the self – annihilate them in Allah's Attribute.

Sayyidi Fudul says:

> All is a mirror for the radiance of His beauty.
> Be annihilated to phenomenal beings
> and you will obtain His nearness.
> He is eternally unconcealed and manifest
> in His creation.

'Be annihilated to phenomenal beings' meaning that you ignore them, you go past them, 'and you will obtain his nearness.'

Amir 'Abdalqadir of Jazayr wrote in his Muwaqif about this Ayat in Surat al-Baqara (2:144):

فَوَلِّ وَجْهَكَ شَطْرَ الْمَسْجِدِ الْحَرَامِ

> Turn your face, therefore,
> towards the Masjid al-Haram.

'Turn your face' – the face of the person is their essence, so the turning of the face to the Masjid al-Haram, in the language of the Sufis, as well as its immediate meaning, has a direct meaning. It has the order of Allah, subhanahu wa ta'ala. But it is also to turn your essence, to turn your face to His Face – to the unreachable place. "Wherever you turn there is the Face of Allah," the Face being the Essence.

The direction, the Qibla, is like the appointing of man to this unique knowledge. So his turning his face to this Haram, this untouchable, unreachable, unknowable is the order also for the Mumin to present his essence to be obliterated in confronting the Masjid al-Haram which, in this interpretation, is the Dhatillah, the Essence of Allah, subhanahu wa ta'ala.

Sayyidi Hammud continues:

> Cling to the Shari'at,
> and the Haqiqat as well
> With the help of a scholar
> who will put its disorder right.
> Submit all states willingly to its lover.

Sayyidi Fudul says:

> Do not drink the pure wine
> of the Haqiqat alone.
> Mix its red wine
> with the water of the Shari'at.
> Look with the eye of the Truth
> and then with the eye of the Shari'at.

In other words, in all the journey you have to recognise that outside the realm of the Khalwa and the witnessing and the secrets of the sitting on this Carpet of Adab, you return to unconditional confirmation of the Shari'at of Islam because without the Shari'at of Islam you can go wrong. Sayyidi Fudul says: 'With the help of a scholar who will put its disorder right' – disorder in the sense of intoxication, because part of this process by which annihilation comes is like a drowning. It is described as a drunkenness, but in this inward drunkenness, without a guide, a person can misbehave. Even great Awliya can have great ecstasies in which they say things that are forbidden.

The great example in our Tariqa was of Mansur al-Hallaj who went into the Mosques declaring what should not be said. So the 'ulama who wanted to finish off the Sufis had him arrested, and they put him in judgment because what he said was Shirk. In his statements he was identifying himself with the Truth, recognition of the Truth being founded on your non-existence. So he was declaring the Truth as if he were 'another' to It. The 'ulama sentenced him to death, which is the judgment of the Shari'at, and they sent the death certificate to Imam al-Junayd, radiyallahu 'anhu, who was a qadi of Baghdad, saying, "You sign it!" Imam al-Junayd wrote on the death certificate: "In the eyes of the Shari'at he is guilty. In the light of the Haqiqat, Allahu 'Alim." In other words, there is a way this statement can be made, but it cannot be made with consciousness. It could only come out of obliteration, out of a non-existence.

So before that time when al-Hallaj was actually executed, when he had these ecstasies he was very Majdhub, his

Jadhb was stronger than his Suluk. Imam al-Junayd's way was the way of our Shaykh, the way of the seeker being Salik, and outwardly sober. So when Imam al-Junayd saw him going into these ecstasies, because he was in danger of being precisely accused of saying things he had no right to say, he would immediately have two of the Fuqara take him and put him in the asylum in order to save his life! If he said it in the asylum they would just say, "He is majnun! He is cuckoo!" So they kept him alive for some time through this ruse.

In other words, this is a very delicate subject to speak of. The one who expresses a state has not had a state. The one who tells of a state has not had a state. It is a secret, except with the Shaykh or the teacher who is guiding them through the Khalwa. It must be hidden. It has to be kept secret.

That is why Sayyidi Hammud says, 'Cling to the Shari'at and the Haqiqat.' In other words, stick also to its adab. Tasawwuf has these rules, and you must obey these rules otherwise you will come into offence with the Shari'at. Cling to the Shari'at and the Haqiqat as well because all these western so-called Sufis in Europe have a flickering of spiritual ruhani light and then they come out and say, "You do not have to pray, you do not have to obey the Shari'at. Now that you have this knowledge you are above it!" This is not possible, so you cling to the Shari'at and the Haqiqat as well.

In Shaykh ibn al-Habib's song it says:

> Board the ship of the Sunna
> and you will be rescued in it.
> Travel the path of its captain
> in his love.

In other words, follow the way of Sayyiduna Muhammad, sallallahu 'alayhi wa sallam.

Sayyidi Fudul says:

> It is the straight path of His road.
> You will rise to the peak of gnosis,
> striving in travelling it.
> Do not refrain from drinking it
> from His source.

'Do not refrain from drinking it from His source' meaning that when Allah gives the gifts, do not hold back.

Sayyidi Hammud says on the same line of the song:

> Weave from your heart
> the carpets of its diffusion.
> And join your secret
> to the mixture of His Secret.
> Mix the rays in the rising of its sun.

'Weave from your heart the carpets of its diffusion.' So weave from your heart the spreading out, the diffusion of these knowledges. 'Mix the rays in the rising of its sun.' In other words, as your illumination comes, mix it with the Divine effulgence. Of course, what will happen is like when you put the candle out into the midday sun, it is obliterated, it is irrelevant. So you must let the lights coming from Allah overwhelm the light that is coming from you until you have disappeared because there are not 'two'. There is only One. While you think it is you, it is just a mirror reflection of it.

In that sense, Gnosis is the human creature contemplating his creatureness, not contemplating Allah. The creature contemplating his creatureness has in it annihilation which allows the lights of Allah to manifest.

This is commenting on the line:

> Unite the wine with the goblet and be annihilated by it and you will obtain going-on, Baqa', with His Secret and sublimity.

In other words, the goblet is the one calling on Allah. The wine is this light that comes from Allah, but you unite this wine and the goblet until there is no wine and there is no goblet, it is one, it is united. There is not any ittihad, there is not any joining as that is Shirk. The Sufis never, never claim joining, they claim obliteration and vanishing in the light of the manifestations from the Essence.

You will find this language when you turn to the Diwan of Ibn al-Farid. There is a whole Qasida on the Khamr, on the wine, which is very famous. This language of the wine and the goblet you will also find in Peshwiri and Suhur. Great Sufis all confirm what is very significant – especially to those who are ignorant of Tasawwuf and who have to face up to the fact that all these great 'Arifin confirm the same picture.

There are however, differences in Shari'at. There have to be differences in Shari'at because it is dealing with a multitude of things. One qadi will say one thing, another qadi will say another. They can differ in how they view things within the framework of the Shari'at but there is no difference among the people of Haqiqat. What Mawlay 'Abdalqadir al-Jilani says is the same as what Hujwiri says or Sahrawardi. They all confirm the same unfolding reality. Ibn al-Farid's Diwan is echoed in the Diwan of Shaykh Muhammad ibn al-Habib, the Diwan of Shaykh al-Harraq and the Diwan of Shaykh al-'Alawi. They all tell the same truth because it is the Madhhab of Tawhid.

Sayyidi Hammud says:

Cling to the work of the Creator properly.

I

It will bring the Murid near
to His might and sublimity.
Have a broken heart, and keep it in order.

'Have a broken heart, and keep it in order.' That is a very
beautiful thing to say. That is the mark of the great Salihun.
Their hearts are broken but everything is in order.

Sayyidi Fudul says:

See Him in all manifestations:
the secret of mankind and other,
if you have achieved realisation.
A glass, if you wish, in which to take His wine!

This is commenting on:

**See His Tawhid with the eye of inner sight
but separation is His Shari'at
so do not forget it.**

'See His Tawhid with the eye of inner sight' meaning
with the light of the basira, not the outward eye. The
minute there is distinction, the minute there is other,
the Shari'at is there and must be obeyed. When there
is drunkenness and obliteration and vanishing in the
Khalwa, that has what Sayyidi Hammud calls 'clinging
to the Haqiqat', but the minute there is separation, the
minute you know that you exist and that you are there

on that carpet calling on Allah, then the Shari'at in there, and it is also over your tongue. It demands silence on these matters. You may not say these matters because ignorant people will think that you are claiming something that, in the eyes of the Shari'at, demands execution.

Make your concerns one,
and by Him, all your needs will be met
and you will enter into His protection.

Sayyidi Fudul says:

Do not let the arrival of phenomenal beings
veil you to the End.
Cut through its intervening illusion and,
my brother, raise your himma above all
that is other-than-Him.

Sayyidi Fudul says:

Concentrate your thought on obtaining His overflowing abundance and settle your heart in the Presence of His nearness.
Drink with your secret the sweetness of His kindness.

Recording the session ended here.

3

COMMENTARY

ON

AYAT AN-NUR

given on November 19th 2005
at the Masjid al-Mahmoud,
Constantia, Cape Town

اللَّهُ نُورُ السَّمَوَاتِ وَالْأَرْضِ مَثَلُ نُورِهِ
كَمِشْكَوةٍ فِيهَا مِصْبَاحٌ الْمِصْبَاحُ فِي زُجَاجَةٍ الزُّجَاجَةُ كَأَنَّهَا
كَوْكَبٌ دُرِّيٌّ يُوقَدُ مِن شَجَرَةٍ مُّبَارَكَةٍ زَيْتُونَةٍ لَّا شَرْقِيَّةٍ
وَلَا غَرْبِيَّةٍ يَكَادُ زَيْتُهَا يُضِيءُ وَلَوْ لَمْ تَمْسَسْهُ نَارٌ نُّورٌ عَلَىٰ
نُورٍ يَهْدِي اللَّهُ لِنُورِهِ مَن يَشَاءُ وَيَضْرِبُ اللَّهُ الْأَمْثَالَ لِلنَّاسِ
وَاللَّهُ بِكُلِّ شَيْءٍ عَلِيمٌ ۝

Allah is the Light of the heavens and the earth.
The metaphor of His Light
is that of a niche
in which is a lamp,
the lamp inside a glass,

the glass like a brilliant star,
lit from a blessed tree, an olive,
neither of the east nor of the west,
its oil all but giving off light
even if no fire touches it.
Light upon Light.
Allah guides to His Light whomever He wills
and Allah makes metaphors for mankind
and Allah has knowledge of all things.

Ibn 'Atiyya's commentary on this is:

> The Light, an-Nur, to the Arabs meant Light
> that is discerned by sight, and from this we
> have Kitab al-Munir, the Clear Book. The poet
> said, "As if the sun of the day, light from dawn,
> morning like a pillar."

In other words, he is confirming that when it says 'light'
it means light. Then he says:

> Allah ta'ala is unlike anything else – laysaka
> mithlihi shay, in Qur'anic language. He makes
> it abundantly clear that He is not like light that
> is discerned. Allah desires to make it known that
> He is the Possessor of the heavens and the earth
> by His Qudra. It is said that the king is the light
> of the Ummah by his attending to the people.

One uses the word 'light' also in the sense to describe something. So the king is the light of the Ummah because he looks after his people.

Allah is the King – al-Malik, He is the One Who brought about existence, creation and intellect by a light and by guidance, by Hidaya.

The appearance of creation is by His Light, and there is no Rabb – no creative organiser – equal to Him. A group say that the Deen of Allah is the Light of the heavens and the earth. Ibn Abbas said, "Guiding the peoples of the heavens and the earth." When the jews heard this Ayat they tried to make a ta'wil of it –

– as if it had a hidden meaning and that it was anthropomorphic and making God like a created phenomenon.

They asked, "How could He be the light of the heavens and the earth?" and Allah revealed 'The metaphor of His Light is that of a niche.'

مَثَلُ نُورِهِ كَمِشْكَوٰةٍ فِيهَا مِصْبَاحٌ

The metaphor of His Light
is that of a niche.

'Mathal' is a very important word. You have to sharpen your intelligence to grasp this, because on this matter alone you divide the Muminun who are on a straight path and the people among the Muslims who have gone off the path because they have failed to understand the nature of the Mithal. I will give you an example of that. I was speaking to some Arabs who had a good, modern education and I said something to which they said, "That doesn't make sense!" They took what I had said literally, and so I said, "No, no! This is just a picture of how I mean it to be." They said, "Oh, it's a Mithal!" and it became as though it was not something to be taken seriously. It was 'only a metaphor' so they swept it aside. They had been taught by their modern education to give no evaluation to a Mithal. In other words, there would be physical language, like that is water and it comprises hydrogen and oxygen and so on, and that is real for them. Another step is that there is an idea about something, and when you come to Mithal it is like it is poetry, it has no importance at all.

You have to understand that the human intellect cannot function unless it can make that leap between the specific nature of existence to the picture that will explain existence to you. Let me give you an example. Among the psychiatrists, when they deal with people who are either brain-damaged or who have lost their sanity, one of the tests to see whether they have the full human faculty of intellect is to say to the patient, "I am going to tell you something and you must explain it to me: people in glass houses should not throw stones." If they say, "Well, it means that if you are in a house of glass and you throw a stone then you will break it," they actually consider that this person's intellect is destroyed, they are not sane. They could not make the jump to interpret the metaphor, which means that in a situation, if you are like that, then you should not say that of someone else.

Interestingly enough, they call that the abstract faculty. It is the faculty to abstract from something a meaning. There is no use using metaphor with a little child because he will only take the real. It is only at a certain stage of his intellectual completion, just as the second teeth complete the formation of the whole skull, so also that this faculty completes the humanness of the emerging child. Thus:

$$مَثَلُ نُورِهِ كَمِشْكَوٰةٍ فِيهَا مِصْبَاحٌ$$

The metaphor of His Light
is that of a niche.

At the point one uses the word 'Mithal' all the modernists fall out of the boat into the water and drown, but this is the very point at which they are about to understand – one cannot say the 'nature of Allah' because Allah does not have nature – but what we can say is that this is the way to understanding Allah. This is the way to have a knowledge of Allah because the Mithal is the door to a higher understanding, not to a lesser understanding and not to a poetic understanding, but it is like a seeing of the thing.

Thus the Mithal, and let us translate Mithal as the 'means to understanding' this, is to say something else. "He is the Light of the heavens and the earth", but the way to understand this is that His Light is like that of a niche. Ibn 'Atiyya says: "That means that His Light is already not what you had thought. He is the One by Whom everything else stands. He is their Creator. Ka'ab ibn al-Akbar ibn Jubayr says: 'The niche refers to Sayyiduna Muhammad, sallallahu 'alayhi wa sallam.' Abi ibn Ka'ab ibn Jubayr and adh-Dhahak said: 'It refers to the Mumin.' Al-Hasan said, 'It refers to Qur'an and Iman.'"

In other words, by this indication that has come, they are jumping to say, "Ah, then in fact, that would indicate this," and it is different things they are indicating because they are having insight into what has been allowed for them to grasp by the Mithal.

Ibn 'Atiyya goes on:

The jews tried to anthropomorphise Allah as

ordinary light which we discern and that is not the way we take it. He is an-Nur, and by Him all things stand – Qawam kulli shay. He is the Guide as in the likeness of His Light in Sayyiduna Muhammad, sallallahu 'alayhi wa sallam, the Mumin or the Qur'an. Iman is of His Light.

$$\text{مَثَلُ نُورِهِ كَمِشْكَوٰةٍ فِيهَا مِصْبَاحٌ ۖ الْمِصْبَاحُ فِي زُجَاجَةٍ}$$

> The metaphor of His Light
> is that of a niche
> in which is a lamp.

Ka'ab al-Jabal says:

The Light is like that of Muhammad and the lamp is his Prophethood, his Nabawiyya, and all that pertains to it with regard to action and guidance. The glass is his heart. The blessed tree is the Revelation. The oil is the arguments and proofs of the Revelation. Those who said that the Light is like the Mumin among them was Abi ibn Ka'ab. The lamp is the breast of the Mumin. The lamp is Iman and 'Ilm. The glass is the heart. The tree is the Qur'an. The oil is the argument and the wisdom. This Mumin is in the best of conditions, like the man who is alive and walks among the graves of the dead. Those who say that the Light is like the Qur'an and Iman refer to the Iman in the breast of the Mumin.

اللَّهُ نُورُ السَّمَوَاتِ وَالْأَرْضِ مَثَلُ نُورِهِ كَمِشْكَوٰةٍ فِيهَا مِصْبَاحٌ الْمِصْبَاحُ فِي زُجَاجَةٍ الزُّجَاجَةُ كَأَنَّهَا كَوْكَبٌ دُرِّيٌّ يُوقَدُ مِن شَجَرَةٍ مُّبَرَكَةٍ زَيْتُونَةٍ لَّا شَرْقِيَّةٍ وَلَا غَرْبِيَّةٍ يَكَادُ زَيْتُهَا يُضِيءُ وَلَوْ لَمْ تَمْسَسْهُ نَارٌ

Allah is the Light of the heavens and the earth
The metaphor of His Light
is that of a niche
in which is a lamp,
the lamp inside a glass,
the glass like a brilliant star,
lit from a blessed tree, an olive,
neither of the east nor of the west,
its oil all but giving off light
even if no fire touches it.

Qadi 'Iyad said that Hasan said: "This tree is not of the trees of the world. It is like Allah striking a Mithal with light even though it is in this world, but it is not of the east nor of the west." This only goes so far. Let us look at it again. So, we have taken this as a Mithal of His Light.

I

$$
\text{اللّٰهُ نُورُ السَّمٰوٰتِ وَالْاَرْضِ مَثَلُ نُورِهٖ}
$$

$$
\text{كَمِشْكٰوةٍ فِيهَا مِصْبَاحٌ الْمِصْبَاحُ فِى زُجَاجَةٍ الزُّجَاجَةُ كَأَنَّهَا}
$$

$$
\text{كَوْكَبٌ دُرِّىٌّ يُوقَدُ مِن شَجَرَةٍ مُّبٰرَكَةٍ زَيْتُونَةٍ لَّا شَرْقِيَّةٍ}
$$

$$
\text{وَّلَا غَرْبِيَّةٍ يَكَادُ زَيْتُهَا يُضِىءُ وَلَوْ لَمْ تَمْسَسْهُ نَارٌ}
$$

Allah is the Light of the heavens and the earth.
The metaphor of His Light
is that of a niche in which is a lamp,
the lamp inside a glass,
the glass like a brilliant star,
lit from a blessed tree, an olive,
neither of the east nor of the west,
its oil all but giving off light
even if no fire touches it.

This is a tremendous Ayat. It is making the Mithal which is preventing the possibility of associating Allah, subhanahu wa ta'ala, with creation, with created forms, while at the same time very specifically giving you a particular physical set of forms. But each one is like a protection from allowing that you should say, "This is giving Allah place." Surat al-Ikhlas (112):

$$
\text{قُلْ هُوَ اللّٰهُ أَحَدٌ ۞ اللّٰهُ الصَّمَدُ ۞ لَمْ يَلِدْ}
$$

$$
\text{وَلَمْ يُولَدْ ۞ وَلَمْ يَكُن لَّهُ كُفُوًا أَحَدٌ ۞}
$$

Say: "He is Allah, Absolute Oneness,
Allah, the Everlasting Sustainer of all.
He has not given birth and was not born.
And no-one is comparable to Him."

It cannot depart from this statement. Yet here is Allah giving away, as it were, the secret. What is interesting is that the Mithal of the Light is not light. It is not its own Mithal. The Mithal of the Light is a niche. So to be able to understand this, there has to be a place. Yet Allah is not associated with anything to do with place. To grasp this with the intellect you have to see that there is place. The place by which Allah, subhanahu wa ta'ala, manifests His power is the whole of the creation. All of creation is that niche in which the evidence of Allah's majesty and beauty manifests, subhanahu wa ta'ala.

Having said that it is a place, in this place there is a lamp. The lamp is that thing which is the container from which light emerges. So it is a lamp, and the lamp is inside a glass. Again, between the ones who take light from this there is another barrier and that is the glass. The glass itself is like a star. The glass itself is a blinding light that is between us and that light which is inside the lamp. This glass 'is lit from a blessed tree, an olive, neither of the east nor of the west.' Do you see the fineness? Every time every physical image is given, Allah then breaks it so that you cannot say, "That is it." So it is an olive, but it is neither of the east nor of the west. Its oil is all but giving off light but no fire touches it, so this oil is not lit, it is not fire in that way.

Nurun 'ala Nur. 'Light upon Light.' If we take it that the place is the world – and again, I am not saying that it is, but it is like it is the world – in the world there is a Nabawiyya from the time of Sayyiduna Adam through all the Prophets right through to Rasul, sallallahu 'alayhi wa sallam. That light is transmitted genetically, because the Prophets all come genetically connected. Sallallahu 'alayhi wa sallam identified himself with Sayyiduna Musa and identified himself with Sayyiduna Ibrahim, and identified himself with Sayyiduna Adam.

Therefore, in this great Qurayshi family of the Bani Hashim came the Rasul, sallallahu 'alayhi wa sallam. In one aspect it is in the genetics, in another aspect it is a secret because every one of these Prophets comes with the same message of Tawhid, and every one of them comes with a different Shari'at for the time that he has come for. So it is not 'of the east nor of the west, it is its oil that is almost giving off light so that the human inheritance of Rasul, sallallahu 'alayhi wa sallam, is almost itself the light – but it is not, because nothing is associated with Allah, subhanahu wa ta'ala. It almost gives off light but no fire touches it. The fire would be the humanness of the family of Rasul, sallallahu 'alayhi wa sallam, but no fire touches it. The light is in the heart of Rasul, sallallahu 'alayhi wa sallam, which, again, is something hidden in this set of metaphors which come between us and trying to physicalise the reality of Allah in the creation.

نُّورٌ عَلَىٰ نُورٍ

يَهْدِى ٱللَّهُ لِنُورِهِۦ مَن يَشَآءُ

وَيَضْرِبُ ٱللَّهُ ٱلْأَمْثَـٰلَ لِلنَّاسِ

وَٱللَّهُ بِكُلِّ شَىْءٍ عَلِيمٌ ٣٥

Light upon Light.
Allah guides to His Light whomever He wills
and Allah makes metaphors for mankind
and Allah has knowledge of all things.

Allah guides to His Light whomever He wants. Allah guides to the path of knowledge, to take the obedience in the following of Rasul, sallallahu 'alayhi wa sallam, to the light of Rasul, sallallahu 'alayhi wa sallam. 'Allah makes Mithals for mankind.' Allah does this. He means to do it and He has to do it in order that you have access to the Secret. If He does not do it you will not have access to the Secret. So He makes the Mithal for mankind to give them access to what they do not recognise by looking at the physical world. He transforms the physical world, He transforms the understanding.

Mawlana Jalaluddin Rumi gives a wonderful example of it when he says that when Rasulullah, sallallahu 'alayhi wa sallam, came among his people, Abu Bakr as-Siddiq looked at Sayyiduna Muhammad, sallallahu 'alayhi wa sallam, and he saw the Rasulullah. Abu Jahl looked, astaghfirullah, and he just saw Muhammad ibn 'Abdullah. He saw the man who was the son of the father, he did not see the reality of Rasul, sallallahu 'alayhi wa sallam. When Abu Bakr looked, radiyallahu 'anhu, he immediately recognised that it was Rasul, sallallahu 'alayhi wa sallam. He recognised the meaning of Rasul, sallallahu 'alayhi wa sallam, in the presence of Rasul, sallallahu 'alayhi wa sallam. He was conscious that this was a person whom Allah had imbued with this knowledge. They both looked at the same man and one recognised the light and the other said, "No, he is just a human being so he is nothing."

The modernists made this mistake because in trying to prove that they were not associating anything with Allah they devalued and denigrated Rasul, sallallahu 'alayhi wa sallam, astaghfirullah, by saying, "He is just a man." One of the poets of the subcontinent said, "To say he was just a man in not enough. Coal is coal, and the diamond is a diamond, but they are not the same. Yet they are both the material world."

Ibn 'Ajiba, the Sufi, the Shaykh of our Tariqa says:

> Allah is the Light of the heavens and of the earth.'
> That is its people are filled with light – that is the
> Nur of Islam and Iman, and the Nur of Ihsan for
> the people of Ihsan. The reality of Nur is that it
> reveals all that it covers by the senses and by the
> meanings. The proof is that Allah guides to his
> Light whomever He wills.

This is the last part that we were looking at. 'Allah guides
to His Light whomever He wills.'

> He reveals the Ahkam of 'ubudiyya by clear
> mu'amala. This is the Nur al-Islam. When He
> reveals the Attributes of His High Essence, of
> the Dhat, and perfection by clear proofs, this
> is called the Nur al-Iman. When he reveals the
> reality of the Dhat, of the Essence, and its secrets
> from the way, this is called the Nur al-Ihsan. The
> first is called the Light of the Stars, the second,
> the Light of the Moon, and the third, The Light
> of the Sun. The Sufiyya say, 'The Star of Islam,
> the Moon of Iman and the Sun of 'Irfan.'

Ibn 'Ajiba then says: 'Allah strikes a Mithal with the
Light.'

مَثَلُ نُورِهِ كَمِشْكَوْةٍ فِيهَا مِصْبَاحٌ

The metaphor of His Light is that of a niche.

Shaykh Ibn 'Ajiba says that what takes place in the heart of the Mumin – the Mithal of His Light is the happenings in the Mumin's heart – is that of a niche, as the Mithal of a niche which is like a hole in the wall, but is not a window. The lamp in it gives light to everything. It becomes clear and filled with light. 'In which there is a lamp – he says it is a lamp which kindles. 'The lamp inside a glass,' in it is a candle of pure light-giving glass. The glass of the lamp is the strength of the Mumin's Sifat, of the Mumin's attributes. 'From a blessed tree,' the oil of the olive tree grows on the earth and is a benefit and a blessing for all the world. The oil of the olive tree is like the oil of Syria, because from there, from that earth, Allah blessed us with seventy Prophets.

The olive is the metamorphosis of dry earth. From that dry earth comes this dry tree which produces this fruit, the olive, which is dry, dry, dry and which has to be crushed. When it is crushed then oil is extracted. Thus we would take the metaphor that it is not until the olive is crushed completely that there is extracted an oil, and from that oil comes the light. In that sense, one sees that it is the condition of the Mumin who, in the language of Sufiyya, is the one who is on the Path. In going on the Path he gets crushed, and he has to get crushed in order that this oil is extracted. But this oil is what gives light.

Here we have exactly: 'A blessed tree, an olive, neither of the east nor of the west, its oil all but giving off light even if no fire touches it. Nurun 'ala Nur.' So from this human creature's heart, through being crushed by all the events of life, and all the trials of Suluk, and all his battles with himself – not battling with the world but battling with himself – to make himself realise himself to the fullest, there is extracted this precious oil and that oil is giving off light even if no fire touches it. These are the Salihun. They give off light even though no fire has touched them. Nurun 'ala Nur.

Thus, this is a very blessed Ayat. I wanted to go on to the following Ayats but this is such a tremendous Ayat. To the Sufis, of course, it is the most important Ayat in the Qur'an because it explains to them how they can understand Allah, subhanahu wa ta'ala, and what the Path to knowledge of Allah is, and what the Secret is which they themselves carry in themselves, the way the olive tree carries the olive and the olive carries the oil, just as the land of Arabia carried the family of Rasul, sallallahu 'alayhi wa sallam, in the loins of this family, to arrive at the point of Sayyiduna Muhammad, sallallahu 'alayhi wa sallam. And from him came this Revelation and this spark that lit this lamp that lit up the whole world and has been doing so ever since, and will continue to do so.

This is not a visible thing, it is the Nuri Muhammadi.

I

The Nuri Muhammadi is something that is not seen, but it is that which dazzles. You might say that it is a light so powerful that it blinds. This blinding is what is called in the language of the Sufis, Fana' fillah.

4

COMMENTARY

ON

THE KHAMRIYYA

– of Shaykh ibn al-Farid

Four commentaries
given between
February 4th and 25th 2006
at the Masjid al-Mahmoud,
Constantia, Cape Town

I

FEBRUARY 4TH 2006

شَرِبْنَا عَلَى ذِكْرِ الحَبِيبِ مُدَامَةً

سَكِرْنَا بِهَا مِنْ قَبْلِ أَنْ يُخْلَقَ الكَرْمُ

لَهَا البَدْرُ كَأْسٌ وَهِيَ شَمْسٌ يُدِيرُها

هِلالٌ وَكَمْ يَبْدُو إِذا مُزِجَتْ نَجْمُ

We will look at a commentary on the Khamriyya of Ibn
al-Farid, the famous song of which you have just heard
the opening four lines. This commentary is written by
Shaykh Ibn 'Ajiba who is one of the 'ulama of Tasawwuf
in our Tariqa. He is a very great Sufi of the same rank as
Imam al-Ghazali, if not higher. He says:

Praise belongs to Allah Who allows the hearts of those He loves to drink from the wine of His Love, so that they become among those who are enraptured and intoxicated by His Love. He made them withdraw from witnessing other-than-Him by witnessing His Secret, and they walk in the meadows of His Malakut while their spirits are attracted to the Presence of His Purity. They are familiar with Him in their retreat. He prepared their secrets to bear the burden of His Gnosis and they dived into the sea of His Jabarut, swimming with the ships of their reflection.

He is using terms which you have to find out about and learn as you cannot advance on the Path without knowledge of these terms. For this you need 'The Hundred Steps' because these terms are all defined very clearly in that book and you really must get access to it and study it because without it you are ignorant and there is no use sitting in ignorance. You have to work and acquaint yourself with these terms.

Shaykh Ibn 'Ajiba has used two terms here. He has used the term 'Malakut' and the term 'Jabarut'. If you look in The Hundred Steps you will see that there are triads of terms and these terms are like a further development, a further unfolding of the knowledges of the people of

Tawhid. In the Shari'at you have the terms Islam, Iman and Ihsan. You must know what Islam, Iman and Ihsan mean, and if you are asked you must be able to say what they are from the Hadith that opens Imam Muslim's collection of Hadith: Sallallahu 'alayhi wa sallam was questioned by the Angel, "What is Islam, what is Imam and what is Ihsan?" Afterwards he said, "That was the Angel Jibril who came to you to teach you your Deen."

Then you find these terms Mulk, Malakut and Jabarut. I am not explaining these to you but just giving you the headlines. You have really got to acquaint yourselves with these terms if we are going to continue with this. This is just a preliminary first glance at the matter. Mulk is basically the creation, the cosmos, the whole cosmic creation which is the known, visible universe. Malakut is its unseen equivalent. In other words, where there is Mulk there is Malakut. But there is a third term which is Jabarut which is, you could say, a non-existent reality. It is between the Mulk and the Malakut, not above it, but it is that between the Seen and the Unseen there is a barrier. There is in the Ayat of Qur'an in Surat al-Furqan (25:53):

وَهُوَ ٱلَّذِے مَرَجَ ٱلْبَحْرَيْنِ هَـٰذَا عَذْبٌ فُرَاتٌ
وَهَـٰذَا مِلْحٌ أُجَاجٌ وَجَعَلَ بَيْنَهُمَا بَرْزَخًا وَحِجْرًا مَّحْجُورًا ۝

It is He Who has unloosed both seas –
the one sweet and refreshing,
the other salty and bitter –
and put a dividing line between them,
an uncrossable barrier.

This is Allah, subhanahu wa ta'ala, using the language of opposites like the Jalal and the Jamal, the Majestic and the Beautiful. He has put a division between them, a Barzakh, but it has not get 'there-ness', it is that which allows things to be identified as separate. In geometry, if you draw a line they say that the line has not got spatiality but by it you define the thing on this side and the thing on that side. The line has not got width in physical geometry. I remember a man at Cambridge who was studying the living cell and for two years he just studied the wall of the cell. Then they came to the discovery that the cell did not have a wall, but if they physically intervened then that cell had an exteriority, it had an outsideness if there was intervention. It is like the observer adds to the reality of what is there by his looking at it. He put the knife to it and suddenly there is a wall, but properly speaking the cell does not have contours except once you become the observer looking at it and then it manifests this way. It is the same with creation.

Thus the Mulk and the Malakut are not separate, there is no separation, but when Allah begins to open an understanding of existence to the 'Arif, he sets a Barzakh between these two. He allows him to understand Mulk. He allows him to understand Malakut, and it is by Barzakh. Barzakh is light. Barzakh is power, it is Jabarut. Ibn al-'Arabi says, "If you say it is there, it is there, and if you say it is not there, it is not there." Because it is only to allow us to understand.

Jabarut is light, but it has not got location. It is not physical light. It is the means by which Allah allows us to understand not only the physical world, but the whole process of existence. So he uses these terms. He speaks about the 'Arifin, and how Allah has given them these gifts. He says:

> He has made them withdraw from witnessing other-than-Him,

and witnessing other-than-Him is witnessing existence, witnessing the creation,

> by witnessing His Secret. And they walk in the meadows of His Malakut,

meaning, in the meadows of His unseen reality,

> While their spirits are attracted to the Presence of His Purity.

They are attracted to the Essence, in other words to be obliterated, to be wiped out in this knowledge.

And so they are familiar with Him in their Khalwa – their retreat.

There is an intimacy, and this is what is called in the language of Tasawwuf, the Maqam al-Uns – the Station of Intimacy. We will see in the Diwan of Shaykh Muhammad ibn al-Habib how Allah says to him, "Draw near." This is speaking with intimacy from Allah, subhanahu wa ta'ala, to His 'Arif.

He prepared their secrets to bear the burden of His Gnosis.

In other words, what the 'Arif has to find out are burdens! It is a gnosis which has a burden in it because the more Allah gives to the 'Arif, the more he has to hide it. This is why our Path is a path which Imam al-Junayd called, and which later became known by the scholars as, the Path of Sobriety. It does not mean that they were sober and the others were drunk. It meant that they covered over what came to them which is very hard to bear because it takes you to understanding the ultimate secret of existence which is the Qadr, and the relationship of the Qadr to the qadar – to the event of what is determined. Out of 'apparent' chaos comes the moment which was determined from before time. Thus:

He prepared their secrets to bear the burden
of His Gnosis and they dived into the sea of
His Jabarut.

They dived into this Barzakh of lights which is that
secret which separates the Mulk from the Malakut,

Swimming with the ships of their reflection.

Swimming with their Tafakkar. Shaykh Muhammad
ibn al-Habib says in his Diwan: 'Reflect upon the
beauty of the way in which both the land and sea are
made.'

**Blessings and peace be upon the one who
helps beings by the secret of his Nasut,
while the realities of Gnosis shone from the
light of His Lahut.**

Here you have another three terms which are Nasut,
Lahut and Rahamut. Again, you must look this up for
yourselves. You have to do it if we are to continue. Look
at it in The Hundred Steps where it is explained very
clearly. For the moment, we can say, Blessings and peace
be upon the one who helps beings by the secret of his
Nasut, the secret of his humanness, while the realities of
gnosis shone from the light of His Lahut, from the light
of Allah's Godness, the Ilahiyya of the Divine Reality.

May Allah be pleased with his Companions and the noble people of his house, sallallahu 'alayhi wa sallam.

Before and after everything is the knowledge of Tawhid which is the most majestic of knowledges and the most true of the fruits of understanding spent in it. How could that not be the case when its subject is the Sublime Essence and its radiant Attributes and pure Names?

Again, you have to understand that you cannot approach the knowledges of Tasawwuf without it being firmly embedded in the Shari'at. This aspect of the Shari'at is not the Shari'at of approval or the Shari'at of legal judgments, but the Shari'at of the correct adab of how we may speak about Allah, subhanahu wa ta'ala.

Shaykh Muhammad ibn al-Habib explains in his Diwan: 'Praise Him with what He has praised Himself.' In other words, do not make assumptions about Allah. Do not invent things about Allah. When you want to speak of Allah, take it from what He has told us about Himself. You can only draw your knowledge of Allah, subhanahu wa ta'ala, in what may be spoken, from what He has spoken, which is the Revelation of Qur'an. In other words, you need the Qur'an and there is an adab to the matter of Tawhid in the Qur'an.

For this we find that there have been great scholars of Islam who have helped set up barriers, as it were, against a wrong adab to knowledge of Allah, and also to resist philosophy. Philosophy is a trick. Philosophy is a sophisticated phenomenon which pretends to ask very high questions like, "Why is there something rather than nothing?" "What is the meaning of stuff?" and so on. In fact, when you examine it, it is not actually really wanting to know the Haqiqat. Philosophy is really getting at a means to set up the Shari'at. So the real business of the philosopher is not in the question he is asking, but what follows from asking these questions, or what he proposes – and that is politics.

If you look at Plato, in the end he writes The Republic. When you look at Aristotle, he writes The Polity. At the end of the day they are setting up what you might call 'State'. That State is not the State based on worship but the State based on the idea that this brain can work out how to do the whole process. We are paying the price because what they want to rationalise, as we have seen, is not to bring mercy and compassion but to bring enormous wealth to an elite by means of subduing everybody else whilst giving it a beautiful name. Take the name from Plato and take the whip from the body-guards.

So, these two great 'ulama are of course the ones we use and know: one is Al-Ash'ari, who is also significant because he was encountered by Ibn al-'Arabi so that Ibn al-'Arabi writes about Al-Ash'ari. He does not criticise him but extends and enriches his defence against wrong-thinking about Allah, subhanahu wa ta'ala. The other, who is his equivalent in the world of Imam Abu Hanifa, is Al-Maturidi. He is really performing the same service, but Al-Ash'ari uses, in his way of speaking about Allah, subhanahu wa ta'ala – and deriving it totally from Qur'an – three things. He talks about Allah, subhanahu wa ta'ala, in His Names, His Attributes and His Essence. Or you could say, in His Acts, His Attributes and His Essence.

This is very important because he is not talking about ideas. He is talking about how we understand Allah. Without this language, this protecting language, the process of a sober and sublime illumination of the 'Arif is not possible. It is not possible unless it is grounded in the Shari'at. That is why you find with the great 'Arifin of the Diwans like Ibn al-Farid and of course Shaykh Muhammad ibn al-Habib, that they use this language to describe the process of what happens experientially in Khalwa on what Muhiyuddin Ibn al-'Arabi calls 'the Carpet of Adab', where you sit with Allah in courtesy.

Then you begin to find, if you study the Diwan of Shaykh Muhammad ibn al-Habib, Fana' in the Act, Fana' in the Attributes and Fana' in the Essence. Look

I

at 'Fana' Fillah' in the Diwan of Shaykh Muhammad ibn al-Habib.

$$\text{فَوَحْدَةُ الفِعْـلِ تَبْدُو}$$
$$\text{فِي أَوَّلِ الذِّكْـرِ لله}$$

So the oneness of His Action first appears
at the beginning of doing dhikr of Allah.

The Shaykh is telling you what will happen. In the process of the Khalwa there will come a point where the oneness of the Action will appear, in other words, will manifest itself to the seeker so that he understands the unification of all action because all actions are in the power of the One. All actions are of the Act of Allah, subhanahu wa ta'ala, because Allah is One in His Acts, His Attributes and His Essence.

$$\text{وَوَحْدَةُ الوَصْفِ لَـهُ}$$
$$\text{تَاتِي مِنَ الحُبِّ فِي الله}$$

And the oneness of His Attributes
comes from the love of Allah.

The oneness of His Attributes comes from the love of Allah, so the one who is sitting calling on Allah and calling on Allah, what is awakening in him by his himma,

151

his yearning, is love of Allah, subhanahu wa ta'ala. It is that love which opens to him the understanding of the oneness of the Attributes. Remember that while you see the world in dual terms, the things that make us suffer and the things that make us happy are of course seen as opposites. Things that are terrible are terrible and things that are delightful are delightful.

Shaykh Muhiyuddin Ibn al-'Arabi said to one of the 'Arifin, "How did you reach Allah?" He said, "I reached Allah by the opposite Names," in other words, by the opposite Attributes. "I reached him by joining the Jamal and the Jalal, the Beautiful and the Majestic." This knowledge changed him and gave him opening to Allah, subhanahu wa ta'ala. He Who Raises Up and He Who Brings Low. He Who Advances things Forward and He Who Holds things Back. They are the One, Allah. So by putting the opposites together he achieved his Ma'rifat of Allah, subhanahu wa ta'ala.

I have proof of the effect of this adab on the character of the man. There was a very great Sufi who was one of my first teachers under Shaykh Muhammad ibn al-Habib, Sayyidi Hammud of Blida who has one of his songs in this Diwan of ours. We were sitting in his garden and a man came with the news that both of his sons had been killed in a car accident. When he received the news he said, "Al-Hamdulillah." We did not know what had happened but what we heard was Al-Hamdulillah. So

I

he received this terrible news, praising Allah. He put it
before any way in which he was going to handle this
terrible news. It was from Allah, it was not something
that interfered with or broke the rules of existence. The
Sufi says, "Al-Hamdulillah 'ala kulli hal." Praise belongs
to Allah in every state. If you praise Allah in every
situation then you have Tawhid because everything is
from Allah. The Act is from Allah, the means to it, the
Essence of the Attributes of empowerment in existence
and the Secret itself is from Allah.

$$وَوَحْدَةُ الذَّاتِ لَـهُ$$

$$تُــوَرِّثُ البَقـــا بِاللهْ$$

The oneness of His Essence
gives Baqa' with Allah.

Remember that the knowledge of the oneness of
the Essence is that which obliterates the one who is
experiencing these knowledges. It means that after that
the only thing he can do is return. Baqa' is returning
to existence, because after this knowledge, after this
death, you come back into life and you have to go on
living. Someone said to Imam al-Junayd, "Where did
it take you?" He answered, "Back to the beginning."
Another time he was asked, "What have you achieved?"
He said, "I think I got two rak'ats I once did under
the stairs." So looking at his incredible life which has

changed our whole knowledge of existence, Imam al-Junayd thought he had got two rak'ats right, he felt he had truly worshipped Allah with these two rak'ats done under the stairs.

This is Baqa'. He had gone back to being the humble slave, being hidden. That is why the Sufis say that the Sufi is like a black insect on a black stone in a darkened room. The Sufi is invisible because he has found out, yet he has hidden everything. He realises that Allah is powerful, Allah decrees, Allah determines and so when he moves, he moves by Allah, and when he speaks, he speaks by Allah. This is the knowledge that comes from this circle of dhikr, of singing, and of the Hadra.

The Shaykh then says 'congratulations' to the people who have taken this path:

$$\text{فَهَنِيئاً لِمَـنْ مَشَى}$$
$$\text{فِي طَرِيقِ الذِّكْرِ للّه}$$

Joy to the one who walks on the Path of Allah.

Speaking about this knowledge of Tawhid, Shaykh Ibn 'Ajiba continues:

How could that not be the case when its subject is the Sublime Essence and its radiant

Attributes and pure Names. By it one will
be forever in the bliss of the Garden and will
be granted nearness to the Generous Giver.
It is divided into two categories: the Tawhid
of the proof and evidence which is for the
common people of belief, and the Tawhid of
witnessing and eye-vision, of direct seeing,
which is for the Elite of the people of Ihsan
among the people of tasting and ecstasy.

Thus he defines two sorts of knowledge of Tawhid.
One is by proof and evidence which is for the common
people of belief, and the Tawhid of witnessing and
direct seeing. Of this latter group he says:

They drink the cups of love and are
intoxicated and withdraw from existence.
Then they become sober after their
intoxication.

This is why people misunderstand when they talk
about Imam al-Junayd having this school of sobriety
while these other people get all intoxicated and jump
up and down, and tear their clothes and pass out. This
is not the point. The point is that the former move
from intoxication to sobriety. At the same time there
is an adab in the intoxication that the person, their
body being overwhelmed, does not become so violent
that it affects the experience. The Sufis say, using the

metaphors of the physical world: "A drunkenness with a remembrance is not the same as a drunkenness with forgetfulness." They take the metaphor from alcohol, from drinking – the man who gets drunk and cannot remember what has happened is not the same as the one who remembers what a good time he had.

This metaphor is that the one in the ecstasy of calling on Allah does not behave badly so that the physical dominates, but instead it is equilibrating so that the physical and the spiritual become the same and then he passes out. He loses outward consciousness. This is the matter of sobriety and drunkenness. Shaykh Muhammad ibn al-Habib explains sobriety in the same song:

$$وَاذْكُرْ بِجِـدٍّ وَصِدْقٍ$$
$$بَيْنَ يَـدَيْ عَبِيدِ اللهْ$$

Do dhikr of Him with gravity and sincerity
in the presence of the slaves of Allah.

In other words, in the circle of dhikr in the Zawiyya you do not express yourself, you do not sway about and swoon and tear your clothes, and get up and jump up and down. Whatever is happening inside you, the more you 'do dhikr with gravity and sincerity', the more intoxicated the Faqir is going to be because he has put it all inside, not showing off. He is not saying, "O, I am this person having such an experience," he does not want anybody to know. It is a secret.

> Then they become sober after their intoxication. They enjoy the sweetness of the look and witnessing. How sweet a drink and how excellent a Path!

It is the same as it says in the Diwan: Joy to the one who walks on the path of Allah.

> Offering one's life to achieve it is paltry, and expending spirits and lifeblood to obtain it is a mere trifle. How excellent is what the speaker said:

> > If my blood is spilled
> > to achieve what You desire,
> > a mere glance from You
> > makes shedding my blood not dear.

> Among those who have obtained precedence in this area, and who had a portion and importance in this Secret, were the Prophets and the Messengers, peace and blessings be upon them. The greatest of them in that was the master of mankind, our Lord, the best blessings and purest peace be upon him,

since the secrets overflowed from the sea of this secret and their lights spilt from the sun of his light. All of them took a handful from the sea of the Messenger of Allah or a drink of his rain.

Then the elite Awliya and pure friends inherited that from him. They strove against their lower selves with various forms of discipline and exerted themselves in seeking their Beloved to the utmost. They were true to their Lord in their behaviour and refused their portions and appetites, and so they obtained the greatest legacy after realising the ascription of spiritual kinship, clear evidence of witnessing the contract of love and the rulings connected to company – the rulings connected to company being the adab necessary among the people doing the dhikr – and the emergence of the sperm drop of concern from the loins of Wilaya whose veins are in the placenta of the will and then the manifestation of the foetus of happiness.

In other words, it is like a giving birth to something completely new, which is this gnosis.

Then it grows in the nest of the people of

gnosis between the parents of watchfulness and striving. Then it is nourished by the milk of the knowledge of certainty to the time of his weaning by witnessing the Lord of the Worlds.

So he makes a complete metaphor of this to the birth and growth of a child.

This is the knowledge inherited from the Prophets, peace be upon them. It is not the Tawhid which is a result of proof and evidence and subject to increase and decrease since doubts and illusions occur to such a person which are impossible in respect of the Prophets, peace be upon them.

One of those who grasped this high legacy and splendid Secret was the Sultan of the Lovers and Imam of the intelligent, the sovereign gnostic and eternal sage, the honour of the Deen, Abu Ja'far 'Umar ibn 'Ali ibn al-Murshid known as Ibn al-Farid as-Sa'di, Egyptian by residence, birth and death. He was the wonder of his time and unique in his age and among his contemporaries. He was born in 576 AH in Cairo and he died there in 632 AH. He is buried at the foot of the Muqattam outside

Cairo. There is an immense tomb built over him and it is a well-known site for people to visit. May Allah give us the benefit of his blessings.

His Qasida in Mim which we want to discuss is known as the Khamriyya, the Song of Wine. Indeed its words are sweeter than wine and it has a more fluid style. Only a Malakuti tongue and a Jabaruti tongue could articulate it. In it the poet goes to great lengths to praise the pre-eternal wine, and in it he displays the secrets of the unseen reality – the unseen Haqiqat – and removes the cover of protection from the secrets of His Jabarut and the lights of His Malakut. May Allah repay him with the best repayment! He made perceptions easier to understand and clarified the paths using the most succinct expressions and most eloquent indication.

We desired by Allah's help to explain its words in brief and to unravel its meanings after doing the Istikhara of the Prophet and spiritual Ishara. This is the time to begin this composition relying on the strength and power of Allah and what Allah has opened of the gifts of His grace.

I start by Him. Ibn al-Farid said:

شَرِبْنَا عَلَى ذِكْرِ الحَبِيبِ مُدَامَةً
سَكِرْنَا بِهَا مِنْ قَبْلِ أَنْ يُخْلَقَ الكَرْمُ

After remembering the Beloved,
we drank a wine by which we
were intoxicated before the vine
was created.

This is the very famous opening line of the Khamriyya.

The words 'mudam' and 'mudama' are both
names for wine, because the Arabs used to
like to have it constantly with them and
so they called it that for good luck. The
root of the verb means 'to last'. The word
'karm' is used for the vine and the grapes
themselves. He, may Allah be pleased with
him, said, 'After remembering the Beloved,
with our hearts and spirits we drank a pure
wine in the station of purity by which we
were intoxicated, and so we were absent
to sensation and we saw the lights of the
Beloved in everything.'

This intoxication involves the vanishing of the body,
of the experience of the body – the body contains the

evidences of the Attributes, because we have speech, hearing, sight, will, life, knowing, touch – all the senses, all the sensory reality, and like the one who is getting drunk, they leave him, they slip away from him. Thus the one calling on Allah with love for Allah, begins to lose all his attributes. He begins to lose his seeing and his hearing and his touch so that step by step he becomes disembodied. He leaves the body behind. Then he has to leave consciousness behind.

So, he says:

> **After remembering the Beloved, with our hearts and spirits we drank a pure wine in the station of purity –**

– the station of purity being in other words where there is no other. If there is an 'other' then there is not the station of purity. The station of purity means that you are vanishing –

> **by which we were intoxicated, and so we were absent to sensation and we saw the lights of the Beloved in everything.**

What has been otherness, becomes manifest lights of Allah. Otherness is illusion. Everything masiwallah, everything other-than-Allah is illusion. The only reality is the reality of Allah. He has made this appear bil-Haqq, so when the things disappear the Haqq manifests. This is not like the hindus who think it is all illusion, no, because Allah has created everything bil-Haqq but He is not in it. He is not in it, He is not above it, He is not under it – nothing is associated with Him, but He has related it bil-Haqq and it is into this knowledge that the 'Arif is able to step without putting one foot wrong because the slave is the slave and the Rabb is the Rabb. Ibn 'Ajiba comments:

> **We were absent to sensation and we saw the lights of the Beloved in everything. He is with everything and before everything and after everything. Intoxication made us absent to the darkness of temporal beings –**

– the reality of people and temporal beings and things which exist in the world –

> **and we saw the lights of enduring timelessness.**

Shaykh Ibn 'Ajiba gives his poem on the same subject:

> **I indicated this meaning in my poem in 'Ayn in which I said:**

We were intoxicated and wandered
    in the radiance of His beauty
And withdrew from sensation
    while the light was shining.
The sun of the day
    appeared to us and shone:
The light of the star does not remain
    when the sun is shining.

The shining sun is Divine light.

Ibn al-Farid, may Allah be pleased with him, said that this intoxication by the pre-eternal spiritual wine occurred to us before the existence of the vine from which physical wine comes. Ash-Shustari, who was a great Sufi from Morocco, indicated this meaning when he said:

Not the drink of past cups
    passed around.
They are terrestrial.
Its wine is other than my wine:
    my wine is pre-eternal.

All these Americans now take this Sufic poetry and try to make out that really these Sufis were lovely Muslims who used to get drunk. There are books in universities published to this effect! Whereas here, ash-Shustari is not talking about the drink of past cups passed around which are earthly. **Its wine is other than my wine: my wine is pre-eternal.**

Again, Shaykh Ibn 'Ajiba says:

> **This intoxication by the pre-eternal spiritual wine occurred to us before the existence of the vine from which physical wine comes.**

We go back to the first line of the Song:

> **After remembering the Beloved, we drank a wine by which we were intoxicated before the vine was created.**

His words, 'by which we were intoxicated before the vine was created', can mean that this intoxication was after the appearance of the world of forms and that the spirit became intoxicated at the mention of the Beloved with pre-eternal wine before the manifestation of the vine from which comes the terrestrial sensory wine. What is meant is that he was intoxicated with the spiritual wine before the manifestation of the matter of physical wine. It is possible that this intoxication was experienced by the spirit before time in the world of spirits before the manifestation of the world of the forms, and so his words, 'before the vine was created' mean its manifestation, i.e. before the manifestation of the matter of physical wine. That is supported by his words that come later, "I had rapture from it before I was formed."

So when this thing happened to the Faqir in his calling on Allah, at that moment in time of whatever age he may have been in, he was actually tapping in to something that had already happened to him before the existence of the world. His dhikr is his remembering his worship of Allah, subhanahu wa ta'ala, before the creation of existence. This goes back to the Ayat of Qur'an where Allah called all the spirits of the human beings and said to them (Qur'an 7:172):

$$\text{أَلَسْتُ بِرَبِّكُمْ}$$

"Am I not your Lord?" And all the spirits replied, "Yes." So it is a remembering of this pre-existent glorification of Allah. Shaykh Ibn 'Ajiba says that we will go into this when this other line appears.

The first interpretation is more apparent, and Allah knows best. Absence in Allah is called intoxication because it shares with physical intoxication in being absent from sensation. As the light of the intellect is veiled by the darkness of clay – that is the body – which is the intoxication which grows from physical wine, so it is veiled by lights of meaning which come to him suddenly from the pre-eternal wine and renders him absent from sensation. That is why they called that absence "intoxication", and Allah knows best.

That is the beginning of this subject and, inshallah, we will pursue it. In the meantime I want you to acquaint yourselves with these terms that are in The Hundred Steps and in other places, so that you know Mulk, Malakut and Jabarut, and Nasut, Lahut and Rahamut. Now we will sing 'Reflection' from the Diwan of Shaykh Muhammad ibn al-Habib.

REFLECTION

Reflect upon the beauty of the way in which
both land and sea are made,
and contemplate the Attributes of Allah
outwardly and inwardly.

The greatest evidence
of the limitless perfections of Allah
can be found both deep within the self
and on the distant horizon.

If you were to reflect on physical bodies
and their marvellous forms
and how they are arranged with great precision,
like a string of pearls –

And if you were to reflect on the secrets
of the tongue and its capacity for speech,
and how it articulates and conveys
what you conceal in your breast –

And if you were to reflect
on the secrets of all the limbs
and how easily they are subject
to the heart's command –

And if you were to reflect on how the hearts
are moved to obey Allah
and how at other times
they move darkly to disobedience –

And if you were to reflect on the earth
and the diversity of its plants
and the great variety
of the smooth and rugged land in it –

And if you were to reflect
on the secrets of the oceans and all their fish,
and their endless waves
held back by an unconquerable barrier –

And if you were to reflect
on the secrets of the many winds
and how they bring the mist,
fog and clouds which release the rain –

And if you were to reflect
on all the secrets of the heavens –
the Throne and the Footstool
and the spirit sent by the Command –

Then you would accept the reality of Tawhid
with all your being,
and you would turn away from illusions,
uncertainty and otherness,

And you would say,
"My God, You are my desire, my goal
and my impregnable fortress
against evil, injustice, and deceit.

You are the One I hope will provide
for all my needs,
and You are the One Who rescues us
from all evil and wickedness.

You are the Compassionate,
the One Who answers all who call upon You.
And You are the One Who enriches
the poverty of the Faqir.

It is to You, O Exalted,
that I have raised all my request,
so swiftly bring me the Opening,
the rescue and the Secret, O my God."

By the rank of the one in whom we hope
on the day of distress and grief –
that terrible day when people come
to the Place of Gathering.

May Allah's blessings be upon him
as long as there is an 'Arif
who reflects on the lights of His Essence
in every manifestation,

And upon his family and Companions
and everyone who follows
his excellent Sunna in all its prohibitions
and commands.

II

FEBRUARY 11ᵀᴴ 2006

We will continue where we left off last Saturday. I would just like to emphasise to you that what we have been doing is not just something that we started last week. What we have arrived at is a point where you must recognise that this gathering is not the same as it was when we began in Al-Jami'a Mosque in Claremont. In other words, in that time, we have studied together in great depth the Qur'an in finding a correct definition of what is Tawhid. At another time we examined the Surat al-Waqi'a.

Now we are beginning to go into the depths of what you might call the Sufic doctrine, the Sufic sciences.

This gathering, this process of the dhikr from the beginning of the recitation of Qur'an and then the Wird, then the singing of the Diwan and the Hadra and the Discourse – all these begin to alter the state of the Faqir. You should be taking advantage of this and using this so that now, in the practice of the dhikr, you should not be like the youth who is looking here and looking there distractedly by whatever movement of whoever comes in and goes out, but instead you should be watching inwardly to your own heart. Unless that is happening, in a sense, it is of no value.

The Sufis of the east tell different stories about how the people of the Path have different levels. Some like the Path because of the robes and the tasbihs, some like it because of the beautiful singing, but among them are those people who want that their heart should come to life. When Shaykh al-'Alawi went to his Shaykh, Shaykh al-Buzidi, he said to him, "Construct me a heart." This is what this is for. This is like a scientific arena where you have to shut out the world. You cannot have telephones ringing and people twitching and moving and watching. You have to have people who are sitting still.

One of the Shuyukh used to say, "Lower your eyes. Fold your hands. Bow your heads. If one of you moves I will get up and leave you." It was his need that the Fuqara should reach a state of intensity in their concentration in order that they get benefit from the dhikr. What you want now to happen is that the heart, which has been pumping blood to the head, should now begin to awaken for the highest of things. The heart is always awake for the things of dunya. The heart is a magnet which draws the things of dunya, halal or haram, whatever they are – it draws them to you and they come to you by the destiny. But the Fuqara are the ones who want to become enlightened, to be filled up. This is what this gathering is for.

Now we are looking at the science of it, the explanation of it, so that you will benefit from it in the singing of the dhikr. In continuing his commentary, Shaykh Ibn 'Ajiba says:

> There are some terms which are used by the Ahl as-Sufiyya. We will mention some of them upon which the understanding of the words of the poet depend.

In other words, you need these words to understand Ibn al-Farid's Khamriyya which we have been looking at.

> These words include: Dhawq, Shurb, Sukr, and Sahw, as well as the Sensory and the Meaning, Power and Wisdom, Wajd, Wujdan and Wujud, and Jam' and Tafriqa.

We will look at these terms.

> Dhawq is Tasting. It is the shining of the lights of the timeless Essence on the intellect so that it withdraws from seeing temporality in the lights of timelessness, but that does not last. It sometimes shines and flashes and at other times is hidden. When it flashes, he withdraws from his senses. When it is concealed, he returns to his senses and seeing himself. They call this Dhawq.

> If that light lasts for an hour or two, it is called Shurb – Drinking. When it continues and lasts, then it is called Sukr – Intoxication. It derives from the annihilation of forms in witnessing the Living, the Self-Sustaining, and withdrawing from effects, in other words, from existent things, by witnessing the Effector – the One Who makes things happen. You withdraw from what there is by witnessing the One Who makes what is, be. It is also called Fana' – Annihilation.

These are processes. Ibn 'Ajiba says that Dhawq is Tasting. It is the shining of the lights of the timeless Essence on the intellect so that it withdraws from seeing temporality in the lights of timelessness.

What he is indicating is the whole process, both in the circle of the dhikr and in Muraqaba, when you are alone calling on Allah in the night on what Ibn al-'Arabi calls 'the Carpet of Courtesy.'

What overwhelms the seeker is this illumination that sometimes shines in flashes and then is sometimes hidden. When it flashes, the person gets to where he loses the five senses of sight, hearing and touch and so on, but also the sense that he is there at all. But when it is concealed then he comes back to his senses and he sees himself. This is called Dhawq. Shaykh Ibn 'Ajiba then expands it and says: **If that light lasts for an hour or two, it is called Shurb – Drinking.** In other words, in that state of losing the body and losing the presence of the dunya in the presence of the lights, if that continues it is called Shurb – Drinking.

What is interesting is that he uses these terms at this depth. You will find in al-Hujwiri for example and the great writings of these other Sufis, that they apply these terms to what you might call lighter states of experiencing the Presence of Allah. But he sees it as going deep into the loss of the nafs. He then goes on to say about Dhawq becoming Sukr:

It derives from the annihilation of forms in witnessing the Living, the Self-Sustaining and withdrawing from effects by witnessing

the Effector – withdrawing from all the stuff by the One Who makes the stuff happen. It is also called Fana' – Annihilation.

Thus he sees it as being something that takes one directly to that condition in the Khalwa when you are completely alone and you lose all consciousness, and you lose the consciousness that you have lost consciousness.

If he returns to the establishment of things by Allah and their being sustained by Him, and he sees them as one of His lights, having no existence with Him, that is called Sahw – Sobriety. It is also called Baqa' – Going-On – in other words, you are annihilated, then you return. The return is that you go on, and that is slavehood, that is 'ubudiyya – since things go on by Allah after they have been annihilated by His Light as insight in Allah. The author of the Hikam, Shaykh Ibn 'Ata'illah, the great Sufi of Egypt, indicated this meaning when he said: 'The light of the inner eye, the basira, lets you see His nearness to you. The source of the inner eye lets you see your non-existence by your existence. The truth, the Haqq of the inner eye lets you see His existence, not your own non-existence or existence. Allah was and there was nothing with Him. He is now as He was.'

This is the core of the Sufic experience. Let us look at it again. **The Nur of the basira lets you see His nearness to you. The 'Ayn, the source of the basira lets you see your non-existence by your existence.** That is that you have your existence, but by it you see that you are non-existent. **The Haqq of the basira lets you see His existence, not your own non-existence or existence.** So both of these knowledges vanish in the Haqq of the basira. In that he says, **Allah was and there was nothing with Him. He is now as He was.** This was also called by al-Hujwiri and the Sufis of the east Fana' in the Fana'. The annihilation has in it a knowledge that you are annihilated and then there is a complete disappearance of the experiencing locus, you might say. This is where Mawlay al-'Arabi a-Darqawi says, "If the universe disappears, Allah has to appear." Nothing exists except the Haqq. Shaykh Ibn 'Ajiba continues:

> **He also says in explanation of intoxication and sobriety and clarification of the Shari'at and the Reality:** – referring back to Shaykh Ibn 'Ata'illah – **Then there is the one who possesses inner reality. He has withdrawn from creation by seeing the Real King. He is annihilated to causes by seeing the Maker of causes. This is the slave who is face-to-face with the reality and its radiance is manifest on him. He travels the Path and**

has mastered its dimensions. However, he is drowned in the lights and the traces of creation have been wiped out to him. His intoxication dominates his sobriety. His gatheredness dominates his separation.

Gatheredness is that all the things are just one thing. If you take again the metaphor of the drunken person, he loses awareness of the separateness of things. If you take the opposite, separation, it is our consciousness that the glass is the glass and the jug is the jug. Remember that pain, which is a kind of opposite of all this, is when you are acutely separate. You are acutely aware of the finger or the knee that has been wounded. It is like you are utterly aware of its otherness to the rest of your body. That is an acute example of separateness. But separateness is that which knows that each person who is sitting here is different. The one who is in the dhikr begins to get this loss of the nafs so that the nafs becomes illuminated, then slowly all the people become undifferentiated, they become the same. It is like when you are at sea, everything is just ocean. **His intoxication dominates his sobriety. His gatheredness dominates his separation.** Then he says:

His annihilation dominates his going-on. His absence dominates his presence. More perfect than him is the slave who drinks and is increased in sobriety. He withdraws,

and it increases him in presence. And here
we have the key sentence – **His Gatheredness
does not veil him from his separation and
his separation does not veil him from
his gatheredness. His annihilation does
not keep him from his going-on and his
going-on does not divert him from his
annihilation. He gives everything with a
due its due and he gives everyone with a
portion his full portion.**

What Shaykh Ibn 'Ata'illah is seeing is a perfection of
a knowledge. Let us go back a step. In the ordinary
experience of ordinary life, we have, as it were, ninety-
nine percent consciousness of the outward things and
one tiny percent is aware that there is another dimension.
The most you go from the seen to the Unseen is in
perception of character – that when you face a human
being, if you have any quality of an intellect and an
inwardness, when you see that person you get some
knowledge of something that is not visible. You have
just one crossover into what we call the earthly Unseen.
Not the heavenly Unseen, but the earthly Unseen.

The whole process of the circle of dhikr and the whole
process of the Khalwa is because we are so drenched in
dunya that the only break we actually get from dunya
on a quotidian basis is Salat. The Salat is the break. Every
Muslim, the minute he makes Salat, that is what the

Sufi is. He has put the world behind him when he says: "Allahu Akbar." The great example is of Sayyiduna 'Ali, karamullahu wajhahu, who was in sajda and the wall of the mosque collapsed, and he did not know it until he made the taslim and saw it. He had turned from the world completely in his worship of Allah, subhanahu wa ta'ala.

What we are saying is that one has to arrive at a point where this outward reality that is so dominant vanishes. The interesting thing is that it does not 'vanish' as such, it does not disappear, it is there. So look what happens – to reach a successful result of the science of Tasawwuf, the annihilation that is desired is to put the outward and the inward in absolute balance. If you just make everything vanish, declaring that 'this is all unreal', then you are a Majdhub, you are a like a madman. There is a nothingness because the world does not exist any more!

What we are talking about is a consciousness that by its withdrawal, withdrawal and withdrawal into the lights, the outward and the inward become balanced. When they are completely balanced then they are not opposite. They are not there. That is why saying "Men and women are equal" cannot be true, because if men and women are equal then there are no men and women. There are just human units. There has to be difference in order for there to be existence. What is desired is this balance between the two, so that after the annihilation there is an understanding of the Mulk which is created existence, and the Malakut which is the unseen existence, having become perfectly balanced, and this is what the interspace is. It is the Jabarut, which is the power of Allah, subhanahu wa ta'ala, and the knowledge of Unity. We go back and read again Shaykh Ibn 'Ajiba quoting the Hikam of Shaykh Ibn 'Ata'illah:

> Then there is the one who possesses inner reality. He has withdrawn from creation by seeing the Real King. He is annihilated to causes by seeing the Maker of causes. This is the slave who is face-to-face with the Reality and its radiance is manifest on him. He travels the Path and has mastered its dimensions. However, he is drowned in the lights and the traces of creation have been wiped out to him. His intoxication dominates his sobriety. His gatheredness dominates his separation. His annihilation dominates his going-on. His absence dominates his presence. More perfect than him – here we have the science of Imam al-Junayd of our Tariqa – is the slave who drinks and is increased in sobriety. He withdraws, and it increases him in presence.
>
> His gatheredness does not veil him from his separation and his separation does not veil

> him from his gatheredness. **His Fana' does
> not keep him from his Baqa', and his Baqa'
> does not divert him from his Fana'. He gives
> everything with a due its due and he gives
> everyone with a portion his full portion.**

This means that when he comes back from this
experience, he then has a completely other relationship
to existence. **He gives everything with a due its
due and he gives everyone with a portion his full
portion.** This is why the cleaning of the nafs and the
dominating of the nafs is the duty of the Faqir, because
if you have resentment, if you have enemies you will
be held back. I am not talking about people who are
the enemies of Allah and that you have to fight them
because you know that everything will be given its due.
If you obey Allah then you will take on your enemies
by Allah. The modern people are not taking on their
enemies by Allah, they are taking them on for the causes
they care about.

He gives everyone with a portion his full portion.
Therefore he sees that the other in his otherness is who
he is, and you have to accept that that is who he is. It
does not mean that the Shari'at will not take its place –
the murderer will be arrested and judged, but you will
see everyone with a clear eye. Do you understand the
difference of this? This is why there can never be someone
you cannot forgive. You can never have something that

is unfinished, unless you leave it unfinished and don't care, so that you spit on it. It has to not matter. When it does not matter, it will anyway right itself in your own life, in your own existence. The test of the nafs is if it matters to you. If the nafs has conquered it, then it is the same whether it is a yes or a no. It is the same if they go or if they stay.

The importance of the Shari'at is that the Shari'at dominates the Haqiqat, not the other way around. The Shari'at must be given its due. The Shari'at must be given its weight. Otherwise you would make personal judgments, and not the judgments of what Allah has decreed as acceptable and not acceptable, what is approved and what is not approved and so on.

We go back to these terms. He says:

As for Wajd – Ecstasy –

Remember that the purpose of reciting the Wird is in order that you should receive Warid. By the end of the Wird, already the heart should have started to move. There should be commotion of the heart by the recitation of the Wird, because the Wird is what leads to the Warid, and the Warid is an opening.

As for Wajd – Ecstasy, it is a Warid that comes and moves the hearts and unsettles

**them. It is either an unsettling anxiety that
provokes expansion and joy, or a disquieting
fear that provokes contraction and sorrow.**

In the first stages of the Faqir's Path, the effect of the
dhikr will be this unsettling. He will be unsettled. This
may make him delighted and full of joy, or it may
make him troubled and contracted. He will either be
in contraction or expansion. There were two Fuqara
in the Zawiyya of Shaykh Muhammad ibn al-Habib,
rahimahullah, and one was white as though he had
had a shock. He was the whitest man you have ever
seen! And the other was jet black. They were the closest
friends and they always sat together – the whitest white
man and the blackest black man. In the dhikr, the old
gentleman with the white beard and the white face
would always start to cry, and his friend who sat with
him, this black gentleman, the minute the dhikr began
he began to smile and a look of absolute joy came over
his face. As the dhikr went on, as the singing of Diwan
went on, the one would be weeping and weeping and
the other would be smiling and smiling, and the Fuqara
used to debate which one had a higher place with Allah,
subhanahu wa ta'ala, because it was such a powerful
condition which came over them, but they were in what
is called the Wajd, which is that thing which happens in
the Faqir in this stage of his journey. Shaykh Ibn 'Ajiba
continues:

As for Wujdan, it is the enduring of the sweetness of witnessing and its connection to the one experiencing it while intoxication and astonishment predominate. It is Wujud. Imam al-Junayd, radiyallahu 'anhu, indicated this when he said, "My existence is that I withdraw from existence by what appears to me of witnessing."

So when illumination comes to him, his existence is his withdrawing from existence.

Know that what causes Wajd is listening to the words of the Beloved – to Allah, subhanahu wa ta'ala – and the cause of Wujud is witnessing the beauty of the Beloved. The state may dominate them, and their forms are compelled and dance, following the agitation of the heart. An illustration of that is a child in the cradle. It becomes still when the cradle moves and weeps when it is still. That is how it is with the heart that is at rest when the heart is moved. Otherwise it is unsettled. The stillness might leave it immediately.

As for someone in ecstasy, he is firm and settled. He is intimate with the Presence and so astonishment and confusion departs and he is like a firm mountain. Imam al-Junayd was asked, "What is it with you? You used to show ecstasy when listening to the dhikr, to the Diwan, to the singing, and you used to do the Hadra, and then you changed so that nothing of you moves?" He replied with this Ayat of Qur'an from Surat An-Naml (27:88):

وَتَرَى ٱلْجِبَالَ تَحْسَبُهَا جَامِدَةً وَهِىَ تَمُرُّ مَرَّ ٱلسَّحَابِ

You will see the mountains you reckoned to be solid going past like clouds.

In other words, he was outwardly like the mountain that appears to be solid, but inside he was being blown away like clouds. This is the state of this great Wali of Allah. Thus the metaphor of the child in the cradle is the metaphor of the Fuqara in the Hadra. The Hadra is to bring this sweetness and enchantment and delight to the heart so that these knowledges can begin to enter.

Evidence for that is found in the companions of Yusuf, 'alayhi salam. When he appeared to them suddenly with his radiant beauty, they lost their senses and "they cut their hands and said, 'Allah preserve us! This is no man.'" Surat Yusuf (12:31) When that continued with Zulaykha, she did not do any of that. That is the case with the masters of Wujdan. When they looked towards the light of the Presence, they were astonished and withdrew from their sensation. When they were firm in witnessing it and at home in it, not one of its lights moved them. The witnessing of beauty dominates the 'Arif and he dances and delights, but that is rare, and Allah Almighty knows best.

The dance is in order to allow the heart to reach these conditions of delight, but he is indicating that there is a point at which, precisely with this knowledge, the condition of Imam al-Junayd becomes your condition, where, if you are sitting still you are the mountain, while in fact you are being blown away like clouds. This is part of the knowledge of Tasawwuf.

III

FEBRUARY 18TH 2006

We were looking at the technical terms which Shaykh ibn 'Ajiba defines in his Commentary on the Khamriyya of Ibn al-Farid, radiyallahu 'anhu. We were looking at Dhawq, Shurb, Sukr, Sahw, Wajd, Wujdan and Wujud, and we will come to Jam' and Tafriqa. Let us first listen again to the opening four lines of the Khamriyya:

شَرِبْنَا عَلَى ذِكْرِ الحَبِيبِ مُدَامَةً

سَكِرْنَا بِهَا مِنْ قَبْلِ أَنْ يُخْلَقَ الكَرْمُ

لَهَا البَدْرُ كَأْسٌ وَهِيَ شَمْسٌ يُدِيرُها

هِلالٌ وَكَمْ يَبْدُو إِذَا مُزِجَتْ نَجْمُ

189

All that we have been looking at is the Commentary on the very first two lines of the Khamriyya:

> **After remembering the Beloved, we drank a wine by which we were intoxicated before the vine was created.**

Now we come to two very important terms. Again, you will take benefit from this gathering if you are studying them in 'The Hundred Steps'. The book will give you a deeper and more considered definition of these terms. These terms are Jam' and Farq, in the form of Tafriqa. Shaykh Ibn 'Ajiba says:

> **As for gatheredness and separation, gatheredness – Jam' – designates the disappearance of the temporal into the affirmation of the timeless, or you could say that it designates the adding of the branches to their roots, and so what is not is annihilated and what goes on continues.**

Gatheredness – Jam' – designates the disappearance of the temporal into the affirmation of the timeless, in other words, Jam' is that condition of the Faqir in the Khalwa or in the circle of dhikr where the experience of the stuff of existence, of the bodies, of the things, all begins to become like just one thing, as if you were under water, and everything under water is part of the water like the fish and the seaweed and all these things – they are all in one unified experience. So the Faqir begins to feel himself stop not at the ends of his fingers and his knees, but that he is somehow connected to all of it. It does not stop with his body, it is as if he fills the whole thing.

In the circle of dhikr, it is love that is awakening. The heart of the seeker of knowledge is moving towards the Janna he is yearning for. He breaks the bonds of separation and there awakens in him, love.

The healthy love of the child is for himself. If a child knocks on your door and you say, "Who's there?" he says: "Me!" Because that is the station of the child. But the kafirun keep that station until they are dead. There is a point where this love spills out and the first love is for the Fuqara. Abu Madyan the Ghawth said of the Fuqara: "When will my ear hear news of them, when will my eye have sight of them? They are the Sultans, they are the Kings!" This love of the Fuqara dominates.

So this first stage of intoxication is really just the coming out of the body. But then it is also the keeping of the beard. The beard is the badge of Nabawiyya. So it is at this point where, as it were, when you look at the Fuqara, every Faqir has the face of Rasul, sallallahu 'alayhi wa sallam. It is like you are aware of the Muhammadan presence among all the Fuqara. They only have this by love of Rasul, sallallahu 'alayhi wa sallam. This is what lets you come out from yourself and into the sea of the presence of the Fuqara. And this is just the beginning of this drowning, of this Jam', this gatheredness.

It happens in stages and I want to give you an example of this – I have never told anyone this: I was once in the circle with Shaykh Muhammad ibn al-Habib, rahimahullah, and at the mealtime he told me that after the dhikr people should not be frivolous. They should not laugh with their mouths open and talk silly talk – they can talk about serious or light-hearted matters but they should not come out from themselves and lose their intellect. They must guard what happens in the dhikr. Again, many of the secrets of knowledge come when you are eating together with the Fuqara. They say that the Baraka is in the food. If people come to the dhikr and leave before the meal, then there is actually something they have not tasted and it is not the food. This is the fact of the unity of the brotherhood.

Now, I was sitting at the table, as I told you, with Shaykh Muhammad ibn al-Habib, and there came upon me this state where I began to feel this extraordinary love for all the people who were there at table. Then I suddenly looked and I saw that one man didn't have any grapes. We had all been given some grapes but he did not have any, so I took my grapes and I put my grapes in front of him, but the minute I did that, Shaykh Muhammad ibn al-Habib, without looking, took his grapes and FLUNG them across the table and they landed right in front of me, so the grapes had gone to my brother and the next thing they were there in front of me. And at that point I was gone. Do you see? Gone. There is a trigger moment and it comes from your concentration. It comes from the concentration in the Diwan, concentration in the Wird, an intensity of inner concentration on your own heart that allows the possibility that Allah may choose to manifest lights to the Faqir.

So this is Jam', that point where you and the brothers and the Shaykh – it is all one unified state of existence, and that continues and continues until all the phenomenal beings, all the stuff, all these people are in the end like dust in water, and you do not differentiate anything any more. Those are the stages of Jam'.

You come to another point where these conditions of togetherness and separateness and unification are joined.

> Gatheredness – Jam' – designates the disappearance of the temporal into the affirmation of the timeless, or you could say that it designates the adding of the branches to their roots, and so what is not is annihilated and what goes on continues.

That is where knowing that we are in the world of separate things, and also this intoxication, become balanced.

> Separation – Tafriqa – or Farq – is an expression that designates the affirmation of rulings and wisdom, establishing the form or slavedom and the adab with lordship. The place of gatheredness is the inward and the place of separation is the outward since lordship without slavedom is imperfect and slavedom without lordship is impossible. That is why they say, "Gatheredness without separation is heresy since it invalidates rulings and wisdom, and separation without gathering is deviance since it removes the person from the definition of perfection. Combining them is the source of perfection."

You must recognise that the underlying statement of the people of Tasawwuf, the underlying statement of the people of Al-Ash'ari, the underlying statement of the Imams of the Fiqh, is that the Shari'at dominates but there must be Haqiqat. You must also remember that the Shari'at dominates because the Shari'at is low and the Haqiqat is high, and what is low always dominates what is high. Ibn 'Ajiba says that **combining them is the source of perfection.** He continues:

III

I heard the Shaykh of our Shaykh say, "Some people have Shari'at and no Tasawwuf, some people have Tasawwuf and no Shari'at, and some people make the Shari'at a door and the Haqiqat several doors.

أُوْلَٰٓئِكَ حِزْبُ ٱللَّهِ أَلَآ إِنَّ حِزْبَ ٱللَّهِ هُمُ ٱلْمُفْلِحُونَ ٢٢

Such people are the party of Allah.
Truly it is the party of Allah who are successful.
(Qur'an 58:22)

These are the first words I heard from him when I met him. He said to me, "You are part of the third category." May Allah make us realise their love and provide us with adab with them. Amin.

As for the physical, it is an expression about what is dense and appears among created things. The meaning designates the subtle internal light in them. As for the secret by which things are established, the sensory is a description of the meaning.

This is very important. The sensory is a description of the meaning.

Created beings are vessels that bear meaning.

This again is a very important aspect of understanding what happens to the Faqir when he starts to call on Allah. And that is that everything that is created in the sensory world is a meaning set up in a form. We live in a world where the form contains the meaning. In the Next World, in the Unseen, it is the opposite. The unseen world is a non-spatial reality where the meaning manifests as form. After your death and when we are risen on the Yawm al-Qiyama – the rising of the spirits in the bodies of men is in the realm of meanings but those meanings are experienced as sensory. Every thing in Qur'an tells you that the experience of the Afterlife is tasted, does it not? Gardens under which rivers flow, youths, beautiful girls – all these things are experienced in the realm of meanings as sensory. This means therefore that as you live in THIS realm, which is all sensory, you have to recognise the meaning. You have to interpret the whole of existence because it is all meaning set up by Allah for you to discriminate between the things and know what they mean.

Now, the point is that it is not something you project as if in a fantasy. It is that every experience in life has a meaning to it. Every encounter has a meaning to it. Remember that the Sufis say that the murderer and the murderee go into the same mosque and they find each other, they don't find someone else. The meaning of the one is the other. They find that reality.

In every Hadra I did with Shaykh Muhammad ibn al-Habib in Meknes and all the places we travelled to in Algeria and so on, I always considered that whoever was on my right and on my left, that was the condition I was in. I could not complain about it, I could not have bad feelings about it because that was me – this one and that one, that was 'me'. One day I found myself in the front of the Hadra between this Faqir and that Faqir and I was content because I knew: that is my condition. But if I am at the back and there is this funny one here and that funny one there then I must not complain: that is also for you to have adab and courtesy, and deal with that and bear with that and not push it away.

You have to interpret all the things that happen in an intelligent way, with furqan, because discrimination – that is wisdom – is discriminating between things. The foundation of wisdom is the Shari'at: this is halal and that is haram and then there are things where you say: Now look, that is dangerous. It is not forbidden but it is disapproved of. So there are zones, and you are moving all the time in various zones, and there are times when you have to say, "I have to get out of here!" for the protection of your heart.

Is there not an admonition of Rasul, sallallahu 'alayhi wa sallam, that you put something right by your actions?

If you see something wrong you put it right by your actions, and if you cannot do it by your actions you put it right by your tongue, and if you cannot put it right by your tongue then you have to deal with it in your heart. But what is important is not to be conquered by it. If you are not able to deal with it, it is because you should not be there in the first place.

Sometimes there is a great need in the heart. The heart in Arabic is 'qalb' and it comes from 'qalaba' which means to turn over. It is an instrument which is magnetic and it is turning over all the time, and what it is doing is drawing to you what you need. Now if you decide you need the haram it will bring you the haram, but if you desire a wise companion then it will bring you a wise companion. Then you begin to touch on the meaning of the destiny because the thing may be happening by your energy and by your actions but it is also what has been written for you in your destiny.

On one occasion I was coming home to the hotel in Tangiers from the Siddiqi Zawiyya and it was very late at night. We came down through the Kasbah, very hungry, and we got lost. It was two in the morning. Suddenly there was a door open and there was a room and in it there were three men, and there was a table set, and the man said, "Come in! Come in!" and he called us in. And so the two of us went in and the man said: "We've been waiting for you! We couldn't start until you came." But I had never seen them in my life! Then he said, "This food has been written for you since before the creation of the world. How could we start without you? Please, sit down. Bismillah." And we were fed. And I realised that every meal is like that.

This is an engagement you have with phenomenal beings, with the stuff of existence. This is certainty – certainty about Allah and certainty that in this world with its masses of different things, you are going to be alright, you are going to be safe. Allah is going to look after you more than you deserve. This understanding of the discrimination among things is the foundation of Tasawwuf.

> **Created beings are vessels that bear the meaning. Allah knows best.**
>
> **Power designates actions that issue from the Sublime Essence – from the Dhat – whether they are according to norms or outside of normal patterns. Wisdom designates the connection of causes to effects. Customs are those which normally occur.**

This is a very interesting thing he says. He says that custom is what usually happens. Certain things happen in a certain way, that is how they happen, but he then says, about the customs which normally occur:

They are the cloak of power and its covering.

The sameness of certain things happening in existence is the covering over with a cloak of power that makes things that way. Do you follow? So the things that happen, happen in the physical world. Allah has set up the whole physical universe according to laws, and these laws are in operation all the time. We take them for granted.

It is like the earthquake in Kashmir. These Muslims are calling on Allah, and not recognising His Decree. The laws of geophysics are HIS laws, and He set it up that way. And He set it up that at a certain time it would crack and at that point that He sets it up to crack and for thousands to be killed, is the point at which the kafir is about to sign a treaty with India of adjoining and collaborating to give peace to Kashmir and to start this thing by which Pakistan will become the Northern Province of the Indian mushrik State. And Allah shakes the earth to destroy thousands of people to stop the loss of the Muslim enclave of the Indian subcontinent. It is like the story of Sayyiduna Musa where thousands of little children had to die in order for Musa to be put in the little basket. That had to happen.

So he says that **wisdom designates the connection of causes to effects. Customs are those which normally occur. But what normally occurs represents the** cloak of power and its covering.

> Whoever stops with the cloak of wisdom is
> veiled from witnessing the power. Whoever
> is veiled from the attribute is veiled from
> what is described since the existence of
> both is obliged. Recognition of these things
> in incumbent for the understanding of the
> Sufis.

You have to understand this. Now we come to the third
and fourth lines of the Khamriyya. Ibn al-Farid says:

> It has the full moon for a goblet,
> being a sun encircled by a crescent.
> When it is mixed, how many
> stars appear!

This is extraordinary. It has the full moon for a
goblet, being a sun encircled by a crescent. When
it is mixed, how many stars appear!

> He is saying, may Allah be pleased with
> him, that this pre-eternal wine has a goblet
> which is the moon of a special Tawhid.
> Anyone who is a mushrik by affirming
> otherness or by seeing things along with
> the Master does not drink from the wine of
> passion.

At this point, again, he is now talking inside the language of Tasawwuf for the people of Tasawwuf: **Anyone who is a mushrik by affirming otherness** – in other words, in this stage of knowledge, in this stage of the condition of the Faqir, he cannot affirm otherness. There is no 'other'. There is no otherness. There is no 'masiwallah'. In the famous question put to Rasul, sallallahu 'alayhi wa sallam, "Where was Allah before the creation of the universe?" he, sallallahu 'alayhi wa sallam, said: "Allah was, and there was nothing with him." And Imam al-Junayd added: "Is, as He was." So **anyone who is a mushrik by affirming otherness or by seeing things along with the Master does not drink from the wine of passion.**

> **You could say that whoever has a heart which is filled with love of things or is tempted by the goods of this world does not taste anything of this wine.**

In other words, for the Faqir it is not that there are all these lovely things and that he is denying himself. To be free of the dunya is not to deny it, it is that it does not matter. If you get it it does not matter, and if you do not get it it does not matter. It does not mean you are not going to weep at bad news, but although you may weep at the bad news, it is the same as the good news.

I was with Mawlay Abul-Qasim, and he said something

to me to which I replied lightly, "Alhamdulillah!" But it was like I had struck him in the face, because I had said it flippantly – "Alhamdulillah!" like that. Now if anyone else says it to me like that I get ill. He grabbed me by the arm, and he looked into my eyes and said with great gravity: "Na'am Sidi: AL-HAMDU-LI-LLAH!"

I remember Si Hammud of Blida who was a great Sufi and my first teacher when I was with Shaykh Muhammad ibn al-Habib, and whose song is in our Diwan, and he was brought the news that both his two sons had been killed in an accident. The first thing he did was to say, "Alhamdulillah." Then he got up and did two rak'ats. But he made himself praise Allah for the loss of his sons. It does not mean that the bad news is the same as the goods news. But it does mean that the good news is not made frivolous. You do not open your mouth and laugh so you can see the back of the throat. Someone used to say, the Sufi is the one who laughs at the funeral and cries at the wedding. This is the same meaning. He laughs at the funeral because the dead man is freed of all the troubles of the world while at the wedding, which is the heart of life, all the troubles are going to come. Over all this is the dhikr of 'Alhamdulillah 'ala kulli hal' – Alhamdulillah in every state.

Ibn 'Ajiba says:

This wine is the sun of gnosis. When it shines in the horizons of the heaven of the heart, it covers the existence of all beings and forms, and eye-witnessing occurs in which sources are absent. The crescent of happiness passes it around to the drinkers in the rising of the happiness and the will. If it is drunk pure, then intoxication withdraws from forms and only the lights of the Living, the Self-Sustaining remain seen. If it is mixed with sobriety and Suluk, then he becomes perfect.

In other words, the separation does not veil him from gatheredness and the gatheredness does not veil him from separation. He is then in the condition of Jabarut which is the Interspace between the Mulk and the Malakut. You balance the two worlds and then they have to disappear and that is what is called 'Fana' fillah.'

Then how many stars of knowledge will appear to him and how many of the treasures of understandings will be opened to him! When he has permission to express that, then hearts hear his words and his indication is disclosed to them.

This is what is called the Red Sulphur.

III

Shaykh Abul-Hasan ash-Shadhili, may Allah be pleased with him, said when speaking about love: 'The drink is the radiant light from the beauty of the Lover. The cup is the subtle kindness bringing that to the mouths of the hearts. The cupbearer is the one who undertakes that for the elite of the great and righteous – the Salihun – among Allah's slaves. It is Allah Who knows the decrees and the best interests of His slaves. Whoever has that beauty unveiled to him or is given something of it, a breath or two, and then has the veil lowered on him, tastes and yearns.

In other words whoever gets a bit of it, from then onwards you taste it and you want it, you want it, from then on you want it.

Someone who has that last for him for an hour or two is truly a drinker. Someone who has the matter continue for him and has the drink continue for him until his veins and joints are filled with the hidden lights of Allah, that is quenching. He may withdraw from the sensory and intellects and not know what is said nor what he says. That is intoxication. The cups are passed to him and the states vary for him. They are

returned to dhikr and acts of obedience, and they are not veiled from Attributes so that matters decreed are in conflict with one another.

Now this intoxication is illumination. When Shaykh Muhammad ibn al-Habib, rahimahullah, whose first Shaykh was in Tafilalet, at the point when he completed his journey he was in Khalwa, and when it happened to him he was like this description: **he had the drink continue for him until his veins and joints were filled with the hidden lights of Allah, that is quenching. He may withdraw from the sensory and intellects and not know what is said nor what he says. That is intoxication.** The Shaykh then staggered out into the streets. There were Fuqara sitting in the mosque near to the Zawiyya and someone rushed in and said "Shaykh Muhammad ibn al-Habib is mad! He is in the market place saying all these things!" And one man – nobody knew who he was until that moment – got up and rushed into the square where he was and took him, took him forcibly. The Fuqara did not know what to do. But this man took him to his house, shut the door and locked them out. He kept him there and then one day he came out. Allah puts these people there to complete the affair.

They are returned to dhikr and acts of obedience, and they are not veiled from Attributes so that

matters decreed are in conflict with one another.
Now, not being veiled from the Attributes is a seeing into
events, because events are matters which are in conflict
with one another. But if he discerns the Attributes – the
Divine power that lets these things happen, that makes
these things happen – he can see them. Therefore what
looks like conflict to everybody in the world does not
look like a conflict to him. Everybody in this day and
age wants to 'do' something. It is like this business
when they insulted Rasul, sallallahu alayhi wa sallam,
in those cartoons – the people went rushing into the
streets and there is chaos, but they make more chaos.
The real matter has to be decided by the Haqq of the
Shari'at so that from one aspect you cannot lift your
finger, so you do not do anything. The Sufis are tuned
to doing nothing because doing nothing may be the
right thing at that moment because the ones who are
doing something are not doing the right thing.

> That is the time of their sobriety, expansion
> of their sight and increase of their know-
> ledge, and so they are guided by the stars
> of knowledge and the moon of Tawhid in
> their night, and illuminated by the suns of
> their gnoses in their day. "Such people are
> the party of Allah. Truly it is the party of
> Allah who are successful." This is like the
> words of the poet. Then the poet, Ibn al-
> Farid, said:

**If it had not been
for its sweet fragrance,
I would not have been guided
to its tavern.
If it had not been
for its radiance,
imagination would not have
conceived it.**

We will stop there and, inshallah, we will continue. Now, we will open our Diwans and sing from The Lesser Qasida.

THE LESSER QASIDA

In the tavern of the Presence we drank a wine
of the lights that totally dispelled the darkness.

Through it we grasped that the act in every atom
is through its Creator
Who is worshipped everywhere.

We realised that Allah is manifest in everything
through His most Beautiful Names
and the secrets of power.

However, the states of existence are numerous,
and because of this great veils have fallen over wisdom,

And the Merciful has sent
the flower of His creation
as a bringer of good news and warner,
a guide with inner sight.

If you wish to obtain the gift of true happiness
then make him the guide
of your every thought and move.

Tell the impulses of the self: 'Do not come with me.
Do not cut off my path to the Lord of creation.'

Whoever has got dhikr, reflection and himma
will in every moment transcend otherness,

And he will attain gnosis beyond what he desires
and fast realise the secrets of existence.

He will see that separation is pure Shari'at,
which, properly speaking, is the source of Haqiqat.

This is why the Qur'an
commands mankind to reflect
and brings a Tawhid which eliminates any doubt.

The Merciful is only to be seen
in manifestations like the Throne, the Footstool,
the Tablet, or the Lote-Tree.

The intellect cannot grasp the nature
of the Attributes of the Lord
through unveiling, let alone realise
what nature itself is.

So attack the attributes of the self and efface them,
and you will be helped
by the lights of the eternal attributes.

Thus you will see lovers
who have become intoxicated by the lights,
and the drunkest lover is the one
who is given special licence.

There is no restriction
on what those utterly overwhelmed by Allah
may reveal, or on the people of idhn.

Here are ones who have obliterated their selves
and plumbed every depth in the oceans of love,

So submit to them for what you see
of their ardent love,
and the dancing and the singing
in their dhikr of the Beloved.

If you had but tasted something
of the meaning of our words,
you would already be experiencing every state

And, my brother,
you would have borne your troubles patiently,
and you would have rent the robes of shame
and self-importance,

You would have said to the leader of the people,
"Make us love His name!
There is no shame in that song, nor in that love!"

Unfortunately, whoever becomes subject
to his own self
remains aloof towards the secrets of this path.

The most hostile enemy of man is his self,
which hinders him from fully grasping the Haqiqat.

So become greater than the common people
if you desire reunion with Him,
and do not be satisfied
with a mere reputation of nobility.

Oh, the triumph of a people
who have answered the great call of the Beloved,
and so obtained the Garden!

By that I mean both gnosis
in the presence of nearness
and gnosis of the garden of rivers,
houris, and delight.

Let the one whose heart
has become devoid and empty
of gnosis in every thought weep over himself.

The joy of life without trouble, by my Lord,
is only found in the realisation of reunion.

Perhaps a glance will cure the sick man
of his sickness,
for the perception of the Essence of Haqiqat
is mighty.

My best time is when I am characterised by humility,
incapacity, poverty, and negation of the will.

For these are the foundations of our perfect path.
So follow it and avoid reputation
and self-importance.

Flee to the opposite of the Attributes of the Lord,
then by Allah's favour, you will be
the richest of creation.

His Attributes are encompassing knowledge,
and power,
and our attributes are ignorance
and less power than a particle of dust.

If you desire to reach the goal of all the gnostics,
then, O my companion, set out for it with himma.

Being a slave of Allah is sincere when it goes
along with giving the Lord what He wants
at every moment.

By slavedom I mean
being stripped of every power and strength
and any means, even getting things for yourself.

Because in this way the heart is purified of blindness
and is filled with lights in every thought.

The song is over.
Praise is due at the beginning and the end
for the gift of help from the Best of the Community.

May the blessings of Allah be upon him
and his family,
and his Companions, the people of Allah's care.

Its writer is known,
I mean Muhammad ibn al-Habib,
who seeks perfect slavehood.

So convey a fragrance to it, O Master of Generosity,
from You that will spread the effulgence of Haqiqat
over all beings.

IV

FEBRUARY 25TH 2006

We have been looking at the text of the Khamriyya by Ibn al-Farid and the commentary on it by Shaykh Ibn 'Ajiba, rahimahullah. You must understand that Shaykh Ibn 'Ajiba is one of the Shaykhs of our Tariqa. He was from Shaykh Mawlay al-'Arabi ad-Darqawi and of the same time as him. After all this time, he is only now beginning to be appreciated. He is actually one of the great giants among the scholars of Tasawwuf. He has written a very great commentary on the Qur'an which is a traditional commentary, while adding to it Ishara, ruhani insights into the Ayats, but he never plays with it. There is no Ta'wil in it, there is no interpreting things which should not be interpreted. In other words, the Shari'at laws he leaves alone to be the laws of Ahkam.

He also wrote a two-volume book just on the Fatiha, and then of course these very famous commentaries. He wrote the commentary, Al-Futuhat al-Ilahiyya fi Sharh al-Mabahith al-Asliyya – 'The Basic Research', on the great song of the Andalusian Sufic poet, Ibn al-Banna of Saragossa, which our people have already published and which you know.

The line we have come to in the Song of Ibn al-Farid is:

> If it had not been
>   for its sweet fragrance,
> I would not have been guided
>   to its tavern.
> If it had not been
>   for its radiance,
> imagination would not
>   have conceived it.

Shaykh Ibn 'Ajiba says:

> 'Shadha' is the perfumed breeze – the sweet fragrance. It says in the dictionary that Shadha is the strong scent. The tavern is the place in which wine is sold or drunk. The dictionary says that the 'Khan' refers to both the shop and its owner. The Khan is the merchant and the radiance is luminescence and light.

What he really means is that if it had not been for its radiance, the intellect could not have conceived it. It is not something that the intellect could have thought up or imagined, it is another kind of experience. He continues:

> This wine has a high value, and is sublime, subtle and hidden. So the spirits caught its scent and were attracted to the presence of the Knower of hearts. If it had not been for that, we would not be guided to its place nor have directed ourselves to seeking it, but when the crescent moon of guidance shone to us in the rising of prior Divine Concern, the breeze of election – this Divine awakening, you might say, of Allah's choosing the ones who will have this experience – **blew on our hearts from the immense Presence of Lordship, the Hadrat ar-Rabbani. Then we continued to follow its traces and inhale what diffuses from it until it brought us to witnessing of the lights of the Beloved and the intimate conversation of the Near – the Qarib, in the place of witnessing, direct speech, peace, and being face to face. We** said in that state:

> Time obeys you
> and people are slaves.

Live every day of your lives
like an 'Eid.

Then he refers to the second line of that verse which is:

If it had not been for its radiance,
imagination would not
have conceived it.

This means that this wine is hidden from
weak thoughts, beyond the perception
of intellects and understanding. If it had
not been for its lights which shine on the
hearts after they are pure from other and
purified of trouble, the intellect could not
conceive of it nor could understanding
grasp it since it is not perceived by intellects
nor is it obtained by transmission. It is
perceived by keeping the company of the
Men of Allah, the people of realisation and
perfection, because it is tastings which are
not perceived from pages, as Ibn al-Banna
says in Al-Mabahith – and he is referring to
Ibn al-Banna's poem which he comments on
in the book we have published called The Basic
Research:

Beware of desiring to obtain it
from a book, a poem or a verse.

He goes on to the next line of the Khamriyya:

> Time only retains its last gasp,
> As if it were a secret hidden
> in the breasts of the intelligent.

'Hushasha' is the final breath of the spirit in the sick person. 'Nuha' is the plural of 'nuhya', and it is the intellect. It has something elided, that is, 'the people of intelligence.'

This is very much in the spirit of The Basic Research. He continues:

This wine has left the hearts of people and vanished with the departure of its people and died with the death of its masters. It has slipped from the hearts of people as the ruh slips from the dying body. In this time nothing remains of it except a weak drop, like what is left of the spirit of the dead person in his last breath What the Shaykh said about the rarity of the existence of this knowledge and its disappearance has been said by more than one, both before him and after him. That is only because of its rareness and might. Imam al-Junayd, radiyallahu 'anhu, said, "The carpet of this knowledge of ours has been spread out and we have spoken about it for twenty years, and yet only spoken about its fringes." He used to say, "I have sat with people for two years while they were conversing about knowledges which I did not understand nor know what they were. I was not concerned by lack of knowledge at all. I used to accept it and love it without understanding it." He used to say, "We were conversing with our brothers of old about various knowledges which we do not know in this time of ours and no-one asked me about them. This is a chapter which is as if it is locked and barred."

This is very, very important to understand. First of all, all the great Shuyukh in every age have made the same statement. In a sense, they are facing the reality of the time they live in, and at the same time they are recognising the fact, nevertheless, that Allah has always left in the world people with this knowledge. It is not an accident that we are sitting in this room. It is not an accident that the people in this room have come from all different parts of the world. But from behind all this, one could say that this is from a du'a of Shaykh Muhammad ibn al-Habib, rahimahullah. The stone that was dropped in the water of supplication made these ripples, so that I have come here from a place that if I had travelled north from where I had been living and gone by sea I would have continued until I reached the North Pole. Now I am living in a place, where, if I took a boat and travelled south, I would continue until I reached the Antarctic which is the complete opposite!

All this has come from the inevitability of this teaching continuing. Shaykh Muhammad ibn al-Habib said, "I have divided my light in two. I have put one light in the Sahara with Sayyidi Muhammad bil-Qurshi, and I have put one in the West, meaning Europe.

When I sat with Shaykh Muhammad ibn al-Habib, I can say the same as what Imam al-Junayd said then, because there were people sitting with Shaykh Muhammad ibn al-Habib conversing on things at a level that other people did not understand, if they were able to attend it. There were men who were illiterate, who could not read or write, yet Shaykh Muhammad ibn al-Habib said of them, "My high Fuqara can discourse on Tawhid at a level at which the professors of the Qarawiyyin Mosque do not understand what they are talking about." They could not read or write but they had this knowledge.

In the Qut al-Qulub, which is one of the first texts written by a great Sufi, Abu Talib al-Makki, he says: "One of our scholars said, 'I know that those before had seventy knowledges. They used to come together to discuss them and would acquaint one another with them in this science. Today, all we have left is one knowledge, and the knowledges I discern now consist of falsehood, delusion and claims calling themselves knowledge.'" I would also mention that Sayyiduna 'Umar ibn al-Khattab said when one of the Sahaba died, "When that man died, one half of all knowledge went with him." This is at the time of the Sahaba!

So this is something you have to recognise, and you also have to examine why that is the case. Why this is the case is because the Shari'at has slipped out of the hands of the Muslims, and the defence of the Haqiqat is the Shari'at. If there is no Shari'at, the Haqiqat cannot survive. The desperation of our time, and you see it in Iraq, is that nobody knows how to act, and nobody knows what is the outrage. For example, the outrage yesterday in Iraq was not people being killed in the streets, the outrage was that the authorities that run a whole nation closed off the streets and barred the Muslims from attending the Jumu'a. This meant that at that moment they had declared war on Islam.

The Shi'a do not celebrate the Jumu'a so it was no offence to them – they have the documents to justify it in times of crisis and so on, but it is not a Fard of their Deen. At that point, it meant that the powers of the country had sided with them and were now governing the country, and had stopped the Fard act of the Muslims of Iraq. That is a war on Islam. It is not terrorism. It is not an occupying army. It is not 'winning hearts and minds' and all this language – it was war on the Shari'at. When the Shari'at is blocked, the Haqiqat cannot move. This is how, as we will see in a moment, this matter is explained, but it is the difficulty of the time we live in.

Without the Shari'at, the Haqiqat cannot breathe. This is because it is based on the basic material of the men. Men must have a quality of Insaniyya, of humanness which must be wholesome in order that they can have access to this understanding. The Shari'at has a visible face, which is the 'amal, that people behave in a certain way and are seen to behave in a certain way, so that if someone crosses a line in their behaviour, at that point the Shari'at of judgments and Ahkam fall into place. But there is an invisible aspect of that which is not understood by the kuffar which is the very essence of the thing that is actually the Muslim Community, which is adab. The Sufis say: "At-Tariqa kulluha adab." The Tariqa is all adab.

The Tariqa is adab. It is the courtesy, and by that I do not mean 'thank you' and 'you're welcome', but I mean the attention to others, and giving everyone their due and recognising who everybody is: recognising the person of intelligence, recognising the person of weakness who needs help. All that awareness of the other is what adab is. It is making room for someone. The basis of adab is that the Rasul, sallallahu 'alayhi wa sallam, said, "Make way in your assembly." If someone comes in, the Muslims know that they move to make way for that person to sit down. It is second nature. It just happens, because from the beginning we have been trained to do so.

In order for you to arrive at this knowledge, you must have developed the proper adab. The proper adab begins with the child. Al-Umm al-Madrasa. The mother is the university of the child. Modern Arab idiots say that she teaches them things, but it is not that she teaches them, but that her behaviour with the child is an attention, and that attention is what gives sanity to the child. It is the glance of the mother on the child that makes it know that it is a separate entity. Thus the look between the mother and the child is the beginning of the education of the nafs that is to make the child a whole human being. Now you have the child being fed with a bottle and the mother goes out of the room! The look has gone. I have seen the child being breast-fed and the mother watching the television! This is not making a human being. This is not constructing a human being.

I sent one of our Fuqara to the Zawiyya of a Shaykh up in the mountains, and he came back with an enormous impression having been made on him. I asked him, "What was it?" He said, "The Shaykh would sit down, and the children would come in, they would kiss his hand, and then he would say, 'Now, go along!' and they would say, 'I want to stay!' He would say, 'Go along!' Then one child would go down to his feet and the child started to massage his feet, and by doing this for his grandfather he was permitted to stay." So it was this attention, this manner, this courtesy that was the making of this person who one day would be an adult. The modern father says, "Leave me alone, I'm busy on the computer!" But it is that attention, that physical attention between the grandfather and the child that was so important for the learning of this adab. Do you understand? This is VERY important. THIS IS WHAT MAKES A HUMAN BEING.

Nowadays it looks as though whole sections of society are dying out. All they give are explanations about viruses and microscopic examination. Everyone has a destiny, but they have moved the destiny slowly, slowly from the Unseen, and it has ended up in the genetics of the person. So the destiny is now in the DNA and it is in the microbic infection. They do not understand the harmony of existence in which this formation of the person, if its main building blocks start to fall apart, is itself going to fall apart. Whole sections of communities in South Africa are being wiped out, and I am not saying that it is not happening at the level of the biological structure, but what has happened is that people are not living like human beings any more. If you do not live like human beings, you will not die like human beings. Thus the whole of society is as though it is falling apart.

I am sorry to expand on this but it is germane to what we are studying. Capitalism has made people have these factory farms for chickens and now they are saying in India that before there was any official documentation about this 'bird flu' disease, there were thousands of chickens dying in these factories. Then you see the factory and it is just as shocking to look at these chickens as it is to look at concentration camps. It is a lower level of life but it is the same procedure. You can treat existence like it was just stuff that you move about for your benefit – just as the concentration camps were to save money and to provide cheap labour, it is the same for the chickens.

Now people are terrified that it is going to be a world epidemic, but what you have is that people are not full human beings. The Insaniyya has started to collapse. They have not got concern. The essential element of the human is concern. The difference between the child and the adult is concern. The child says that his concern is "Me!" That is right for the station of the child, but once it becomes adult, the concern is, "What's the matter?" It is to reach out to the other. If that crossover does not take place as the evolution of the child grows, if that does not take place and the adult is saying, "Me!" then the whole human transaction has gone. The adab has stopped. There is no adab any more. This goes for the parents with the children, and the husband with the wife, and the brother with the brother.

Remember that in the understanding of the human creature, Shaykh Ibn Taymiyya said, "If you want to understand what is wrong in the human situation, go to the story in the Qur'an of the first humans. If you want to understand what is wrong in the Deen, go to the story of the First Community of Rasul, sallallahu 'alayhi wa sallam, and his Sahaba, and everything you see there is what is happening in our time," which was our Middle Ages.

If you go to the first humans, the first crack in the breaking of the contract of accepting Divine protection, Divine support, Divine love and the Divine generosity of giving a Garden to the human beings, is that the brother kills the brother. Thus the essential, fundamental thing that indicates the crack is when the brother turns on the brother. This is why Imam Malik said, and I cannot remember the exact ratio, but it is like two years of tyranny is better than one hour of civil war, because the most terrible thing is when the brother turns on the brother. Every country that has had a civil war has been marked irrevocably and has never recovered. Spain has never been the same. Honour has never recovered its place in a country that was once a Muslim country. America never recovered from its civil war. The issues around why it happened do not matter, because what was broken was this trust that was between the brothers. However, it is of the nature of man to fight his brother, and he will fight his brother before he fights anybody.

The significance of Islam, the importance of Islam as a Revelation from Allah, subhanahu wa ta'ala, and the sending of Rasul, sallallahu 'alayhi wa sallam, is that he said, "O Abu Bakr, I would take you as my friend, but Allah has made us brothers in Islam." That is why there is nothing more repellent today for the Muslims than people who call themselves the Ikhwan al-Muslimun, because if you do not belong to the 'Ikhwan al-Muslimun', then although you are Muslim, it is as though you do not belong to the brotherhood of the Muslims! They say to you, "Ya akhi!" But let us confirm one thing: no-one ever said to his brother, "Ya akhi!" Ever! It is a lie. These things are not on the tongue. I never once said to my brother, "O brother!" He is my brother, and I call him by his name. I might even call him by names I should not call him! But I do not say, "Brother!" That is theatre, it is acting, and it is a lie. It means the brotherhood is broken because what should be hidden has become apparent.

In the age in which we now live, the human contract has been so radically broken that the bringing together of people to approach this knowledge is rare, in a very special way that never was before. What I am saying is: you have to understand the importance of this gathering. It has been brought together by a ruhani secret that we cannot even map the geographics of, let alone the impulses of the hearts that moved the hearts to be here. It is not possible! The matter of how we are all together in this room has a ruhani secret: Allah wanted to bring this group of people together to praise Him in order that He should pour out on them lights of illumination and knowledge. This is what we are participating in.

Let us go just a little further with Shaykh ibn 'Ajiba's commentary:

> Our Imam, Sahl at-Tustari, used to say in 369 AH, "It is not lawful to speak of this knowledge of ours." This is due to its few number of people, because there are people who listen to people and innovate and dress up things with words. Their artificial ecstasies are their robe and their inward is darkness, and their devices their words. Abul-Qasim al-Qushayri said at the beginning of his Risala – and this is one of the first key documents of Tasawwuf, along with Al-Makki's Qut al-Qulub – "Know, may Allah have mercy on you, that most of those who have realisation among this group have passed, and only their trace remains in this time of ours." Shaykh Abu Madyan said in his Qasida:
>
> Know that the Path of the People
> is effaced

And today the state of those
who claim it is as you see.

He then goes on to say:

The Shaykh of our Shaykhs, Sayyidi 'Ali
al-Jamal, the great Shaykh of Fes, said:
"This does not indicate that the men by
whom Allah shows mercy to His slaves are
cut off in any time. The known number
will not end until the Deen ends." We read
in Lata'if al-Minan: 'One of the Gnostics
was asked about the numbered Awliya and
whether they reduce in number over time.
He said, "If any of them had been reduced,
the heaven would not release its rain nor
the earth let its plants grow. The corruption
of time is not due to the departure of their
number, nor the decrease of their help, but
rather, when the time is corrupt, then Allah
desires to conceal them. When the people of
the time turn away from Allah, preferring
what is other-than-Allah, admonition does
not save them, and reminder does not make
them incline to Allah. Then they are not
worthy to have the Awliya appear among
them. That is why they said, 'The Awliya
of Allah are brides and the criminals do not
see the brides.'"

Then the Rasul, sallallahu 'alayhi wa sallam, said, "When you see avarice being obeyed, passion being followed, this world being preferred and everyone admiring his own opinion, then you must guard your own ruh." They heard the words of the Messenger of Allah and preferred concealment. Rather, Allah preferred it for them because some of them were in the time of teaching, establishing the proof by the words of the Messenger of Allah, sallallahu 'alayhi wa sallam: "A group of my Community will continue to openly support truth. They will not be harmed by those who oppose them until the Day of Rising."

These Imams exist in our Community now. They appear as the sun appears on the horizons of the one who enjoys Divine concern. Then Allah bestowed on us recognition of them and keeping their company, and we found them to be among the people of Prophetic instruction, travelling the Path and recognising the Source of realisation. They travelled the lands of Tajrid and dived into the seas of Tawhid, calling to Allah by himma and the halal, recognising the technical terms and words, rising to Allah by the state, and directing to Allah by words. They travelled through the station of attraction and annihilation and returned to the station of going-on. Allah has guided a large number at their hands, and taught many people by them. However, the sun must have a cloud and the beautiful woman a veil, so Allah has veiled their secret with some of what appears from some of their companions of dark states and shaytanic actions while they themselves are free of that. The command of Allah is decreed and success is by Allah, and there is no strength nor power except by Allah, the High, the Immense. Then Ibn al-Farid says:

> It rises from the inwards of
> the wine jars, while in reality,
> nothing but its name
> remains of it.

What we want to conclude with is that you are these people whom he is talking about. You must recognise that Allah has elected you for knowledge. It has nothing to do with me. It has nothing to do with any transmission, as he says, but it is that Allah will give you illumination in the heart. You must use the time in which we gather together for this inner awakening which is like when you wake up from sleep. It is to feel inside you with the recital of the Wird, and to feel inside you with the singing of the Diwan of our Shuyukh, that the meanings of what we are singing are for you. It is about your condition, and you must more and more realise that this aspect of your existence, however crowded your existence is, however busy it is, whatever an agenda you have – this has to run right through it so that you do not forget it.

Thus you will be people whom neither commerce nor trading distracts from the remembrance of Allah. Whatever you are doing, you are remembering Allah. The best way is to have the tongue supple with the Name of Allah, and that is the secret of the People of Tawhid. They say that Shaykh Chisti was in a gathering in India with all his Fuqara and some great hindu sage came with all his people and announced, "We know more about the Divine than you, and I will show you that we know more of the Divine than you!" Shaykh Chisti said, "No, no, no, there is nothing to show! I will demonstrate that my people have the knowledge of Allah," and he took a stone and threw it at one of the hindus. The hindu turned around and said, "What was that?" The Shaykh then took another stone and flung it at one of his Fuqara and it hit the Faqir who exclaimed, "Allah!" That has to be your condition – that everything is returned to Allah, whatever the situation.

Alhamdulillahi 'ala kulli hal. Praise belongs to Allah in every state.

5

COMMENTARY

ON

KNOWLEDGE OF GOD

– Shaykh al-Alawi's commentary on
the Murshid al-Mu'in of Ibn 'Ashir

Four commentaries
given between
March 11th and April 8th 2006
at the Masjid al-Mahmoud,
Constantia, Cape Town

I

MARCH 11ᵀᴴ 2006

On 'Author's Introductions' and
'The Nobility of the Knowledge of the Sufis
above other Knowledges'
pages xiv–xxii

We were making commentary on Shaykh Ibn 'Ajiba's notes on the Khamriyya of Ibn al-Farid, and I feel we need to go back to the same material as explained by Shaykh Mustafa al-'Alawi, radiyallahu 'anhu, in his book 'Knowledge of God'. This book is a Sufic commentary on the Murshid al-Mu'in of Ibn 'Ashir, the famous poem which outlines the Deen: the Fiqh of Imam Malik, the 'Aqida of Al-Ash'ari and the Tasawwuf of Imam al-Junayd, radiyallahu 'anhum. He takes every single one of its propositions and whilst he does not deny their outward meaning, he gives an inward insight that these material things inspire in the Sufi. He will later explain how he is able to do that and not be incorrect in doing it. He says:

> The obliterated slave in his Lord, Ahmad ibn Mustafa ibn al-'Alawi, says that when Allah had been generous with me, He gave me the helping spring, and He allowed me to open the closed doors of this extraordinary poetry that encompasses outwardly the pillars of the Deen, and inwardly a road from the roads of indication. I found that a lot of people of the outward have come to its outward. The people of the inward have stopped from search in its inward through their jealousy of giving away its secrets.
>
> Bliss has carried me away to this art, and immense yearning for arrival at it. Without any weapons and ready to bear the burdens, I have invited myself to it because I have found that it is not haram to do so. I have become like the generous, because to become like them is a great gain.

He goes on in his Introduction to what he calls 'The Nobility of the Knowledge of the Sufis above other

1

Knowledges.' It is what we were looking at through the commentary of Shaykh Ibn 'Ajiba, but I think this is also of great benefit for you. He says:

> Know that this knowledge is the best of knowledges, and the most generous when understood, and no-one denies it except the one who is deprived of its blessing. You can do without all knowledges after a certain time except this knowledge, which by obligation you cannot do without at any time. No-one says he can do without it except the ignorant who has been deprived of reunion. One who ignores a thing becomes the enemy of that thing. Allah knows best. 'Izzuddin al-Arbili said, rahimahullah:
>
> > Perfect your reality
> > which has not been perfected,
> > and leave the body
> > in the lower area.
> >
> > Do you perfect the obliterated
> > by work and leave the remaining?
> > You did not celebrate His order.
> >
> > The body is to the precious self
> > an instrument.

If you do not get hold of it
(the body) by it (the self),
you cannot get it (the body).

The body will be annihilated
and you will remain after it
with immense joy, or with a
suffering that does not leave.

You gave your body a servant
and you became its servant,
and you forgot your contract
from the First Age.

He means by 'You gave your body a servant and you became its servant' that you gave your body your appetites, and you became the servant of your appetites. 'And you forgot your contract from the First Age.' This is the contract of "Alastu bi-Rabbikum?" which the human creature made before the creation of the world with Allah, subhanahu wa ta'ala.

You possess your freedom with
your perfection still incomplete.
Does the better own the best
as a slave?

Very often Al-Ghazali used to repeat the two verses of Abul-Fath al-Bisti, rahimahumullah:

O slave of the body! How much
you yearn to serve it.
You want to gain
from what is in it a loss.

Go to the self,
and perfect its happiness,
because you are by the self,
not by the body, a human being.

This is the very core of the Sufic perspective. You are by
the self. You have reality and exist by the self, not by the
body, as a human being.

We understand from these verses that
this knowledge is the most noble of all
knowledges, and its nobility is the nobility
of the known. Its value is attached to the
value of the essence of the Eternal. By Allah,
this knowledge has encompassed nobility.

The knowledge of the people is taken from
witnessing. Knowledge of others is taken
from directories and proofs. And after the
explanation, explanation. News is not like
witnessing.

Rasul, in a very famous Hadith, said that the one who
has news of a thing has a lesser knowledge than the one

who has witnessed it, because witnessing is over report. The Sufis take enormous importance from this Hadith. **News is not like witnessing.**

> **The Doctor of the Sufis said: "There is a lot of difference between the one who is guided by it and the one who is searching for it." Differences and misunderstandings spring up between the possessors of every other knowledge – different views, different explanations – except in this noble knowledge because it is placed above argument and alteration.**

Shaykh Muhammad ibn al-Habib has always said that the people of Shari'at, the Fuqaha, have differences, and they must have those differences because they must clarify the matters of decision, of law, of what concerns the world. But the people of Tasawwuf have no disagreement. They are all agreed because they have all witnessed. So they all confirm what they have experienced and seen. If you look in Ibn al-Farid's songs, and if you look in the Diwans of Shaykh Muhammad ibn al-Habib, of Shaykh al-'Alawi, of Shaykh al-Harraq, they all speak of this extraordinary moment where they are made welcome in the Unseen world when their self has fallen away, when the body has become as though it were dead and they are without a body, and they are without the senses. Then Allah says, "Welcome. Come near." It is exactly the same experience in every case and it is confirmed if you go to Afghanistan or Bangladesh – you will find the same description there, over ages, stretching over centuries. Shaykh al-'Alawi quotes Ibn al-Farid, saying:

> **How much it is discussed**
> **among skilled debaters,**
> **while there is no disagreement**
> **among the lovers of the Beloved.**

> **The knowledge of the branches is taken from**
> **directory and proof and from transcription,**
> **but the knowledge of the People is taken**
> **only from discovery and witnessing.**

This means that the Sufi becomes transmuted into a different kind of person, a different quality of person, which is also why you cannot judge by the outside. Someone may just see a miserable beggar, but the Sufi will see a Wali of Allah. Another one will turn away from a king saying, "Well, he is a king so he is of no spiritual significance," whereas the Sufi will say, "This king is Sufi." Ibrahim ibn 'Adham of Afghanistan was a king who was Faqir. That is why Rasul, sallallahu 'alayhi wa sallam, taught one of his Sahaba the 'Ilm al-Farasa, to read the face. The ruh is not written on the outside of the face, but it can be seen by the one who knows how to read the story it has to tell, what is, in fact, hidden.

Shaykh al-ʿAlawi continues:

> He who does not have a portion of this knowledge has no portion of the understanding of the inward of the Qur'an. His lot is the outward of the expressions. It is reported that Imam ʿAli Abu Talib, karramullah wajhahu, said, "If I wanted, I would draw forty meanings from the commentary of Al-Fatiha." All this is because of what he was given from the understanding of indications and the precise expressions of the knowledge of the inward. He could take out even more than that because the short phrase includes the meaning of the whole of the News. All that is in the Torah is in the Evangil, and all that is in the Psalms and the Evangil is in the Qur'an. All that is in the Qur'an is in the Fatiha of the Book. All that is in the Fatiha is in the Bismillah, and all that is in the Bismillah is in the Ba, and all that is in the Ba is in the dot of the Ba.

Abu Yazid al-Bistami said, "I am that dot."

We understand by this that all the
Books that descended on the Prophets
from Sayyiduna Adam, 'alayhi salam to
Sayyiduna Muhammad, sallallahu 'alayhi
wa sallam, with their words and meanings
and wisdom, are gathered in the dot of the
Ba, even though it is small. Who is capable
of drawing these meanings and these
indications from the dot of the Ba? No-one
– except the gnostics of Allah, possessors of
the inner eye. They are the ones who know
what the tradition means, and they believe
the one who said it by way of witnessing
and vision, not by way of trust.

If this meaning lodges in your mind, O
reader with a core – with a 'lubb', in the
Qur'anic language – that the dot of the
Ba gathers all the wisdom and forms and
gnoses and understandings – then give
yourself up to the People of this knowledge
and do not marvel if you see them taking
many meanings from one meaning, and
from one word many words. It is theirs to
take whatever they want from whatever
they want. By Allah, if one of them wants
to take honey out of vinegar, he will!

وَتُخْرِجُ ٱلْحَىَّ مِنَ ٱلْمَيِّتِ وَتُخْرِجُ ٱلْمَيِّتَ مِنَ ٱلْحَىِّ

You bring out the living from the dead.
You bring out the dead from the living.
(Qur'an, 3:27)

All this is a proof of what Allah has given them from the secret and the gnoses and the lights. O brother, do not be deluded by the words of the people of illusion, the ones who defame the friends of Allah and stir up trouble in their circles. They think they have a degree over them, but they are like children compared to them. They do not know from which ocean they have drunk and they do not know from which direction they have taken. As Shaykh Muhiyuddin Ibn al-'Arabi has said:

> We left behind us
> the awesome seas,
> So how can people know
> where we went?

By this they have become the most noble of the people, undeniably. Their knowledge is the most noble of knowledges by agreement. So work hard, O brother, to attain it. Believe

I

the People of this knowledge, and you will win booty, or surrender the matter to them. Imam al-Ghazali has said in the Ihya 'Ulum ad-Din, from some of the Gnostics:

> He who does not have a portion of this knowledge, I mean the knowledge of the inward, I fear for him a bad seal. The smallest portion from it is to believe it and to surrender to its possessors.

Abul Hassan ash-Shadhili – one of the Shaykhs of our Tariqa – radiyallahu 'anhu, says:

> The one who is not steeped in this knowledge dies concealing his arrogance, and he does not know it.

An example of arrogance in the view of the People is to witness otherness. No-one is free from this vice except one who stands humbly at their door, even if they are from the men skilled in outward knowledge and ascetics who are worshippers. Be humble to them, O brother, so that you may gain their affection, or it not, believe their knowledge.

Al-Junayd, radiyallahu 'anhu, said:

> To believe in our knowledge is
> Wilayat. And if this escapes you,
> do not let belief that others believe
> in it escape you.

Abu Yazid al-Bistami, radiyallahu 'anhu,
said:

> If you see the one who believes in
> the Way, then tell him to supplicate
> for you to Allah, because his
> supplication is answered.

Siqilli said, radiyallahu 'anhu, in his
book 'The Light of Hearts in the Gifted
Knowledge':

> Everyone who believes in this
> knowledge is from the elite. And
> everyone who understands it is
> from the elite of the elite. And
> anyone who expresses it or talks
> about it is a star that cannot be
> reached and a sea that cannot be
> left.

The Tabib, who wrote 'The Courtiers of

Unveiling' used to say:

> The scholar must not be satisfied
> with his knowledge, even if he is
> the most learned scholar of his
> time. He is obliged to find the
> People of the Way so that they
> can guide him to the Straight
> Path, until he becomes one of
> the ones in whose hearts Allah
> speaks, because of the extreme
> purity of their inward until, as it
> is said, he starts to take from the
> light of the Prophets.

And I say, how can the man of outward
knowledge be independent with his
knowledge, when he falls short in his
understanding?

Remember that Imam al-Ghazali himself was the Sultan
of the 'Ulama of his time. He was on the Minbar, and in
the middle of his Khutba he was absolutely overcome
with this fear of Allah, and he could not continue. He
withdrew and he vanished from the sight of all the
cultured, educated people, and went off into the desert
and began his path to Allah as a humble Faqir. This is
something that happens, and when it happens nothing
can be done. You cannot undo it, you cannot change

it because it is something that comes down, and once that happens to the person they cannot turn back, they have to go on.

> We have heard that Imam al-Ghazali, radiyallahu 'anhu, when he occupied himself with the purification of his inward, following the People of Allah, said: "We have wasted all of our life. Oh how worthless my purpose in those days!" And they said to him, "Did you not become the Proof of Islam in those days?" He said, "Leave this nonsense! Have you not heard that the Prophet said, sallallahu 'alayhi wa sallam, said, 'Allah strengthens the Deen by it enemies'?"

So look, brother, at the humility of this great man of outward knowledge and his acknowledgement of what he was doing before he met the People of Tasawwuf. Do not think that he made this statement to slight the Shari'at. He said it in exaltation of it because he knew the Shari'at, and he was among the idle ones in it before he met them. Even though he researched the outward of it, he was short-sighted in its inward. In conclusion, he had gathered the form and ignored the knowledge and the

Known. When Allah gave him the opening
of meeting the Sufis, his knowledge
became knowledge of Allah, where before
it had been knowledge of the laws of Allah.
'Izzuddin Ibn 'Abdussalam said, radiyallahu
'anhu:

> The Sufis have settled for the rules
> of Shari'at that can be destroyed
> neither in this world nor the
> Next, and others have settled for
> the forms.

This is proven to you by what comes
from their hands including miracles and
guidance to the creation, and by what
comes from their mouths of wisdom and
guidance until the one who sits with them
benefits. Imam Nawawi, radiyallahu 'anhu,
has reported from the explanation of the
Shafi' School:

> I have benefited from sitting with
> the Sufis by two sayings of theirs:
> Time is a sword. If you do not cut
> it, it cuts you.

What does this mean? 'Time is a sword. If you do not
cut it, it cuts you.' In other words, if you do not take

the Path of Knowledge, you will not come to that point where the in-time experience is obliterated in the beyond-time experience. So if you are trapped in time, then it cuts you because it passes and passes and passes, and then it is all over. The other saying he took from the Sufis was:

> If you do not occupy your self with good deeds, it will occupy you with bad deeds.

So he is saying that you have to move between deeds, not states of consciousness and psychology – there is no psychology. If you are not occupied in good actions, the self will get you occupied in bad actions. There are two zones of action, and you choose which one you want.

> Reflect, O brother, on the sincerity of this great Imam and how he became a witness for the Sufis, and confirmed their seriousness and struggle. Shaykh Sharani, radiyallahu 'anhu, said:
>
> > Reflect on how Shafi' has taken this from the Sufis and not from others. It is by this that you know their superiority over others, the men of knowledge of the outward, the ones from whom he once learned.

In conclusion, it is agreed that this knowledge is the knowledge of the truthful ones and he who has a portion of it is one of the Muqarrabun, above, in degree, the People of the Right. Oh, how happy is the one who has a small portion of it! How unhappy is the one who is in conflict with its people in ignorance and rigidity! He tries to prove that what he has is correct, and he argues with them about what he does not know. This man we call insane, because he is fighting one who is stronger than him. Some of the wise have said, "The one who fights a stronger opponent, brings trials on himself."

So the one who opposes the Sufis brings trouble on himself.

So brother, have a good opinion of Allah and His noble slaves, and especially the People of this Path, because meddling in their affairs is deadly poison. May Allah protect us and all the Muslims from it.

We will continue, inshallah, with this next week.

II

MARCH 18TH 2006

On 'Book of Doctrine'
pages 1-8

We have been reflecting on the matter of Ma'rifa and on the famous Qasida of Ibn al-Farid – the Khamriyya. Then to clarify this we looked at Shaykh al-'Alawi's commentary on the poem of Ibn 'Ashir. However, I was thinking that to go deeper into the matter of Ma'rifa, which is the real affair of Tasawwuf, demands the education of your own nafs, the mastery of you own self. This strange teaching of the Sufis, which is contrary to all kafir psychology, teaches that your selfhood is an enemy to you. It is not actually your ally. This strange idea has of course always produced among the Muslims and among the Sufis a strong trend, if you might say, of zahids. In fact, in some of the classical literature, the word zahid is a kind of code-name for 'Sufi'.

At the same time the matter of the conquest of the nafs is not really a matter of doing-without, so much as an understanding of mastery by knowing how the nafs works. Again, it is not about being introspective about yourself. The healthiness of the Faqir is his busyness with good actions. We saw the other day that you replace wrong actions with right actions, and this is the tilt that is necessary to be healthy. In other words if you examine yourself, as Shaykh Muhammad ibn al-Habib, rahimahullah, says in the Diwan, there is nothing in the self that is any good. So if you keep examining and examining yourself, that becomes its own sickness. The point is that you busy yourself with right actions, with Birr. Birr is right action, and that is the Path of the Sufi.

This matter of living in correct and good action means that you have, as it were, good manners. You have to have good manners with creation. The Sufic way is that you have good manners with the creation because you cannot look at the creation and see that it is masiwallah, that it is other-than-Allah. Allah is not the creation, but its reality is Allah. So wherever you look you are confronting the reality of Allah, and your confronting the reality of Allah is your recognition of your destiny, because you are where you are and not somewhere else.

In the Fatiha we say: 'Ihdina Sirat al-Mustaqim' – Guide us on the Straight Path, and Sirat al-Mustaqim is that you go with good intention, with good niyyat, because our science is achieved by niyyat, not by study. The Path of the Sufis is achieved not through study and research, but it is achieved through intention, because "Amal bin-Niyyat' – action is by intention. For the intention to be pure, the heart must be pure and this is what the dhikr is for, it is to purify the heart. By the recitation of Qur'an and the Wird and the singing of the Diwan, the heart is slowly, slowly alchemically being changed and transformed. But you must remember that you have to have these good manners with creation.

Shaykh Muhammad ibn al-Habib, radiyallahu 'anhu, says in the Diwan: "Take care – you cannot despise even the lowest atom." Again, the Shari'at is sent to steer us through all the myriad things, through all the complex things of existence, because it has shown us that these actions are wrong, those actions are right, these actions are disapproved of, those actions are approved of. There are delineations so that you can go through the maze of existence making right judgments.

When new things appear to the Shari'at, they do not throw us because the system of the Fuqaha has a mechanism. Thus we have in the School of Madinah, Masalih Mursala and Sadd adh-Dhara'i'– we have two kinds of pincers which pick up and look at new things and ask, "What will the outcome of this thing be? Will what it results in be good for us, or will it be harmful for us? Is there any component of it which is intrinsically bad and dangerous?" In a sense, the new things are not new. There is not anything we cannot apprehend by the process of intelligence and examining things to see the outcome of the action. This is why the Faqir who follows the Sirat al-Mustaqim and submits to the Shari'at has an open path to the Haqiqat because he is safe, he is secure, and he has a confidence by his confirmation of Shari'at, whereas other people make wrong assumptions of Shari'at, as in the modern day where there is no 'Amr, there is no command among the Muslims. So the 'ulama have retreated from their heavy responsibility of protecting the morality and the behaviour of the Muslims because they do not have the means to do it. They have retreated into this matter where they start to give licence to the chicken – "Is it halal?" and so on, and from there they say, "Well, has the biscuit got some sort of pig fat in it?" "Is there alcohol in this medicine?" when the medicine is going to save your life! They got lost. They have become superficial. But the Shari'at is a mighty thing and it is there to open this way for you to allow you to have a safe path to knowledge of Allah, subhanahu wa ta'ala.

Now, we will look at the very beginning of the Murshid al-Mu'in, and Shaykh al-'Alawi's commentary on it:

'Abdalwahid Ibn 'Ashir says,
beginning in the Name of Allah,
the Most Powerful.

This is the affair of the Gnostics, to start
with His Name, and to end with it. It is
not possible for any one of them to begin
by any other than Him in speech or in
action. This is why he said, "I started my
verse taking the Name of Allah." Meaning,
obliterated in it, and disintegrated, until it
became the beginning in speech, not me. "I
have put down verses by the Name of Allah,
not by myself, fearing that the reader will
imagine that I am the one who speaks, and
be veiled from Allah and chased from Allah
because he considered me." This station is
the station of the people of annihilation
and the Supreme Name. In most cases the
one who remembers sees himself like an
instrument or a pen. Some of the Gnostics
have said:

You see me like an instrument
and He moves me.
I am a pen and the Power of Allah
is the fingers.

This is if the Murid is in the state of

annihilation, drowning in the Name, away from the circle of his senses, and nothing remains for him except the Name, mixed with his blood and flesh so that when he stands up it is by it, and when he talks, it is by it. Shaykh Shibli, radiyallahu 'anhu, said, "I was on a journey in the countryside when I saw a woman. Her colour was yellow and her clothes were dusty, and she was walking very fast. I said to her, 'Be gentle to yourself, O creation of Allah,' and she said, 'Huwa! Huwa!' and I said to her, 'Where did you come from?' and she said, 'From Huwa!' I asked her, 'What is your name?' and she said, 'Huwa!' And I said to her, 'What do you mean by saying Huwa, is it Allah you want?' And she screamed when she heard the Name of Allah, and her self overflowed from her, she died, may Allah be merciful to her and to the like of her. I ask Allah that He put us on the Path of those who remember by His generosity." Then Ibn 'Ashir said, radiyallahu 'anhu:

Praise be to Allah who taught us knowledge of our responsibilities.

Praise, here, goes back to the Name, because the Name, in the People's view, is the source of the Named. When the speaker of these verses drowned in the Name until his attributes were annihilated in the Attributes of his Lord, and the bad in him was annihilated in what is praised in his Master, and he became a man of knowledge after being tied down by his ignorance, he said, "Praise be to Allah who taught us knowledge of our responsibilities."

Before that, he did not have any knowledge because he acquired knowledge by him himself. But when his speech was through his Lord, then he was not to blame, because his attributes were annihilated in His Attributes, and his existence unfolded in His Existence, and he gave news of himself with knowledge. If he did that before, his knowledge would be ignorance. The one who says, "I am a man of knowledge" is ignorant. The ones who have knowledge of Allah do not say, "We have knowledge" until they reach the mentioned station.

Know that knowledge is of two types: acquired knowledge and knowledge that is a gift.

You hear this again and again in the things we are doing

and it will make sense to you. This is why there is no debate about Tasawwuf. There is no argument. People say things about Tasawwuf, but have you experience of it? Have you knowledge of it? No? Then you must not speak. It is something about which you can only speak by having experienced it. Have you experience of it? If you have experience, then you may speak. Thus Shaykh al-'Alawi says:

> Know that knowledge is of two types: acquired knowledge and knowledge that is a gift. Acquired knowledge is attached to the rules of wisdom and the gift of knowledge is attached to the station of the rules of wisdom. We know that knowledge is ennobled by the ennoblement of the known. He said, radiyallahu 'anhu,

>> Prayers and Peace of Allah upon Muhammad and his family and Companions, and the one who follows.

> 'Prayers' in the view of the People mean the manifestation of Lordship. That is because if Allah the Blessed and Exalted becomes manifest to one of His slaves and attracts him, then He brings him to His Presence, He is seen to him sometimes and

other times He is not seen. The slave yearns for that manifestation and every time it appears to him, turbulence ceases and his heart becomes calm. This does not happen except to the Prophets and to the Elite of the Awliya and this why it is not permitted for any of us to pray on anyone except his prophets – on Awliya, for example. It is a noble station and no-one gets it except the Elite of the Gnostics of Allah. Prayer means manifestation if it is from Allah, or if not, its meaning is supplication. If you say, "O Allah, pray and give peace to our Lord Muhammad and his family," it is as if you say, "O Allah, be manifest to Muhammad, and his family," and if it did not mean manifestation, the Prophet, sallallahu 'alayhi wa sallam, would not have asked for it.

Do you follow that? It is very beautiful. If you say, "O Allah, pray and give peace to our Lord Muhammad and his family," it is as if you say, "O Allah, be manifest to Muhammad, and his family," and if it did not mean manifestation, the Prophet, sallallahu 'alayhi wa sallam, would not have asked for it.

He ordered us to pray for him at all times and in all states. He desires from it the manifestation of Essence which has Names and Attributes in it, until he withdraws from seeing all that is made by that manifestation until this is his state most of the time, and until nothing replaces Allah for him in this station. The Prophet, sallallahu 'alayhi wa sallam, said, "I have a time in which nothing satisfies me except my Lord." This time is the time of the prayer of Allah on him, meaning the manifestation of Allah to him.

Do you see what he is saying? He is saying that in the Qur'an, Allah, subhanahu wa ta'ala, makes this Salli on Rasul, sallallahu 'alayhi wa sallam, and he is saying that that means the manifestation of Allah to him.

He is still asking for that manifestation, and the community is asking the manifestation for him until the Yawm al-Qiyama. If the meaning of the prayer was mercy, the following would have been enough for him:

$$ وَمَآ أَرْسَلْنَٰكَ إِلَّا رَحْمَةً لِّلْعَٰلَمِينَ ۝ $$

We have only sent you as a mercy to all the worlds.
(Qur'an 21:107)

The one who seeks its essence does not stop with attributes. In conclusion, the prayer of Allah on His slaves is his extensive affection, and their nearness to Him. If one of the slaves receives a prayer from Allah, he receives everything. With it Allah pulls his friends from the prison of their selves to the witnessing of their Lord. He said, subhanahu wa ta'ala:

$$\text{هُوَ ٱلَّذِى يُصَلِّى عَلَيْكُمْ وَمَلَـٰٓئِكَتُهُۥ لِيُخْرِجَكُم مِّنَ ٱلظُّلُمَـٰتِ إِلَى ٱلنُّورِ}$$

It is He Who calls down blessing on you,
as do His Angels,
to bring you out of the darkness
into the light.
(Qur'an 33:43)

This means that He takes you out of the darkness of the cosmos to the light of the Maker of the cosmos, or from the chains of otherness to the open space of secrets.

'The chains of otherness' means everything that connects us to created existence, to the forms which are visible and touchable and known. He takes you out from that to the open space of secrets. 'The open space of secrets' means when you are in the Presence of Lordship by which all that is left is that awareness, and the body and its senses are all gone – they are non-existent as though dead – then you are in the open space of secrets.

This is why no-one has enough of the prayer, and everyone asks for its continuation. This is why it is said that the Prophet, sallallahu 'alayhi wa sallam, benefits from the prayer on him, and the gardens do not open without it.

وُجُوهٌ يَوْمَئِذٍ نَّاضِرَةٌ ۝ إِلَىٰ رَبِّهَا نَاظِرَةٌ ۝

Faces that Day will be radiant,
gazing at their Lord.
(Qur'an 75:22-23)

This is the meaning of the prayer on the Prophet, the Salat an-Nabiy, sallallahu 'alayhi wa sallam, and Allah knows best.

Allah has been generous to his slaves by the security and the firmness in that manifestation which they undergo. This is why man should not ask for prayer alone but also for peace. He should not ask for firmness and fixity in that manifestation.

Allah, subhanahu wa ta'ala, prays on a group
of His slaves and His manifestation becomes
for them fear, trembling, unsettling – and
they become nervous, and they cry out
more often, and they disclose some words
to other than the people of their station.

In other words, they say things in that state that they
should not say.

Then these people accuse them of lies and
they judge them to be malicious. The cause
of that is the prayer only without the peace
from Allah on them. If Allah wants to guard
them, and to guard others from them, He
follows the prayer with the peace on them.
Then their turbulence ceases and their
path straightens. Their outward is with the
creation and their inward is with the Real.

This is the completion of the human creature, this is the
completion of man when this condition adheres: their
outward is with the creation and their inward is with
the Real. In the words of Ibn 'Ata'illah in the Hikam,
'The outward does not veil him from the inward, and
the inward does not veil him from the outward, and he
gives every creature in creation its due.'

They have the two opposites. They have

knowledge of the two stations, and these are the inheritors of the Prophets. From this noble station –

And here he is saying that from this noble station comes the whole language of Tasawwuf –

From this noble station they talk about drunkenness and sobriety, annihilation and going-on, and other terms. Drunkenness stands for prayer from Allah on them, and the peace stands for sobriety after the drowning in the witnessing of their Lord. Then know that the Prophets, peace be upon them, specialised in joining the prayer and the peace from Allah on them at once, or one after the other. But as for the Awliya, radiyallahu 'anhum, some of them have the prayer without peace, and this station is called drunkenness. Some of them die in this state. Some of them return to the sensory and their inward is firm in drunkenness.

كُلّاً نُّمِدُّ هَـٰٓؤُلَآءِ وَهَـٰٓؤُلَآءِ مِنْ عَطَآءِ رَبِّكَ وَمَا كَانَ عَطَآءُ رَبِّكَ مَحْظُورًا ۝

We sustain each one,
the former and the latter,
through the generous giving of your Lord;
and the giving of your Lord is not restricted.
(Qur'an, 17:20)

In conclusion, a prayer from Allah on his loved ones stands for reunion and arrival in the same way that a curse for His enemies stands for distance and separation. May Allah protect us and the Muslims from that. Amin. And Ibn 'Ashir said, radiyallahu 'anhu,

> And then, help is from acting by Allah, the Praiseworthy, the Magnificent, in setting down these verses which are of benefit to the illiterate.

He said in this verse that help is from Allah, and that is in every action, good or bad, sweet or bitter, by choice or by discovery. This is why he said, "By Allah, the Praiseworthy", because if there was no help from Allah, He would not be called Praiseworthy. The meaning of Magnificent is the one who has reached the goal in nobility. That is why the poet, radiyallahu 'anhu, sought help from the Allah the Magnificent in actions both few and many, the small and the big, the noble and the humble, the long and the short, the inward and the outward, even in verses. If it was not Allah the Blessed and Exalted who put down the verses, they would not be there. Know that this composition has indications and extraordinary secrets and precious meanings. No-one knows its inward except the Gnostics of Allah, and this is why he said, "It benefits the illiterate."

In other words, what he is taking is the fundamental 'schoolboy's book' of a summary of the Deen: the Fiqh of Imam Malik, the 'Aqida of Al-Ash'ari and the Tasawwuf of Imam al-Junayd. He is not denying that all that it contains in outward instruction is the purpose of the book – what he is saying is that to the Sufis it is full of indications and extraordinary secrets and precious meanings. He said in his second preface entitled 'Clarification of how the people understand many meanings from one word': 'We are a people who take many meanings from one thing.' And for example, he said:

It has reached us from the Shaykh of our Shaykhs, Mawlay al-'Arabi ad-Darqawi, radiyallahu 'anhu, that he was touring with a group of Fuqara and suddenly a popular singer sang: 'The turbulence has gone, the open space has remained.' Then the Shaykh went towards him and his head was bowed down. The Fuqara were astonished by the action of the Shaykh. When the singer finished, the Shaykh gave him all the money he had, and he was pleased with what he heard. Some of the Fuqara said to him, "O master, how can you allow yourself to hear what is not permitted?" The Shaykh replied, "And why not? Since the one who sang said, 'The turbulence has gone and the open space has remained,'" and he pointed to himself. It had gone from him and now he was relaxed and free from curing it.

We return to our text. Shaykh al-'Alawi continues:

This means no-one benefits from its reality except the one who has the station of unlettered because unlettered in the view of the People is the one who has the prophetic unletteredness.

The prophetic unletteredness is that the Rasul, sallallahu 'alayhi wa sallam, took his knowledge directly from Allah. Allah taught him. The prophetic unletteredness is that he is educated by illumination and by indication from Allah which gives him discrimination – one of the names of Qur'an is The Furqan, The Discrimination. Sayyidatuna 'Aisha said of the Rasul, sallallahu 'alayhi wa sallam: "He was Qur'an walking." So he was Discrimination walking. He could discriminate. He knew who was in front of him. This is the condition of this knowledge.

> It is the following of the Rasul, sallallahu 'alayhi wa sallam, in his sayings, and his actions, and his states – this is the real unletteredness – even if he was versed in all knowledges. Do you not see that some of the men of outward knowledge, before entering the Path, had a great station and degree and authority and high position and leadership and they loved this world and they boasted of their knowledge?

He is thinking of Imam al-Ghazali and Mawlay 'Abdalqadir al-Jilani for example.

> But when they took the Path, their states changed and they became sharers of the prophetic unletteredness, and their behaviour and all their attributes became those of the Prophet, sallallahu 'alayhi wa sallam. Then he is unlettered by station, humbled in his nobility, low in his high

position, weak in his strength, poor in his wealth – this is what is called the Qutb – the Pole, the gatherer, the beneficial – he understands the hidden minuteness of things, and he takes out of words the meanings of practice. The one who cannot smell the fragrance of this station has caught a cold! He cannot expect to understand the minuteness of knowledges while he is held by the bridle of separation, and he is forbidden the encounter with the people of Allah.

So someone who is completely held by a specific, particular knowledge, it is like a bridle that holds him back, and it holds him back from having access to the people of this circle, the People of Tasawwuf.

The people of Allah – the Rijal, said, radiyallahu 'anhum, "No-one understands our words except the one who is like us." This is what proves that the knowledge of these people is not dependent on reading or transcription – but it is a gift from the Lord.

مَا كُنتَ تَدْرِے مَا ٱلْكِتَٰبُ وَلَا ٱلْإِيمَٰنُ وَلَٰكِن جَعَلْنَٰهُ نُورًا نَّهْدِے بِهِۦ مَن نَّشَآءُ مِنْ عِبَادِنَآ

You had no idea of what the Book was, nor faith.
Nonetheless We have made it a Light by which
We guide those of Our slaves We will.
(Qur'an 42:52)

This is the meaning of his saying 'unlettered'
and Allah knows best.

In the 'Aqida of Al-Ash'ari, and
the Fiqh of Imam Malik, and in
the Tasawwuf of Imam al-Junayd
as-Salik.

In this verse he says what is obligatory for
the Sufi to take on, which are these three
degrees. What is meant is that he should
behave according to these states. He should
wear in his actions and his worship the Fiqh
of Malik or the Fiqh of one of the Imams,
radiyallahu 'anhum, and in his inward
drown in the witnessing of the Path of
al-Junayd or one of the Sufi Imams. The
meaning of it is that he should not see in
existence anything but the One Who made
it exist. He gets this by way of witnessing
and seeing, not by way of knowledge.

He is saying that the task of the Sufi is to make himself
available, to make himself open, to make himself ready

for gifts coming into the heart from Allah. So the Hizb
is recited, the Wird is recited, the Diwan is sung with
the expectation that during that time the heart is going
to be flooded to such an extent that the person will think
that they are passing out. They will be open to it.

> If he has firmness in this station, he should
> not speak except by what the intellect of
> creation can understand about doctrines,
> like that of Al-Ash'ari, so that his speech
> to them is not a disturbance. The news
> has reached us that when Rasul, sallallahu
> 'alayhi wa sallam, was asked, "Do you tell
> the people all that you have heard?" he
> replied, "Do not tell people what is beyond
> their intellect, so it does not become a
> disturbance to them."

What is significant is that he is taking from that famous
Hadith about the matter of Ma'rifa. Of course it was
a wider reference than that, that you should not speak
to people over their heads so that they do not know
what you are saying, but he is taking this at its deepest
meaning which is the subject of his book.

> Imam Shafi', radiyallahu 'anhu, said on
> this meaning, "Speak to the people by
> what they know, and avoid contradicting
> what they are used to. The ignorant have

a tremendous excuse, they see realisation and they cannot recognise it." If you say, "Do people have a doctrine other than the doctrine of Al-Ash'ari?" I would say, "Yes." Al-Ash'ari has a doctrine special to him, in himself, and this is the doctrine of men. It is not possible for it to be seen by children, and it is said that the food of men harms children.

The Prophet, sallallahu 'alayhi wa sallam, said, "There is a hidden aspect in knowledge that only the Gnostics of Allah know. If they show it, the people of ignorance deny them." How far you are from knowledge! If you do not have it, it is as if you were non-existent. Speech does not free you from state, because the Sufis do not say anything to us except what our intellects can grasp. Returning to the tradition, "Speak to the people according their intellect" – know that the three Imams, and they are Al-Ash'ari, Malik and al-Junayd, differ in these states, and every one of them has a specialty on the Path so that he is supported by a station.

Inshallah, we will continue this next time.

III

APRIL 1ST 2006

On 'Book of Doctrine'
pages 21-24

We ask Allah, subhanahu wa ta'ala, to give light in the grave to Shaykh Muhammad ibn al-Habib, and Shaykh al-Fayturi. We ask Allah, subhanahu wa ta'ala, by the Baraka of these Awliya, to give illumination to all the Fuqara of this Tariqa. We ask Allah, subhanahu wa ta'ala, to expand the circles of dhikr in every place. We ask Allah, subhanahu wa ta'ala, to give victory to the Muslims of the Sirat al-Mustaqim.

We are looking at passages from Ibn 'Ashir. Ibn 'Ashir says:

> The obligation of Allah is Existence and Timelessness, also Going-on and Absolute wealth. Distinction from His creation without similitude. The Oneness of Essence and Attributes and Acts, Power, Will, Knowledge, Life, Hearing, Speech and Seeing – all these are obligations.

That is the language of Al-Ash'ari. You will notice how everything that is said in the science of Tasawwuf is actually embedded in the teaching of Al-Ash'ari. If you were to remove the teaching of Al-Ash'ari, the whole science of Tasawwuf would basically not sustain itself. If it is not using that, then it would be the equivalent teaching in the East of Al-Maturidi. Here you may see how Shaykh al-'Alawi comments on this. He says:

> Here he explains what Allah is. Reflect, O slave, on what you have. If you describe yourself with one of these Attributes, then you are in conflict with your Lord, because Allah, the Glorious and Exalted, must exist. And Existence is the source of the Existent, and what is meant is Absolute Existence. It is

impossible that another existence exists with
this existence, because of its independence,
and the strength of its manifestation, and
the greatness of its light.

What he is coming to, what he is getting at, for the
Murid, is an understanding that how he looks on
existence, on life, with all his senses and perceptions, is
actually only true from one point of view. But there
is this other point of view which is the point of view
of these matters in relation to the truth, of how you
may understand the truth. What he is doing is pulling,
as it were, the ground from underneath the Faqir.
He is taking away from him everything he has been
standing on in his understanding of existence. So he has
a completely new way of looking at things.

Know then, that this Existence does not
accept negation in the inner eyes of the
'Arifin, in the same way that the sensory
does not accept negation in the eyes of
those who are veiled.

'Those who are veiled' being people who perceive
existence in the normal manner by which life is led.
What he is saying is very radical, and you have to be
patient with it and follow it.

Existence does not accept negation in the

inner eyes of the 'Arifin, in the same way that the sensory does not accept negation in the eyes of those who are veiled. Maybe because the appearance of meaning to the meaning is stronger than the appearance of the sensory to the sensory, when the appearance of the absolute existence comes to the Sufi and he drowns in glorification, even if he explores the field of timelessness, he will not find an end to it. He looks at going-on and he does not find a boundary to it. He sinks in the mires of the inward and there he will not find a crack. He ascends with the aspects of the outward, and he does not find escape. Then he says, "O my confusion, where do I go?" Then the realities of the Names and the Attributes call to him, "Did you ask to limit the Essence? Or did you try to describe Him by the directions? You are in a station that requires the Names and the Attributes to be hidden. Why do you pay attention to created things?"

So the realities of the Names and the Attributes ask him this: "Why do you pay attention to created things?"

Then he gives himself up to that Existence and he realises that with that Existence there is neither non-existence nor existence. In conclusion, Existence is the self of Essence and timelessness is a negative attribute of the existence of firstness, and going-on negates the existence of lastness, because lastness implies that there is an end to existence. Allah the Exalted is timeless and there is no beginning to His timelessness. He goes on, and there is no end to His going-on. There is to that Absolute Existence a complete independence, meaning that the Essence is independent of all possibilities, even from the Attributes. It stands on its own and it is not impoverished by otherness. It is independent of place. The Real, glory be to Him, does not need a place to show Himself or to remain. How can He need a place when the place needed Him before He needed it? The tongue of this presence spoke in one of my Qasidas, may Allah forgive me:

> I am the absolute in existence,
> not limited.
> My place is that I am from me,
> and in knowledge I am in
> ignorance.

Now you must really grasp the following because it has great beauty and there is great wisdom in it:

Another obligation is that Allah should be the opposite of event.

Think how the kuffar see that their experience of life is that the event is the reality, but here Shaykh al-'Alawi is saying that Allah is the opposite of event.

Another obligation is that Allah should be the opposite of event. The Gnostics do not rely on this attribute because resemblance does not occur in their thought by state.

'Resemblance' meaning something being like something else. That never occurs to them.

They are outside the realm of imagination and 'how' and resemblance. The barriers have been destroyed and the witnesser is enfolded in the Witnessed. Do they see other than the worshipped King? No, and there is nothing existent with Allah, so there is no resemblance. This is a good attribute for the veiled ones, because it is a ship for their escape. It negates in their hearts the existence of 'how' and resemblance and directions and partiality and place and discrimination. The Real is exalted above all the attributes of event, and He unveils the attribute of exaltation to the 'Arifin.

In other words, the thing that the wahhabis fail to understand is that when they say that Allah is One and nothing is associated with Him, they do not, if I may say, actually mean it! In a very definite sense they do not recognise, although they claim Tanzih – they claim Allah being exalted over everything – but what Shaykh al-'Alawi is pointing to is that to the 'Arifin, this is actually the case. So what matters to us cannot be the event. Our attitude to the event, to things happening, becomes different.

The Real is exalted above all the attributes of event, and He unveils the attribute of exaltation to the 'Arifin. They are taken by bewilderment because they find the Real exalted above exaltation. They want to give news of extraordinary secrets, and He forbids them to speak and the words remain hidden on the tongue. Perhaps a word comes out of them that resembles resemblance and it causes great turbulence in the hearing of the people of the veil, even if it is far-reaching in exaltation.

In other the words, the 'Arifin, in a certain state of losing their exaltation they say things, and when they say these things which are true they are misunderstood by the people of the veil because they think it is to do with event and with creation. Do you follow?

No-one is free of 'how' and resemblance except the one who accompanies the 'Arifin. He travels the way of the universe. How can he be free of chains if he sees that the Real is far away? How can he be free of the boundaries if in his view the cosmos exists? If you are not annihilated, O brother, from existence, in the witnessing of the Worshipped, and you take the Companion before you take the Path – then you are in a position where you cannot have any success except by the Lutf of Allah. Allah takes us by His Lutf and He protects us from 'how' and resemblance. O brother, disconnection by the tongue does not benefit you nor does connection by the inward. If you are veiled from Him, you make connection in exalting Him because you do not have knowledge. If you had knowledge of Him, then you would exalt Him above connection because of the annihilation of your existence in His Existence. In conclusion, the connection of the Sufis is better than the disconnection of the common folk.

The basis of connection among the Sufis is that it is founded on this double knowledge. Whereas if the common folk make disconnection it is by their intellect. They recognise it is true but they only know it by the teaching of it.

The veiled one must disconnect Allah above what is not appropriate, and he must not speak about what he does not know. He must strive in seeking the One Who will take him from the existence of himself to the witnessing of his Lord, until he finds that resemblance and 'how' are negated before he negates them, and they are annihilated before he annihilates them.

Another obligation on Allah is Oneness in Essence, Attribute and Action.

This is the basic teaching of Al-Ash'ari.

Another obligation on Allah is Oneness in Essence, Attribute and Action. He cannot be made up or counted. This is why he said, 'Oneness in Essence and Attribute,' so that the hearer would not be deluded if he hears of the existence of the Attributes and of their timelessness and believe in a number of timelessnesses. Allah is above this, and the oneness of the Real can have nothing added to it because it does not accept addition, in the same way that it does not accept imperfection. 'Allah was, and nothing was with Him – and then he quotes the famous addition to this which was made by Imam al-Junayd – and He is now as He was.'

The Attributes do not stand on their own until they are independent by their own existence, or they are separated from what they are attributed to, which is the Essence. This is the meaning of the oneness of Essence and Attributes. As to the oneness of Acts, it means that it is impossible that there is an action along with the action of Allah, subhanahu wa ta'ala.

In conclusion, the Sufis are divided into three groups. The first group see that there is no Doer except Allah, and they become realised by the meaning of oneness of Acts, by way of discovery, not by way of belief. They say that the Doer is One even if the actions are many. These are the children of the Tariqa, according to realisation. The second group has realised the reality of the oneness of the Attributes. When they know this oneness in Attribute, they find that there is no hearer, no seer, no living, no speaker, no powerful, no-one with will, no knower, except Allah. They see the Attributes in all existing things by seeing, not by proof. If we realise that there is no

Doer except Allah, then it is not possible to attribute these Attributes to other-than-Him.

The third group are the ones who have realised the realities of oneness of the Essence. They are veiled from other-than-that, from existing things, because of what they have discovered of the greatness of the Essence. They do not find a place where existing things appear. They say, "In reality, there is no existent except Allah," because they have lost all other-than-Him. These are the people of Essence, the 'Arifin, the unifiers – the Muwahhidun, and other than these are veiled and heedless, and they have not tasted unity and have not smelled the fragrance of isolation, though they thought they were unifiers when they heard of unity. No, they are far from the Real, and they are cut off.

Unity is not carried on paper and is not spoken by mouth. The entire earth and heaven cannot hold it, except the secrets of the 'Arifin and the hearts of the lovers. Rasul, sallallahu 'alayhi wa sallam, said that his Lord said: "My earth and My heaven cannot contain Me, but the heart of My

believing slave contains me." Oh, what a
heart, and what a Lord! Oh, what a lodging
and what a Lodger! O Allah, lodge in our
hearts.

The Fuqara sing 'Fana' in Allah' from the Diwan of
Shaykh Muhammad ibn al-Habib, radiyallahu 'anhu.

ANNIHILATION IN ALLAH

O seeker of Fana' in Allah,
say constantly, "Allah, Allah!"

And withdraw yourself in Him
from other-than-Him,
and with your heart – see Allah.

Gather your concerns in Him and He will be
enough in place of other-than-Allah.

Be a pure slave to Him and
you will be free from other-than-Allah.

Submit yourself to Him and be humble
and you will win a secret from Allah.

Do dhikr with gravity and sincerity
in the presence of the slaves of Allah.

Hide (your awareness)
when He is manifested to you
with lights from the Essence of Allah.

With us, other is impossible,
for existence is the Haqq of Allah.

Constantly cut right through your Wahm
with a pure Tawhid to Allah.

So the oneness of action appears
at the beginning of dhikr of Allah,

And the oneness of attributes
comes from the love in Allah.

And the oneness of His Essence
gives Baqa' with Allah.

Joy to the one who walks
on the Path of Allah,

Believing in a living Shaykh,
who is an 'Arif of Allah,

He holds constantly to His love
and sells his self to Allah.

He rises in the night to recite His word,
longing for Allah.

And so he gets what he seeks of the power
of knowledge in Allah.

Our gifts are from a Prophet who is the
master of the creatures of Allah.

May the purest of blessings be upon him in
quantity as great as the knowledge of Allah.

And on his Family and Companions,
and everyone who calls to Allah.

IV

APRIL 8ᵀᴴ 2006

On 'Book of Doctrine'
pages 26-31

We were looking at the book of Shaykh al-'Alawi, making commentary on the famous Murshid al-Mu'in of Ibn 'Ashir. Remember that he is not saying, 'This is what it really means,' because these are the ruhani insights that the people of Tasawwuf are entitled to make without denying the truth of what its obvious meaning is, which is a direct text on the 'Aqida and the Fiqh and the Tasawwuf.

In the last part we read that Ibn 'Ashir says:

> The obligation of Allah is Existence and Timelessness, also Going-on and Absolute wealth. Distinction from His creation without similitude. The Oneness of Essence and Attributes and Acts, Power, Will, Knowledge, Life, Hearing, Speech and Seeing – all these are obligations.

They are what he calls the obligations of Allah. Then he goes on to describe what you cannot say about Allah, subhanahu wa ta'ala:

> The opposites of these Attributes are impossible – non-existence, occurrence – but they are the Attributes of events, also obliteration, impoverishment. Resemblance, the negation of oneness, incapacity, reprehensibility, ignorance and death, and deafness, dumbness, blindness and silence.

Remember that this is a summary of the teaching of Al-Ash'ari which is the wall of protection that the Muslim Community has set up to protect the knowledge of

Tawhid and the knowledge of Allah, subhanahu wa ta'ala, as revealed in the Qur'an, from being brought down to the ratiocination and mental operation of what is philosophy. Shaykh al-'Alawi says:

> He informs us here that everything that is impossible for Allah is an obligation on the slave. And the slave among the Sufis is the scholar, from the earth to His Throne. It means that everyone who has come from the word, Kun! – Be! is otherness. And other is obligated by everything mentioned in these verses. They are non-existence, occurrence – these are with regard to events, so brother, you must realise your attribute and that you look with the eye of your heart to the beginning of your existence, and the state of its coming-out from nothingness. If you realise your attributes, He will give you His Attributes. One of your attributes is non-existence, and this is the attribute of all the universe. If you are satisfied with your non-existence, He, subhanahu wa ta'ala, will give you His Existence. If you attribute to yourself existence, you oppose Him.

He is now going deeply into what you might call the actual psychology of the Sufi – how he experiences existence, how he looks on existence and how he looks on himself.

How can you attribute it to yourself when there is proof of your non-existence? You have occurred, and you know that yesterday, you were not there.

Then he quotes the Ayat from Surat al-Insan (76:1):

هَلْ أَتَىٰ عَلَى ٱلْإِنسَٰنِ حِينٌ مِّنَ ٱلدَّهْرِ لَمْ يَكُن شَيْئًا مَّذْكُورًا ۝

Has man ever known a point of time
when he was not something remembered?

Shaykh al-'Alawi says:

Where did you get this existence, and who made you witness what you have witnessed? Who brought you forth to witnessing? You are still non-existence and existence is to the Existent, subhanahu wa ta'ala. He made it and He appeared in it, and without His appearance in the appearances the eyes would never set upon them. Some say – and he quotes the Sufi poets – :

He makes things exist,
and He is the source
of their existence.
Without His Existence,
their existence
would not have appeared.

Another of your attributes is annihilation.
You are, brother, annihilated before your
annihilation, you are decomposed before
your decomposition, and removed before
your removal. You are illusion in illusion,
and non-existence in non-existence.
When did you exist so that you could be
annihilated? You are just like a mirage that
is thought by the thirsty one to be water.
When he comes near it, he finds nothing –
and there he finds Allah.

This is a direct reference to Surat an-Nur (24:39):

$$\text{وَالَّذِينَ كَفَرُوٓاْ أَعْمَٰلُهُمْ كَسَرَابٍ بِقِيعَةٍ}$$
$$\text{يَحْسَبُهُ ٱلظَّمْـَٔانُ مَآءً حَتَّىٰٓ إِذَا جَآءَهُۥ لَمْ يَجِدْهُ شَيْـًٔا}$$
$$\text{وَوَجَدَ ٱللَّهَ عِندَهُۥ}$$

> But the actions of those who are kafir
> are like a mirage in the desert.
> A thirsty man thinks it is water
> but when he reaches it,
> he finds it to be nothing at all,
> but he finds Allah there.

When did you exist so that you could be
annihilated? You are just like a mirage that

is thought by the thirsty one to be water.
When he comes near it, he finds nothing –
and there he finds Allah.

He is using this Ayat to show that this amazing thing
that he is saying is actually the foundational teaching of
the Qur'an.

If you search yourself, you will find it is
nothing – and you will find Allah in it.

So what he is saying is that the Muraqaba, the Khalwa of
the Sufi, when he sits alone, calling on Allah by Allah's
name – that is his searching himself. In other words,
if you use all your self to call on Allah, if you search
yourself you will find that the self is nothing, because all
the attributes will disappear, until the consciousness that
you are without attributes disappears, which is what we
call Fana' fillah, "And you will find Allah in it."

That is, instead of finding yourself you find
Him. Nothing remains of you except the
name without shape, because existence is
for Allah, not for your self. If you started
to realise what is, and found that Allah
is, by stripping from yourself what never
belonged to it, you would find it like an
onion – all skins. If you take the skins away
one by one you find nothing, and this is the

example of the slave with the existence of his Lord.

Another of your attributes is that you are poor by essence, because we have pictured your existence and we have said that you exist, but that existence is poor – a total impoverishment of essence. It cannot be confirmed unless you confirm the One Who made it exist. If not, it disintegrates instantly. With all this, meaning the non-existence of the slave and his obliteration and his impoverishment, you will find that he tends to make resemblance to the Real, subhanahu wa ta'ala. He negates the Oneness. This is why the author has said, "He makes resemblance and he negates the oneness." If he confirms his own existence with the existence of the Real, and he knows that non-existence is an obligation on himself, for example, if his self talks to him about existence, then he is making resemblance to Allah.

In other words, if, in the loss of the attributes he recognises that he has lost the attributes, he is still making resemblance between himself and Allah, subhanahu wa ta'ala.

He made himself existence with the existence of the Real. He must not negate the oneness which is impossible to do because he confirms the two existences: the existence of the Real and his own existence. Then where is unity and where is isolation? This is Shirk to the Sufis. In other words, if you stop at the annihilation of the attributes and still, by your own being, identify this as the truth, you are still making Shirk.

> Allah does not forgive that you associate something with Him. This is a wrong action that cannot be measured. It is said that Rabi'a al-'Adawiya, rahimahullah, met one of the 'Arifin and asked him about his state. He said, "I have trodden the Path of the ones who obey, and never have made a wrong action since Allah created me." She said to him, "Beware O my son. Your existence is a wrong action that cannot be measured."

> Go the way of the unifiers, the Muwahhidun, brother. Do not affirm any existent other-than-Allah. If one of the Sufis affirms his own existence, he associates with Allah, may Allah protect him from that. But the common folk cannot escape the affirmation of the existence of other-than-Allah. In this affirmation are all disasters.

In other words, it is the failure to understand the true Tawhid that puts the Muslim people off the Path and that is disaster. So if disaster befalls a Muslim people it is because they have lost the true teaching of Tawhid. If they have the true teaching of Tawhid, as in all the great moments of Muslim history, it is because there has always been at the heart of that community a body of 'Arifin who recognise this and who teach it to the common people.

Another of the attributes of the slave is incapacity, because power is only attributed to Allah, the Mighty and majestic. No-one has a part in it except Allah, even if he was a King who was made near, or a sent Messenger. All that is other-than-Allah is incapable, owning nothing for himself, neither bad nor good, except what Allah wants. Surat al-Hajj (22:73):

$$\text{إِنَّ ٱلَّذِينَ تَدْعُونَ مِن دُونِ ٱللَّهِ لَن يَخْلُقُوا ذُبَابًا وَلَوِ ٱجْتَمَعُوا لَهُۥ}$$

Those whom you call upon besides Allah
are not even able to create a single fly,
even if they were to join together to do it.

Realise your limited capacity, and Allah will give you His power.

Another of the attributes of the slave is the lack of will. As to will, it is one of the Attributes of the Living, Mighty and Majestic. If you attribute it to yourself, then you have attributed the opposite to your Lord, because you have no part in it. Know your position. If not, you will fall in the eyes of Allah. The one who attributes will to Allah lives in security. The one who disputes this with Allah stops with its opposite, which is lack of will. The Real, Mighty and Majestic, says – in a very famous Hadith Qudsi of Rasul, sallallahu 'alayhi wa sallam:

> O slave, you want something and I want something. If you surrender to Me in what I want, I will disagree with what you want, and there will be nothing but what I want.

In the original text it is: 'You want something, and Allah wants something, and what you want is not what Allah wants, but know that what Allah wants will certainly happen.'

Leave will to Allah, and do not choose an action alongside the action of Allah. To surrender the will is the affair of the 'Arifin, and the disputation of the judges is the attribute of the ignorant, the heedless ones.

You find modern Muslims saying, "Inshallah," in the wrong way because they do not understand the Tawhid. In Surat al-Kahf (18:23) we find:

وَلَا تَقُولَنَّ لِشَاْىْءٍ إِنِّي فَاعِلٌ ذَٰلِكَ غَدًا ۝ إِلَّآ أَن يَشَآءَ ٱللَّهُ

Never say about anything,
"I am doing that tomorrow,"
without adding "If Allah wills."

Thus the command in the Qur'an is not to say you are going to do a thing unless you say, "Inshallah." In other words, at the moment you impose your will on events you deny it and give it to Allah. Someone may say, "I hope it rains today," and the ignorant Muslim of today says, "Inshallah." But the rain has got nothing to do with the Mashi'a of Allah! You might say, "I hope all these Americans in Iraq are destroyed!" and someone says, "Inshallah!" But that has nothing to do with the Mashi'a of Allah. The Mashi'a of Allah is: "I will do it, inshallah." Between your action and the event, you surrender your will to Allah, subhanahu wa ta'ala. In other words, you are not the doer. You make the action, but it is not yours. The minute you hear someone say "Inshallah" incorrectly, do not accept it. Reject it! Say, "That has nothing to do with the Mashi'a of Allah." Otherwise you will lose your own Tawhid before this ignorance of the one who says it to you. Shaykh al-'Alawi goes on to a most interesting point:

> At the beginning the seeker has a will, and that is his orientation towards Allah, subhanahu wa ta'ala. The end is to surrender the will to Allah. The one who has will with Allah is off the Path of his Lord at the end of the matter. Beware brother, of your unwillingness, and agree to the will of Allah. As Shaykh az-Zarruq said:

سَلِّمْ لِسَلْمَى
وَسِرْ حَيْثُ سَارَتْ
وَاتَّبِعْ رِيَاحَ الْقَضَا
وَدُرْ حَيْثُ دَارَتْ

> Submit to Salma,
> Go wherever she goes!
> Follow the winds of destiny,
> Turn wherever they turn.

This is a very famous poem. Shaykh Ahmad az-Zarruq was in a very remote place in the middle of the desert called Hadramut. He had been there with his Shaykh for about two years, and at a certain point the Muqaddam came to him and said, "The Shaykh said that he can do no more for you, it is finished. Go!" He said, "But I came to get something from him and I am not complete, I have not reached the goal – I cannot leave!" The Muqaddam said, "That's the orders. Pack up your things and go! I will be back in five minutes and we will lock you out of the Zawiyya. There are bandits outside and we cannot leave the door open."

Shaykh az-Zarruq came out with all his belongings and he was shattered. He said to the Muqaddam, "Please go back to the Shaykh and ask him to give me something that I can take with me for the rest of my life." The Muqaddam told him to wait outside, and he shut and bolted the door and went back to the Shaykh. The Muqaddam came back and he opened the grill and he said these two lines of poetry from the Shaykh:

$$\text{سَلِّمْ لِسَلْمَى}$$
$$\text{وَسِرْ حَيْثُ سَارَتْ}$$
$$\text{وَاتَّبِعْ رِيَاحَ الْقَضَا}$$
$$\text{وَدُرْ حَيْثُ دَارَتْ}$$

Submit to Salma,
Go wherever she goes!
Follow the winds of destiny,
Turn wherever they turn.

'Salma' in the language of the Sufis is used, like 'Layla', to indicate the Essence, the Dhat of Allah. Then the Muqaddam shut the grill, and with that Shaykh az-Zarruq lost consciousness and achieved what he had been waiting for. That is how he became Shaykh – with these two lines: 'Submit to Salma, go wherever she goes! Follow the winds of destiny, turn wherever they turn.'

This is another kind of knowledge that is the opposite of the knowledge of ordinary people, because it is actually understanding how existence works, how existence is set up by Allah, subhanahu wa ta'ala. In it, every object, every event has meaning and these meanings lead you to Allah, subhanahu wa ta'ala. This is the difference between the Sufis and the ignorant Muslims who, if they are taught the proper Tawhid in the mosques, will have a glimpse of this and an understanding of this.

Even the common people among the kuffar taste this for an instant, and for a moment they feel they are in tune with the destiny. While they stay in tune with the destiny, everything goes right for them, but when they lose it, everything crashes and collapses about them. What he is saying here is that if you think that the Will is from you, then the operation of your life is on the wrong basis – you do not actually have any will! Since Will belongs to Allah, if you think you are imposing your will, it is not that you are imposing your will but that you are actually only on a procedure that can only end in disaster because it is not true.

What is interesting is that the nihilists of the nineteenth century, of which we are now getting the backwash in events, came from the point where the materialist, rationalist society reached its nihilism. They were the nihilists in Russia, and Nietzsche in Germany with his main book which was called 'The Will to Power.' He was calling people to have the will to power, to build a will to power on the ego, and what we saw of that destroyed the whole of Europe. The drive to the will to power wiped out millions of people and devastated a whole civilisation. We will continue with the text:

> **Another of the attributes of the slaves is ignorance, and you are, O slave, ignorant of yourself and your origin. How can you ask for knowledge of Allah? You must ask for knowledge of yourself and realise what is your origin. Then you can pay attention to other than that. You do not know what you are and where you come from, but you found yourself in this appearance and you stood up in this place and ran away from the other place. All that you can say is that you are from non-existence, and you do not know what non-existence is. It is like you have attributed a whole world to non-existence from which you came and to which you are returning. If it is so, you have made non-existence an existence because you made it a thing.**

Sallallahu 'alayhi wa sallam said, "Allah was, and there was nothing with Him". There is no non-existent with the Existent. If you affirm something with the Timeless, you have no knowledge, you have no Ma'rifa, you are ignorant and you ignore your ignorance. So seek one to take you by your hand and bring you to the Presence of your Lord. Then your illusion becomes understanding, and your ignorance knowledge.

Another of the attributes of the slave is death. Life is not one of your attributes. You are dead though seeming to live. Your example is one who is inhabited by a jinn: he says, "I am so-and-so," but he is not. If you put your body between the hands of your Lord, like the body of your father Adam, 'alayhi salam, He will blow of His ruh into you and forgive you and He will create your being in His being. Then you say, "I am living" and there will be no harm because you have realised your death. But if you attribute living to yourself, and become independent by your existence, then you become an opponent to Allah, subhanahu wa ta'ala, because Allah has said, in Surat an-Nahl (16:4):

خَلَقَ ٱلْإِنسَـٰنَ مِن نُّطْفَةٍ فَإِذَا هُوَ خَصِيمٌ مُّبِينٌ ۝

He created man from a drop of sperm
and yet he is an open challenger!

He quotes this Ayat as proof of what he is saying.

**So brother, return to your attribute, which
is death, and be firm in your place, and do
not pretend to that which you do not have,
until Allah supports you with His ruh.**

In other words, take the Path of pursuing this knowledge
until you recognise your non-existence. That is why
the Sufis say, "Maut qabla tamut" – Die before you die.
Die the death of meaning before you die the death of
the sensory.

**Another of the attributes of the slave
is deafness. You are now, O slave, deaf.
Hearing is not yours, Allah is the Hearer. If
you attribute hearing to yourself, you will
become deaf – even when you hear you do
not hear. If you were hearing, you would
hear the call of Allah at all times and in all
states. Allah is still speaking, and silence
is impossible to Him. So where is your
hearing, and where is your understanding?**

Commentary on Knowledge of God

You are deaf and you are in the folds of non-existence. If you came to existence, you would hear the call of the Worshipped One, and how can the deaf hear the call? If you heard, you would answer. How can you answer when you are described as dumb? If you are dumb, how can you pretend to speech, which is one of the Attributes of Allah?

He is reminding one that the knowledge comes by the loss of all the attributes in approaching annihilation, so that, for example, you do not hear. Allah is the Hearer. When I was in the Khalwa with Shaykh al-Fayturi, radiyallahu 'anhu, he came each day to see how I was progressing. I said to him, "I could not do the dhikr because I was not able to speak. Then I heard the Name of Allah, but I was not speaking." He smiled and said, "What a strange thing! There were you looking for the dhikr, and there was the dhikr looking for you."

If you spoke, you would be suitable for teaching, and this is why the station of speech and discussion is forbidden to you. If you realise your dumbness, He will give you His speech, and you will speak by the words of Allah. You speak with Allah until your hearing becomes the hearing of Allah, and you hear nothing except from Allah.

308

Another of your attributes, O slave, is
blindness. If you had sight, you would
recognise His manifest Name. You are
blind, you see nothing except appearances.
Where is the manifestation of the Real?
There is no veil to His manifestation, but
your attribute has overcome you, which is
being blind.

What he is saying is that the sensory 'seeing' is actually
a blindness.

You are blind to the existence of sight,
because of what you regard sight to be. If
you realised your attribute, and came nearer
to Him, and did what He expects of you, He
would be your hearing and your seeing. If
He becomes your hearing and your seeing,
you will hear and see nothing except Him,
because you hear Him by His hearing, and
you see Him by His sight, and this is your
nearness to Allah, and your orientation
towards Him.

Again, there is the Hadith Qudsi: 'My slave approaches
Me until I love him, and then I become the sight with
which he sees, the tongue with which he speaks and the
foot with which he walks.'

So reflect, O brother, about your attribute which is blindness. Think of what there is in that of wisdom. Then, you will see the gleams of the inner eye. Then you will hear what you have never heard before, and you will see what you have never seen before. This does not become real to you except by knowing yourself and your attributes.

6

COMMENTARY

ON

STIMULATION OF DESIRE
FOR THE ACT OF DHIKR
and
PURIFICATION

– from the Diwan of
Shaykh Muhammad ibn al-Habib

Given on April 22nd 2006
at the Masjid al-Mahmoud,
Constantia, Cape Town

APRIL 22ND 2006

STIMULATION OF DESIRE
FOR THE ACT OF DHIKR

O you who desire
nearness to Allah immediately
– you must perform dhikr of Allah
openly and secretly.

Fill the Awqat with it
and you will swiftly ascend
to the pinnacle of 'Irfan
with pure Fikr.

Through polishing the mirror of the heart,
the veil is removed,
and lights appear to the heart
from the purity of the dhikr.

By dhikr of the God of the Throne
you will become a zahid among men,
and you will be in Fana' from the self,
which holds you back on the journey.

You will become one who sits with Allah,
without ceremony,
and you will be safe from doubt,
Shirk, and otherness.

You will journey from the cosmos
to the Presence of Purity,
and you will witness the Act of Allah
in the creation and the Command.

You will rise to the Names
and drink of their light,
so the Attributes will appear to you
without a veil.

The meaning of the Essence
will emerge from the perfection of Fana',
so you will gain Baqa', rich with Allah
for the rest of your life.

I

If the breath of His dhikr
were to fill the west
and there was a sick man in the east,
that man would be cured of his affliction.

This is the first part of the Qasida, 'Stimulation of Desire
for the Act of Dhikr.' What these verses describe is
nothing less than what the whole journey of the Khalwa
is. Shaykh Muhammad ibn al-Habib says openly what
will happen in the Khalwa when you call on the Name
of Allah. He describes it step by step.

**Fill the Awqat with it and you will swiftly ascend to
the pinnacle of Divine knowledge with pure Fikr.
Through polishing the mirror of the heart, the veil
is removed.** The Shaykh is telling you every single
step of the way. **And lights appear to the heart from
the purity of the dhikr.** Thus he explains that in the
process of this you undergo a kind of transformation
so that by the dhikr of the Ism al-'Adham, of the Great
Name of Allah, you will become zahid among men.

In other words, things that mattered to you before will
not matter at all, and you will be in Fana' from the
self. The self will fall away, because it is the self which
holds you back on the journey. **You will become one
who sits with Allah without ceremony, and you**

will be safe from doubt and otherness, that is, from thinking that there is anything other-than-Allah. **You will journey from the cosmos to the Presence of Purity, and you will witness the Act of Allah in the creation and the Command.** He is telling you exactly what is going to happen. **You will rise to the Names and drink of their light, so the Attributes will appear to you without a veil. The meaning of the Essence will emerge from the perfection of Fana', so you will gain Baqa', rich with Allah for the rest of your life. If the breath of His dhikr were to fill the west and there was a sick man in the east, that man would be cured of his affliction.**

That whole process is what you would call the Tasawwuf of the knowledge of Allah, subhanahu wa ta'ala, of Ma'rifa. But like a coin which has two sides, there is another face of Tasawwuf which is your preparation for it and this you find in the Qasida 'Purification'.

PURIFICATION

If you wish purification from Shirk
and the claim that you exist,
and to drink from the nectar of union
until you are quenched,

Then wrap yourself in Sabr
and wind on the turban of Tawba.
Wear the shirt of Zuhd
and in it exhaust your strength.

Put on the twin sandals
of Khawf and Raja',
take the staff of Yaqin
and a store of Taqwa.

Take the bridle of 'Ilm
for the horse of himma,
and the protection of companions
who will guard you from Bala.

So struggle seriously and travel quickly on the
journey. Do not be stopped by the contemplation
of created existence – that would veil you from
the place of safety.

Rather reflect on Ihsan
and be sincere in Shukr to Him,
and get up at dawn, be humble,
and hand over your trouble to Him.

And bless the Qutb of existence
and his group with a blessing
that will spread abroad our Secret
and make it known to all.

This is Tasawwuf seen from the other side, so to speak. This is what is required in order for you to make this journey which is described in the first Qasida we looked at. **If you wish purification from shirk and the claim that you exist** – again, remember that what we have been seeing in all the teaching of Tasawwuf is the basic denial of the reality of the nafs. The claim that you exist is a kind of presumption from the point of view of the Tawhid which we have been studying. **Drink from the nectar of union until you are quenched,** and this drinking is something we practise and rehearse, so to speak, in the Night of Dhikr, in the singing of the Diwan and doing Hadra.

Then wrap yourself in Sabr. WRAP yourself in Sabr! This is an age where perhaps the worst thing about modern man is his inability to have Sabr because everything is in order to try to get things done now, and to be impatient. There are times when you have to move and there are times when you must not move. You have to have Sabr to know when the time is to wait, and when the time is to move forward. If you do not know when to wait, you will not know when you must act. So, **Wrap yourself in Sabr and wind on the turban of Tawba.** It is beautiful. In other words, your intellect, or how you are measuring existence has to be illuminated by your Tawba of Allah, subhanahu wa ta'ala.

Wear the shirt of Zuhd and in it exhaust your strength. It is a kind of opposite of everything the modern person would be told for personality development! **Wear the shirt of Zuhd and in it exhaust your strength. Put on the twin sandals of Khawf and Raja'** – one step is Khawf and the next step is Raja'. You are between fear and hope. **Take the staff of Yaqin,** of certainty, because certainty will give you the strength, **and a store of Taqwa.** A 'store' of Taqwa, so that you can draw on that Taqwa again and again.

Take the bridle of 'Ilm for the horse of himma. In other words, you have a longing and a yearning, and at the same time your 'Ilm will hold the horse in the metaphor to a sensible pace. It is not to go charging ahead like the Majdhub who wants to be ecstatic before he has got the basic learning about existence. **And the protection of companions who will guard you from Bala,** from trouble. This is a thing which you must remember. The Mumin is the mirror of the Mumin. When the Mumin holds up to you something and you reject him, what you are really doing is rejecting the mirror because you do not like the mirror. But the Mumin is a mirror of the Mumin, so the protection of the Muminun is in the Jama'at.

It is what Shaykh Muhammad al-Kasabi said in his Khutba yesterday: "There is safety in the Jama'at, and the one who withdraws from the Jama'at and goes

alone has a companion allotted to him from Shaytan."
Whether that is in this place or any other place, it is not
fitting to be alone. The only one who can be alone, and
they are very few, are those among the 'Arifin who have
chosen seclusion and withdrawal, and they do exist in
every place, but there is no doubt then about the light
which they do have and that is something very special.

**So struggle seriously and travel quickly on the
journey. Do not be stopped by the contemplation
of created existence – that would veil you from the
place of safety.** There has to be a kind of jumping
out of yourself to knowing that everything you see, all
the created forms, their reality is meanings. The forms
themselves do not have meaning but they indicate
meaning. All the created forms represent meanings.
That is why, in this world, we move among sensory
things and they are all meanings, and we have to
interpret what they mean. All things which come to
us – the good things which come to us and the bad
things which come to us, the permitted things and the
forbidden things – they all have meanings. We have to
interpret everything in the sensory world with meaning.

This is why without Shari'at you cannot make that
interpretation, you will not know where you stand.
You have to apply it. What you find is that, especially
among us not living under a Muslim Amir, we are in a
position where if we like the Islamic Law we apply it,

and if it does not suit us we dump it. You see it in many things, especially things to do with money and the use of money inside the household, and between Muslims. When you want to use Islamic Law you use it and when you do not want to use it you just turn away. This is a nifaq you cannot afford.

Do not be stopped by the contemplation of created existence. I am saying that everything in the sensory world is actually meanings, and everything in the Unseen world is meanings which we will experience as sensory. In Qur'an you will find that Allah, subhanahu wa ta'ala, describes all the pleasures of the Janna as sensory. It is a world of meanings but they will be experienced as sensory. It is the opposite of the visible world. The Seen and the Unseen are opposite each other.

Rather reflect on Ihsan. Ihsan in the Hadith of Imam Muslim is: "To worship Allah as if you saw Him, and while you do not see Him, know that He sees you." This is Ma'rifa, that you KNOW He sees you. **Rather reflect on Ihsan and be sincere in Shukr to Him, and get up at dawn and be humble, and hand over your trouble to Him.** When people have trouble, the age has taught them and the philosophies of the kuffar have taught them that they have to deal with their trouble, but the Shaykh is saying, "Hand over your trouble!" If you have got a big trouble you should rather go on 'Umra than go to the bank! If you hand the thing over to Allah then you will see that Allah will move all the situation for you. While you try to unravel it, it will just go on tying you up until you are completely, as the Americans say, 'hog-tied'. You will not be able to move.

When the affair is difficult, take it to Allah, the whole thing. It is the truth of every moment but it is in a crisis that you realise it. Muhiyuddin Ibn al-'Arabi tells how Sayyiduna Ayyub, 'alayhi salam, was given all these afflictions, and because he was a servant of Allah, subhanahu wa ta'ala, he did not complain. So more afflictions came and more afflictions came until finally he could not bear it any longer and he called out to Allah, and the minute he called out to Allah, Allah took the afflictions from him. Even he had to reach that point of Ma'rifa that he knew the affair was in the hands of Allah. So even this he had to hand over to Allah, subhanahu wa ta'ala. Sayyiduna Abu Bakr as-Siddiq was asked when he was sick, "Who made you better?" And he said, "The same One Who made me ill." The sickness was from Allah and the cure was from Allah.

And bless the Qutb of existence and his group with a blessing that will spread abroad our Secret and make it known to all. We want this knowledge to spill out, and it spills out from us by our always being the same in every place. When we go out among people who are not Muslim and go out among people who are Muslim but are not Sufi and do not know the knowledges of Tasawwuf – you spread this, and you spread this by the light you have and the courtesy you have.

You have to have adab in every situation, and most importantly, when people serve you, you must recognise them. You must use the eye and look at the people who serve you and not ignore them. You must not take a thing by the hand and not look at the person with the eye. You must acknowledge them. You must not treat people below you as inferior and people above you as superior. The ones who treat the ones below them badly, treat the ones above them over-well. In that sense, that part of you should be withdrawn from the process of these things and this is done by adab. I do not mean oriental courtesy, I mean the adab of Rasul, sallallahu 'alayhi wa sallam. We will now sing the section from 'Stimulation of the Desire for the Act of Dhikr' followed by 'Purification'.

HADRA

We are all very appreciative and grateful for the visit of our brothers from Granada and especially Shaykh Muhammad al-Kasabi, and also Sidi Hamid and Hajj Abdalkabir from Morocco. We want this time to make a reminder for ourselves on this occasion, a reminder for our people in Granada and our people here in Cape Town.

In Granada there are two communities and they are quite distinct. There is the Spanish community of Muslims and there are the Muslims who have come from Muslim lands and they have a separate identity. This is an age without Amr and the people who come from lands which call themselves Muslim are, in this age, the last people in the world to understand the Deen of Islam as a social phenomenon of responsibility. The Deen is Ad-Deen al-Mu'amala, and they have lost the Mu'amala because they have lost the Amr. On the other hand we have a bit of knowledge, but we are pinioned and surrounded by another command that is not based on any sort of wisdom or reality but based on the expansion of the wealth of a very small minority.

Here in Cape Town we have two communities. We have a community in the city and we have another community on the Plains. That is a distinction which is pure injustice. At the moment we cannot right that injustice but we have to nevertheless unify the Muslims of these two places and we must unify them by an adab and by an affection and a concern that does not separate us into the two communities. The principle of this society is to condemn an increasing number of poor people to submit to a decreasing number of enormously powerful and wealthy people. This is a way which can only lead to a most terrible explosion at some point.

In a sense, this also affects Granada. There has to be conciliation between the two groups – not reconciliation but conciliation. There has to be a meeting of them, and there has to be an understanding that what is wrong is not from us but that we have inherited it. We have got it, and now we have to start to emerge in this situation, not as social reformers but as reformed people who will be like the yeast in the flour that makes the whole bread rise and take on its true identity in order to be nourishing.

In the time that I was in Granada, from the day I arrived there, our intention was that there should be a Mosque, and because this community in Granada struggled very hard over these years, eventually the Mosque was achieved. Once the Mosque is there, there has to be the correct 'Ibada of the Mosque and the correct adab of the Mosque. This has to be achieved. We now have Shaykh Muhammad in Granada, but at this point you must all recognise two very important things: one is that the politics of the Muslim community is not run by 'ulama or Fuqaha, it is run by Leadership. But, secondly, everything that is done must be founded on the 'Ilm, on the knowledge of these rightly guided 'alims who protect the Book of Allah, subhanahu wa ta'ala, and the Sunna of Rasul, sallallahu 'alayhi wa sallam. If you do not honour the one who has the knowledge and listen to him, then you will not have success. Worse than that, you will have fitna.

Honouring a Shaykh with this tremendous 'Ilm is not by making him into a kind of icon, it is by taking from him, learning from him and making arenas in which he can speak and teach in a way that suits him and in the way he wants. On these matters his word should be a command. This is not happening. This is not happening because people everywhere today are looking after their dunya and when they start looking after their dunya, the first thing they do is to dump the sublime Shari'at of Islam because it does not fit in with their economics.

Inside the household the finance must be according to the Shari'at. The use of the money and the spending of the money and the responsibilities to wives and children must be correct – not what suits people but what they are ordered to do by Rasul, sallallahu 'alayhi wa sallam. Then they must see that the children are educated properly. They must see that the children are taken from this culture of the streets and protected from the streets. We knew a young man and we asked him, "How were you treated?" and he said, "I was treated like a dog." However, he came here and the people took him in and they embraced him and they recognised who he was and in the shortest time he became one of the finest of our young men in the community. This is how things have to be.

It is the same with business. You cannot play with Islam and pretend that somehow as businessmen you have some kind of emotional connection to Islam. You must start making the building blocks of halal transactions. You must start bringing together those men who want more than just to be capitalists who are unitarian. The jews are unitarian! The Unitarians are unitarian! But it is La ilaha illallah, Muhammad ar-Rasulullah. If it is Muhammad ar-Rasulullah then Sallallahu 'alayhi wa sallam must be in your pocket as well as on your tongue. You must obey what Allah has commanded and you must obey what Rasul, sallallahu 'alayhi wa sallam, has commanded.

All of these things must be undertaken, otherwise it is just nifaq and a waste of everybody's time. The Mosque has to be a place of learning, not a place of teaching Arabic to the kuffar. It has to be a place of learning. Where is the Murshid al-Mu'in? Where is the 'Ajrumiyya? Where is the Tafsir of Ibn 'Atiyya? Where is it being taught? What has happened to the children? What are they doing? What are they wearing? What company are they keeping? This also applies to our people here in Cape Town. You have to guard the children, you have to protect them from what you know is out there. Indeed there are less limits put on the social nexus here in South Africa, which has become a cowboy-country in terms of morality and practice.

You must be concerned. You must be concerned for your children, and concerned for their education and you must also understand what Shaykh Muhammad said in his Khutba, which is that if you are with the Jama'at you are safe because the Muslims are like two hands washing. The Muslims support each other, so if you are not in the Jama'at then you are alone and if you are alone then your partner is Shaytan.

Very quickly you will see results. You cannot shut yourself up in your house. You cannot shut yourself up out of the way of the community. You must take your responsibility. Your responsibility is to see that the Deen is taught. There are more important things. If your life is simply your programme then you are no different from the communists who ended up with enormous concentration camps with millions of their fellow citizens dying in ghastly poverty and suffering because they were so busy looking after their own little situation – seeing that they were alright, that they had the money, that they had what they wanted.

Every man of this community must be a leader of Islam and say, "We are going to do this in our time!" But there is no use him doing it if the wife is saying, "Where is the money, where is the dunya?" I once remarked to a woman, "I think your son is really doing well," and she said, "It doesn't matter as long as he brings in the money." So the one who asks for the money has gone off the Path and will destroy the husband or the son! You must say, "This is where we are going. This is what we want to do," then the woman must help. Without the support of the woman, nothing can be achieved. The woman is the reality of man, so if she is not confirming the reality of the Haqq then he has gone off the Path and he is down the drain.

This is for all of you. You must realise that a household is a worshipping household. There was among our Fuqara a family in Switzerland and they had tremendous difficulties and troubles, yet I arrived once at their house in Zurich and I was to stay with them, and suddenly the whole house started to move. It was a very tiny little apartment, and I saw the man take out his prayer mat, I saw the sons, the daughter and the wife disappear into the bathroom, and they came out again and there was a Jama'at. He was leading his wife and children in Jama'at and I thought, "They are safe, it does not matter what will happen. They will be alright because they are unified." They have had troubles and they have had difficulties, but the bond is unbreakable because that house is the Mosque of Allah, where they worship Allah together. They looked up to the man and there was no conflict in the house. If that is not happening, there will be conflict in the house.

These are your responsibilities. You have the future in your hands. You are going to take the whole thing and you are going to be like the surfers you see in the Pacific, where these incredible waves come and they do not go over the top of the wave but disappear into the tunnel of it and come out the other side. That is how you are going to be when all these fitnas come. You are not going to surf on the top of it, no, you would be dashed to pieces. You will get into that tunnel and when the thing clears up, there you will be at the other side. This is what we want for all of you. You have got to be people of 'Ibada and you have got to be people who make your household a place of 'Ibada. You have got to spend time with your children. You have got to talk to them and tell them what blessings there are, and how when they get bigger they are going to embark on a big adventure and learn things. This is what you have to do. This is your responsibility.

It is almost impossible in the so-called Muslim countries because they have totally betrayed the Deen and so their people are running after the dunya like dogs. You cannot play at Islam. You cannot make little gestures. You have to have Sidq, you have to be sincere. Thus they have their difficulty which is to be sincere, to be true. Yet we are not in a Muslim country. Spain is not a Muslim country. South Africa is not a Muslim country. South Africa is going to be a Muslim country before Spain is a Muslim country, and America will be a Muslim country before Spain will be a Muslim country.

The Muslims of Spain must be a witness to the truth and they must not cut themselves off from the poor people and the Moroccan people around them, because what is in Granada is not what is in Fes or Casablanca, it is another matter altogether. There you have educated and cultured people while in Granada you have an underclass – but among them there will be treasures. The first thing the Sufis know is that among all the rubble there is always a diamond. Among all the dross there is always the piece of gold. The job of the Sufis is to find them and bring them out, to culture them, to educate them and to polish them so that they become the jewels of the crown. This is who the Sufis are. This is what Sufis are for in every place and in every time from the time of Rasul, sallallahu 'alayhi wa sallam.

Al-Hasan al-Basri said, "I sat with forty of the men of Badr and they were all Fuqara, they wore the wool, not the fine cottons of the wealthy families." From this is Tasawwuf. The 'suf' of forty men of the Battle of Badr is where Sufiyya comes from. They all wore the wool, they were Mutasawwifun, they were the people of Tasawwuf and we are just their children.

You have to carry this on, but it is in YOU, each one of you – just as what we did in Granada was the establishment of the Mosque, because that is the beginning. The Mosque belongs to Allah. In that is the correct Jumu'a, the correct Salat, the correct adab to

Allah and to the people of the Jama'at. Here in Cape Town we have established the Mosque. Now we have to do exactly the same – we have got to make it true. There has got to be teaching.

If they were teaching Deen, if they were teaching Tasawwuf, if they were teaching the Haqq of Tawhid in Granada there would be no problems. If people hear the word of Tawhid, the word of Rasul, sallallahu 'alayhi wa sallam, then between the Muslims there is harmony by the love of Rasul, sallallahu 'alayhi wa sallam, and by the yearning for Ma'rifa, for knowledge of Allah, subhanahu wa ta'ala. Then everything changes.

You have this responsibility, but it starts at home. It must be sound. It must not be dunya-oriented. It must be oriented to a great victory in the lifetime so that you reach a point in life where you look back and can say, "It was well-done." This is contentment, this is Rida and this will come to you if you say, "It was well-done and it will continue well-done because I have passed it on." Look what Rasulullah, sallallahu 'alayhi wa sallam, said on the last Hajj: "Have I given you the message? Have I done it? Have I completed the contract?" Is that not right? Did he not? That is what you have to do.

* * * * *

7

COMMENTARY

ON

SURAT AL WAQI'A

Two commentaries
given at the Masjid al-Mahmoud,
Constantia, Cape Town
2003

I

بِسْمِ اللهِ الرَّحْمٰنِ الرَّحِيمِ

يَٰٓأَيُّهَا الْمُزَّمِّلُ ۞ قُمِ الَّيْلَ إِلَّا قَلِيلًا ۞ نِّصْفَهُۥ أَوِ انقُصْ مِنْهُ قَلِيلًا ۞

أَوْ زِدْ عَلَيْهِ وَرَتِّلِ الْقُرْءَانَ تَرْتِيلًا ۞ إِنَّا سَنُلْقِى عَلَيْكَ قَوْلًا ثَقِيلًا ۞

إِنَّ نَاشِئَةَ الَّيْلِ هِىَ أَشَدُّ وَطْـًٔا وَأَقْوَمُ قِيلًا ۞ إِنَّ لَكَ فِى النَّهَارِ سَبْحًا

طَوِيلًا ۞ وَاذْكُرِ اسْمَ رَبِّكَ وَتَبَتَّلْ إِلَيْهِ تَبْتِيلًا ۞ رَّبُّ الْمَشْرِقِ

وَالْمَغْرِبِ لَآ إِلَٰهَ إِلَّا هُوَ فَاتَّخِذْهُ وَكِيلًا ۞ وَاصْبِرْ عَلَىٰ مَا يَقُولُونَ وَاهْجُرْهُمْ

هَجْرًا جَمِيلًا ۞ وَذَرْنِى وَالْمُكَذِّبِينَ أُولِى النَّعْمَةِ وَمَهِّلْهُمْ قَلِيلًا ۞

إِنَّ لَدَيْنَا أَنكَالًا وَجَحِيمًا ۞ وَطَعَامًا ذَا غُصَّةٍ وَعَذَابًا أَلِيمًا ۞ يَوْمَ

تَرْجُفُ الْأَرْضُ وَالْجِبَالُ وَكَانَتِ الْجِبَالُ كَثِيبًا مَّهِيلًا ۞ إِنَّا أَرْسَلْنَا إِلَيْكُمْ

رَسُولًا شَٰهِدًا عَلَيْكُمْ كَمَآ أَرْسَلْنَآ إِلَىٰ فِرْعَوْنَ رَسُولًا ۞ فَعَصَىٰ فِرْعَوْنُ

الرَّسُولَ فَأَخَذْنَٰهُ أَخْذًا وَبِيلًا ۞ فَكَيْفَ تَتَّقُونَ إِن كَفَرْتُمْ يَوْمًا

يَجْعَلُ الْوِلْدَٰنَ شِيبًا ۞ السَّمَآءُ مُنفَطِرٌ بِهِۦ كَانَ وَعْدُهُۥ مَفْعُولًا ۞

إِنَّ هَٰذِهِۦ تَذْكِرَةٌ فَمَن شَآءَ اتَّخَذَ إِلَىٰ رَبِّهِۦ سَبِيلًا ۞

إِنَّ رَبَّكَ يَعْلَمُ أَنَّكَ تَقُومُ أَدْنَىٰ مِن ثُلُثَىِ الَّيْلِ وَنِصْفَهُۥ وَثُلُثَهُۥ وَطَآئِفَةٌ

مِّنَ الَّذِينَ مَعَكَ وَاللهُ يُقَدِّرُ الَّيْلَ وَالنَّهَارَ عَلِمَ أَن لَّن تُحْصُوهُ فَتَابَ عَلَيْكُمْ

فَاقْرَءُوا وَمَا تَيَسَّرَ مِنَ الْقُرْءَانِ عَلِمَ أَن سَيَكُونُ مِنكُم مَّرْضَىٰ وَءَاخَرُونَ

يَضْرِبُونَ فِى الْأَرْضِ يَبْتَغُونَ مِن فَضْلِ اللهِ وَءَاخَرُونَ يُقَٰتِلُونَ فِى سَبِيلِ

اللهِ فَاقْرَءُوا مَا تَيَسَّرَ مِنْهُ وَأَقِيمُوا الصَّلَوٰةَ وَءَاتُوا الزَّكَوٰةَ وَأَقْرِضُوا اللهَ

قَرْضًا حَسَنًا وَمَا تُقَدِّمُوا لِأَنفُسِكُم مِّنْ خَيْرٍ تَجِدُوهُ عِندَ اللهِ هُوَ خَيْرًا

وَأَعْظَمَ أَجْرًا وَاسْتَغْفِرُوا اللهَ إِنَّ اللهَ غَفُورٌ رَّحِيمٌ ۞

I

Surat al-Muzzammil –
The Enwrapped

In the name of Allah, All Merciful, Most Merciful

You who are enwrapped in your clothing!
stay up at night, except a little,
half of it, or a little less,
or a little more,
and recite the Qur'an distinctly.

We will impose a weighty Word upon you.

Certainly rising at night has a stronger effect
and is more conducive to concentration.

In the daytime much of your time
is taken up by business matters.

Remember the Name of your Lord,
and devote yourself to Him completely.
Lord of the East and West –
there is no god but Him –
so take Him as your Guardian.
Be steadfast in the face of what they say
and cut yourself off from them –
but courteously.

Leave the deniers, who live a life of ease, to Me,
and tolerate them a little longer.

With Us there are shackles and a Blazing Fire
and food that chokes and a painful punishment,
on the Day the earth and mountains shake
and the mountains become like shifting dunes.

We have sent you a Messenger
to bear witness against you
just as We sent Pharaoh a Messenger.
But Pharaoh disobeyed the Messenger,
so We seized him with terrible severity.

How will you safeguard yourselves, if you are kafir,
against a Day which will turn children grey,
by which heaven will split apart?
His promise will be fulfilled.

This truly is a reminder, so let anyone who wills
take the Way towards his Lord.

Your Lord knows that you stay up
nearly two-thirds of the night –
or a half of it, or a third of it –
and a group of those with you.
Allah determines the night and day.
He knows you will not keep count of it,
so He has turned towards you.
Recite as much of the Qur'an as is easy for you.
He knows that some of you are ill
and that others are travelling in the land
seeking Allah's bounty,
and that others are fighting in the Way of Allah.
So recite as much of it as is easy for you.
And establish salat and pay zakat
and lend a generous loan to Allah.
Whatever good you send ahead for yourselves
you will find it with Allah as something better
and as a greater reward.
And seek forgiveness from Allah.
Allah is Ever-Forgiving, Most Merciful.

Surat at-Takathur – Competition

بِسْمِ اللَّهِ الرَّحْمَنِ الرَّحِيمِ
أَلْهَىٰكُمُ التَّكَاثُرُ ۝ حَتَّىٰ زُرْتُمُ الْمَقَابِرَ ۝ كَلَّا سَوْفَ تَعْلَمُونَ ۝ ثُمَّ
كَلَّا سَوْفَ تَعْلَمُونَ ۝ كَلَّا لَوْ تَعْلَمُونَ عِلْمَ الْيَقِينِ ۝ لَتَرَوُنَّ الْجَحِيمَ ۝
ثُمَّ لَتَرَوُنَّهَا عَيْنَ الْيَقِينِ ۝ ثُمَّ لَتُسْأَلُنَّ يَوْمَئِذٍ عَنِ النَّعِيمِ ۝

In the name of Allah, All–Merciful, Most Merciful

Fierce competition for this world distracted you
until you went down to the graves.
No indeed, you will soon know!
Again no indeed, you will soon know!
No indeed, if you only knew
with the Knowledge of Certainty,
you will certainly see the Blazing Fire!
Then you will certainly see it
with the Eye of Certainty.

Then will you be asked that Day
about the pleasures you enjoyed.

* * * * *

I

To understand Surat al-Waqi'a there is benefit in looking first at Surat al-Muzzammil and Surat at-Takathur. Surat al-Muzzammil can be seen as a preface, as it were, to the theme of Surat al-Waqi'a. Surat al-Muzzammil is the Surat of Khalwa. The affair of calling on the Lord in isolation and in the night. In it Allah says,

$$وَاذْكُرِ اسْمَ رَبِّكَ وَتَبَتَّلْ إِلَيْهِ تَبْتِيلاً ۝$$

Remember the Name of your Lord
and devote yourself to him completely.

He then goes on to say,

$$وَاصْبِرْ عَلَىٰ مَا يَقُولُونَ وَاهْجُرْهُمْ هَجْرًا جَمِيلاً ۝$$

Be steadfast in the face of what they say
and cut yourself off from them – but courteously.

This indicates the adab of calling on Allah by His Supreme Name, which involves what in the language of the Sufis is called "Turning from all that is masiwallah," all this derives from these Ayats. That is why Allah grants in this Surat the uncompromising confirmation that He is aware of what you are doing and that He is already the Answerer of your call.

341

Surat at-Takathur is important for its introduction of two of three Qur'anic terms, of which the third is found in Surat al-Waqi'a. In this Surat Allah refers to two degrees of knowledge. He says, glory be to Him,

$$كَلَّا لَوْ تَعْلَمُونَ عِلْمَ ٱلْيَقِينِ ۝$$

No indeed, if you only knew
with the knowledge of Certainty.

And then He goes on to say,

$$ثُمَّ لَتَرَوُنَّهَا عَيْنَ ٱلْيَقِينِ ۝$$

Then you will certainly see it
with the Eye of Certainty.

So the Yaqin has a triple reality. The Mulk facing the Malakut, the Malakut facing the Malakut, and the third term is the Malakut facing the Jabarut, the Haqq al-Yaqin. And this last term appears at the end of our commented Sura.

* * * * *

Surat al-Waqi'a is the wird of Shaykh al-'Alawi. This is very significant because it starts with what Hajj Abdalhaqq has translated as 'The Great Event'. But if you look in the Qur'an it is:

$$\text{إِذَا وَقَعَتِ الْوَاقِعَةُ} \quad ①$$

In the Arabic this is like "the time of the time," it is like the famous moment when Rasul, sallallahu 'alayhi wa sallam, said, "Ya Abu Bakr, Yawm al-Yawm." The day of The Day. And by that he meant the Last Day. So "idha waqa'atil waqi'a" is the Event of the Event. It is very important to understand this because it is like saying that everything which is creation is event, and the creation is one event. Allah only has to say to a thing, "Kun fa yakun" – "Be / it is." Between the 'Be' and 'it is' there is no hiatus, no grammatical link. "Kun fa yakun" means "Be / it is." We might use an oblique stroke to indicate it, because there is no grammatical joining. "Be," and then as a result of that it happens, because the in-time and the out-of-time are not separated by a hiatus. In grammar an 'and' or an 'or' or a 'but' or a 'then' is a connection, but there is nothing connected to the Command of Allah. There cannot be any association. "La ilaha illallah, wahdahu la sharikalah." So the "Kun fa yakun" is at the very heart of the nature of our understanding of Tawhid, because it is also how we understand existence to come into being.

Allah, subhanahu wa ta'ala, tells us that this ending of

the creation, which is like the undoing of the "Kun fa yakun", is also like that: it is the Waqi'a of the Waqi'a. So it is the Event of what all event is. It is the equivalent to the whole creational "Kun", it is the "anti-Kun" if you like. This places us in a different understanding of the creation from the kuffar. What it means is that we recognise that the creational event has this other side, which is its unseen reality. That is why Sufis have used a variety of vocabularies which they derive from the Qur'an. They talk of Mulk, Malakut and Jabarut.

The Mulk is the Kingdom. Mulk is everything under the 'Arsh' by the 'Kun'. Malakut is that in its unseen dimension. Malakut is the realm of the unseen realities, and Mulk is the realm of the visible realities. The Malakut has an earthly dimension and a heavenly dimension. For example: you yourself sitting here are a visible reality, but it is not possible for you to continue existing another second in your atomic form as you are, without your unseen reality being along with you. At the moment the Ruh leaves the body all this collapses, does it not? It all goes into disintegration. This form finishes, as Raja of Mahmudabad used to say, "The body is like something you have rented from a wealthy owner. Your job while you are in it is to look after it, keep it clean, see that it is taken care of, that it is not destroyed in any way or corrupted in any way, because at the end of your tenure of the house you have to return the house to its owner." He would say, "When you return the house to the owner, the Ruh goes out of it and like a house which is not occupied, it begins to crumble. Then the phosphates go back to the phosphates, the sulphur goes back to the sulphur, and the sodium goes back to the sodium." The lower processes of existence take place once the house is uninhabited. Do you follow? Another whole set of the realm of the visible takes over, but they are then mineral, lower forms of matter because the animal form and the Ruh leave with the 'Aql.

For instance, the madman, the man who does not know that he has 'he-ness', never gets ill. The mad person never gets ill because he does not use the house. It gathers dust but it does not disintegrate because he is still there. The 'Aql and the Ruh have a connection, and that is understanding, which is also what gives reasonable speech, understandable speech and communication, it means that this higher creature, this one that Allah has set over all created forms, is present. When he leaves it, what is 'man' has gone, and then you go down to these lower forms. But while this body is inhabited, has Ruh, has consciousness, in that condition the whole being of identity is present, and at that point there is someone there, so to speak.

That is the first stage of understanding how the creational process happened, because in the Mulk you have been put on the earth. A representative of Allah, subhanahu wa ta'ala, has been put on the earth, and so you have a presence. The first recognition, therefore, is that your true identity is a hidden reality. We cannot see it.

Allah also explains that one of the gifts of Allah to us is that people cannot see our secrets. They are invisible, are they not? One of the mercies of Allah is that everyone does not know all about you when they meet you. Some people have certain insights and so on, but they are insights from the Unseen. They have little flashes about somebody, because this visible world is sensory and everything that is hidden is meanings, and some people have an insight into meanings. Rasul, sallallahu 'alayhi wa sallam, taught Abu Bakr as-Siddiq how to interpret dreams, because dreams are meanings with a sensory character but not a sensory reality. They take place in the hidden realm. He gave to another of the Sahaba the science of reading the face, of Farasa, so he could look at the face and know from those eyes, and that nose, and that twist of the mouth, whether that person is dishonest, or that person is a coward. He gave to another Companion the knowledge of nifaq, so that they would know nifaq whenever they met it. He taught them how to identify the munafiq whenever they met him. But these are hidden things that the human beings have glimpses of, just glimpses, according to their state and their condition, and the time in which it happens and the place in which it happens.

So there is an unseen reality of the Malakut which is earthly, and which is to do with this hiddenness that you carry with you wherever you go. This hiddenness is present in the dhikr, and the dhikr raises it up and illuminates and strengthens it, and good company raises up and strengthens it, and bad company darkens and covers it over.

This is the earthly dimension of the Malakut. The heavenly dimension of Malakut can be identified by the difference between the true dream and the false dream. In other words, if you have a dream because you have indigestion and you have a nightmare, it is because of the disturbance of your stomach. The people who study this do not take it seriously, it was just indigestion. But 'ruya' is a specific term in Arabic for a true dream. Rasul, sallallahu 'alayhi wa sallam, said, "Anyone who has seen me in a true dream has truly seen me, because Shaytan cannot take my form."

So nobody ever knows what is true and what is not except on the absolute truth of knowing they have seen Rasul, sallallahu 'alayhi wa sallam. But even that has verifications. Someone says, astaghfirullah, they saw the Rasul and they have decided for themselves that they saw him. Then if you question certain things you can verify with knowledge that they did indeed see him.

The example of this with these unseen spiritual realities, is when the Rasul, sallallahu 'alayhi wa sallam, received his first announcements from the angel Jibril. You remember in the Sira that he was terrified, that he thought the worst thing in the world to him would be that he should go mad, because he was a man of the truth. He spoke to his wife, and because she was a very wise woman, she knew what to do. He said, "Well, maybe it is Shaytan," and Khadija said, "Next time he comes to you tell me." So he rushed to her, she was in her apartment and she had a robe on. And he said, "It is here now." She opened the robe and was naked, and it vanished. She said, "It is the truth, because if it had been Shaytan it would have stayed."

So these people had knowledges from the past, they knew how to get verification, how to get the truth. This means that all these things of this elevated nature cannot mingle, they cannot co-mingle with the earthly. The heavenly Malakut is to do with visions, it is to do with places where these things are more prone to happen and so on and so forth. Then you have Mulk which carries with it an unseen dimension of Malakut in the earthly form. This is also in all life forces.

There is one thing no scientific description of existence has ever been able to put into its model, and this is why at the end of the day they do not have the true picture of existence. The philosophers do it by asking a slightly false question: "Why is there something rather than nothing?" but that is not the interesting question. The interesting question is, "What is the pulse of life? What is the dynamic or movement?" This is something meditated deeply, deeply by Muhiyuddin ibn al-'Arabi, and it is referred to in the Diwan of Shaykh Muhammad ibn al-Habib. He says in the Greater Qasida, "He would see the planets and the secrets of their constellations, and the meaning of their tremendously rapid movement," and in the Minor Qasida, "To anyone who withdraws into the lights of the dhikr of the Truth, creation is no more than particles of dust in space." It is more space than particles. It is what Ibn al-'Arabi calls the 'gypsum' foundations of the universe: not the clay, but the plaster of the forms.

All the living forms have a pulse of life. You have seen these beautiful speeded-up pictures of plants growing. It is an extraordinary thing when the plant comes shooting out of the earth and how ivy climbs up the walls as if it had a consciousness, which in a sense it does at its own level. So the pulse that makes the life, from the Malakut, is what we understand as the activity of the angels. In the Arabic language the word 'angels' comes from 'flakes', they are like flakes of light, like a flashing of light. This energy is what makes all the creation move – everything is in motion, everything in existence that is living is in motion. This is part of one's understanding that the heavenly operation of the Malakut is also in all the creational processes, so that one is living in event.

What this extraordinary Sura says is that the in-time event is not the whole thing. It is all in order that this other Event should happen. The unseen reality is one event, in the way that the 'Kun' of 'Kun fa yakun' is one event, which is all the creation of the cosmos and its dusts and its gases. Again, it is commotion which synthesizes into these creative forms of life, and this is the reality in which we live. Allah is telling the Muslims that what they are living is something whose actual reality does not get unfolded until the thing is over anyway. But in fact it is everything that has happened in the in-time, in the Mulk, which is that which bears the fruit, which realises itself, which manifests itself in this Event.

For example, Shaykh ibn 'Ajiba explains: "This reality is sensory but it is experienced as meanings. We interpret everything by meanings. But the Next World is meanings and we will experience them as sensory." The exact opposite. In it, the meanings will be experienced as sensory, that is why Allah, subhanahu wa ta'ala, reveals what it is, that there will be these enormous sensory experiences. They are meanings, but we will know them as sensory, whereas all of this that is sensory we know as meanings. Otherwise we have not got 'Aql, we have not got the higher self of the human creature.

So we are busy in all of this interpreting meanings, but in this Event we will be shown the meanings of all these things we were and did, and we will experience them as sensory. They will be real for us, which is why the kuffar mock the Muslims because of their belief in the Unseen. Right at the beginning Allah says,

الٓمٓ ۞ ذَٰلِكَ ٱلْكِتَٰبُ لَا رَيْبَ فِيهِ هُدًى لِّلْمُتَّقِينَ ۞ ٱلَّذِينَ يُؤْمِنُونَ بِٱلْغَيْبِ وَيُقِيمُونَ ٱلصَّلَوٰةَ وَمِمَّا رَزَقْنَٰهُمْ يُنفِقُونَ ۞

"Alif Lam Mim.
That is the Book, without any doubt.
It contains guidance for those who have taqwa:
those who have iman in the Unseen and establish salat
and give of what We have provided for them." (2:1-3)

This Book is for the people who believe in the Ghayb, the Unseen. If they do not believe in the Ghayb it is a waste of time. The kuffar laugh and think, "Oh, they are going to have a miserable time on earth because they think they are going to have a lovely time in the Next World." That is the mockery of the kuffar. But what they do not realise is that the next stage is an opposite of that. Because they failed with the meanings in this life, the sensory they will taste is a terrible one, because of a misunderstanding they have from the beginning.

Now Allah says:

$$\text{إِذَا وَقَعَتِ ٱلْوَاقِعَةُ ۝ لَيْسَ لِوَقْعَتِهَا كَاذِبَةٌ ۝}$$

"When the Great Event occurs,
none will deny its occurrence."

It is really, "When the Event of events occurs none will deny its eventness." That is really the translation. Their denial of the eventness of this world. The truth is that the kafir comes into this world and thinks everything is a given, while the Muslim is educated to understand that he comes into a world that is from the "Kun fa yakun," that he is already under an imperative, a Divine imperative which involves the immediate and absolute destiny of the individual in order to fulfil his maximum potential and capacity and expansion while on this earth in a manner that is pleasing to his Lord, coming under three categories: the Companions of the Right, the Companions of the Left, and the Forerunners. This is the existential outlook of the Muslim over and against the kafir who comes in and thinks, "There is this thing. It has been going on. Everybody was primitive, they have become sophisticated. We knew a little, now we know a lot. They lived in caves, we have got engineering and structural buildings to surpass them. We can make weapons of mass destruction, we can destroy the world in a second and we are the masters of the situation. Everyone before us was ignorant and had superstition and was primitive, but we are evolved, we have no superstition, and we know the world for what it is." This is the difference, and this is the darkness of the kuffar. And the reality of this becomes that they are the Companions of the Left.

$$\text{خَافِضَةٌ رَّافِعَةٌ} \quad ٣$$

"bringing low, raising high."

He says that, "This event, none will deny its eventness." And He immediately tells us what it is: "It brings low and it raises high." It does not keep high and leave low. It means a complete turnover of the evaluation that the people of the dunya have held. Everything will return to its true nature, which is this division of creatures into the Companions of the Right, the Companions of the Left, and the Forerunners. This involves the bringing low and the raising high. So it is also why the khawf, the fear of Allah, is where you stand in that. Bringing low means you were high and you were brought low, and raising high means you were low and you are raised high. That is why Sayyidi 'Ali al-Jamal is continually quoting one Ayat of Qur'an as relevant to the Sufis which is, "We made you poor, low in the land, because We wanted to raise you up and make you imams in the land." Imams in the sense of leaders of the land. So to do that Allah made them low in order that He could raise them up.

This is the process that is going on all the time and which completes itself in this final stage. All the time Allah is bringing low and He is raising up. Rasul, sallallahu 'alayhi wa sallam, said, "Look for me among the miskeen." He did not say "Look for me among the princes." He wrote letters to the Caesars but he did not spend his time with them or go after them. Apart from these letters that he sent, his action was with the people. He said, "Look for me among the miskeen, because I was only sent on account of the miskeen. I was only sent among you because of them. They are the reason I have been sent." So the transformation that the Muslims activate when they are on the Sirat al-Mustaqeem is that by the fulfilling of the Deen, a body of people do get raised up in the world and rule for a time. This has happened again and again in the Deen of Islam.

إِذَا رُجَّتِ الْأَرْضُ رَجًّا ۞ وَبُسَّتِ الْجِبَالُ بَسًّا ۞ فَكَانَتْ هَبَاءً مُّنبَثًّا ۞ وَكُنتُمْ أَزْوَاجًا ثَلَاثَةً ۞

When the earth is convulsed
and the mountains are crushed
and become scattered dust in the air.
And you will be classed into three:

A very extraordinary revelation you see. You are going
to be classed into three.

$$فَأَصْحَٰبُ ٱلْمَيْمَنَةِ مَآ أَصْحَٰبُ ٱلْمَيْمَنَةِ ۝$$

the Companions of the Right:
What of the Companions of the Right?

It is very extraordinary because Allah speaks very openly.

$$وَأَصْحَٰبُ ٱلْمَشْـَٔمَةِ مَآ أَصْحَٰبُ ٱلْمَشْـَٔمَةِ ۝ وَٱلسَّٰبِقُونَ ٱلسَّٰبِقُونَ ۝$$
$$أُوْلَٰٓئِكَ ٱلْمُقَرَّبُونَ ۝ فِى جَنَّٰتِ ٱلنَّعِيمِ ۝$$

The Companions of the Left:
What of the Companions of the Left?
And the Forerunners, the Forerunners.
those are the Ones Brought Near
in Gardens of Delight.

The Sabiqun are the Muqarrabun, the "Ones Brought
Near". "In Gardens of Delight" is not a proper translation,
because Jannah is not just a garden. Jannah is from the
root Jeem-Nun-Nun, it is something hidden. We are

dealing with the Unseen, and this Garden is a hidden garden, a secret garden. The Jannah is a garden so rich in foliage that you cannot see through it to the other side. It is enclosed. It closes itself in on itself, so that its beauty is contained within the thing that is the Garden. You cannot see beyond it or through it. Majnun, mad, is the one who has a hidden sickness, that when you look you cannot see it. He looks alright, but his sickness is hidden, you cannot see it. The hidden sickness is the sickness of the majnun. So the Muqarrabun are the ones in this Jannah, in this hidden Garden of Delight. "Fi jannatin na'im". 'Na'im' is a very precious word. It is a sensory word, it is something that is pleasing. It is a very sensual word. The 'jannati na'im', then, is in a place of hidden beauty which has in it tasting. It is 'dhawq', it has direct experience. This means that the Muqarrabun are people of M'arifat, of tasting, of ecstasies. And then a very significant thing:

$$ ثُلَّةٌ مِّنَ ٱلْأَوَّلِينَ ۝ وَقَلِيلٌ مِّنَ ٱلْأَخِرِينَ ۝ $$

a large group of the earlier people
but few of the later ones.

Now you have an interpretation of history. This is not the kafir history, this is not dynasties, it is not trade figures, it is not a statistic. Yet it is statistics: "A large group of the earlier people." In other words the earlier people were closer in knowledge than the present people. Rasul, sallallahu 'alayhi wa sallam, said, "There will not be a time from my time until the end of time that will not be worse than the time before it." This means that the time is getting worse. Shaykh Muhammad ibn al-Habib, rahimahullah, said, "In the old days of Tasawwuf," in the early years of Tasawwuf, in Balkh and Samarqand and all the Abbasid world, "The Awliya, like Moulay 'Abdalqadir al-Jilani, set themselves enormously harsh tasks in order to reach Allah. It was so difficult for them because the people already had a high position, the Deen was strong."

In its early days the Deen was enormously powerful, and these people had to struggle to surpass it to be Muqarrabun. He said, "They used to put themselves through a lot of physical suffering and torture in order to break the nafs," because again the breaking of the nafs is the task of the Sufi, it is his business to see it is done. Not other people. So they set about it. He said, "They used to tie themselves by the hair and have themselves lowered and hung by the hair into the well." It was to keep them absolutely conscious, and not lose consciousness and slip down into the well and drown. They used to do these sorts of things to reach Allah. Shaykh ibn al-Habib explained that the time got darker and more ignorant. People's Islam got weaker, the Shari'at and its application got weaker. So Allah was merciful and He made it easier. The Shaykh said, "You could mark the stages at which the Awliya had the task eased for them." He was of course commenting on the well-known hadith in which the Rasul, sallallahu 'alayhi wa sallam, indicated that while in his time the omission of one out of ten commanded things would send a man to the Fire, there would come a time when the performance of one out of ten commanded things would gain him the Garden.

Harith al-Muhasibi was almost like a policeman on himself, and is perfectly named al-Muhasibi because what he did was he took account, on the beginning of the path, at the end of every day. Every day he sat down and said, "What did I do today? What can I take to my Lord?" And he would go through everything he did that day and he would ask, "Was that pleasing to Allah, or is that disapproved of by Allah? Was that forbidden by Allah?" He said, "What have I done?" He made the bill, as it were, of the day. And as he advanced on the path he then said, "This is not enough." He made a reckoning of every hour of the day. So he went through the twenty four hours, asking himself, "What have I done?" Then he made it by the minute, and then at a certain point he said, "I cannot do it. I have got to account for every breath." So then he was watching every breath that it was in remembrance of Allah, subhanahu wa ta'ala.

Moulay 'Abdalqadir al-Jilani was a great 'alim. Do not forget that while he is dismissed by these wahhabis and shaytans like that, was a very great 'alim. He wrote an enormous body of scholarship in the Hanbali fiqh, which is very strict and harsh. First of all he was zahid, he did punish himself. But then in his final stage he became the instigator of Hadra. In fact Hadra is not simply from Moulay Abdalqadir al-Jilani. Hadra is nothing less than what is referred to in the Qur'an in an actual term about people calling on Allah, with 'hamsa'. In Surat Ta Ha, Allah, glory be to Him, says:

يَوْمَئِذٍ يَتَّبِعُونَ ٱلدَّاعِىَ لَا عِوَجَ لَهُۥ
وَخَشَعَتِ ٱلْأَصْوَاتُ لِلرَّحْمَٰنِ فَلَا تَسْمَعُ إِلَّا هَمْسًا ۝

On that day they will follow the Summoner
who has no crookedness in him at all.
Voices will be humbled before the All-Merciful
and nothing but a whisper will be heard.

That is in the excellent translation of the Bewleys. It
is again important as we found with the term Waqi'a,
to get the pure Arabic meaning. In the great Maghribi
Tafsir 'Al-Bahr al-Madid fi al-Tafsir al-Qur'an al-
Majid', Shaykh Ibn 'Ajiba comments on the final phrase
of the Ayat (Qur'an 20:108):

فَلَا تَسْمَعُ إِلَّا هَمْسًا

He says this means that all that can be heard is a gasping
from the throat of "Ha, ha, ha..." It is this state of khawf
in which all that is left is a gasping for breath which
is the core of the Hadra, or 'Imara. Thus Moulay
'Abdalqadir gave this practice of abasement to the
Fuqara. Then at a very important stage Shaykh Shadhili
was given permission by Allah to use the name of
Allah, subhanahu wa ta'ala, and by that naming of the
Supreme Name in a certain way it made a very quick
and very easy path to M'arifat. This is another stage of it
being made easy for the Fuqara to reach M'arifat. Then
Moulay ad-Darqawi also utilised the visualisation of the
name of Allah, subhanahu wa ta'ala, the Alif – Lam –

358

Lam – Ha, because the letters of the Name have secrets.
So the putting the letters in front of one and the calling
on the Name was a further making-easy for the task of
reaching knowledge of Allah, subhanahu wa ta'ala.

Allah says, "A large group of the earlier people," because
they were nearer Fitra, their Islam was strong, but few
of the later ones, because the people had lost the way
and turned against all the prophets, and turned against
Rasul, sallallahu 'alayhi wa sallam.

عَلَىٰ سُرُرٍ مَّوْضُونَةٍ ۝ مُّتَّكِئِينَ عَلَيْهَا مُتَقَٰبِلِينَ ۝

On sumptuous woven couches,
Reclining on them face to face.

"Face to face," because the face is the aspect of the
human creature that indicates the essence, the identity
of the person. It is a realm of M'arifat, it is a realm of
contemplation.

يَطُوفُ عَلَيْهِمْ وِلْدَٰنٌ مُّخَلَّدُونَ ۝ بِأَكْوَابٍ وَأَبَارِيقَ وَكَأْسٍ مِّن
مَّعِينٍ ۝ لَّا يُصَدَّعُونَ عَنْهَا وَلَا يُنزِفُونَ ۝

There will circulate among them, ageless youths,
carrying goblets and decanters
and a cup from a flowing spring –
it does not give them any headache
nor does it leave them stupefied.

Every term in these last six Ayats can be found inside the Diwan of Ibn al-Farid. Ibn al-Farid uses all of these terms to indicate aspects of M'arifat, intoxications, ecstasies, unveilings, secrets, illuminations. He uses all this as a coded language but it is all from Surat al-Waqi'a. The Sufis say, "A drunkenness with memory is higher than a drunkenness without memory." In the sensory world they say, "You had a good time last night!" and he replies, "Oh, I don't remember anything." So in fact he got no benefit from it. But Allah says that the spiritual ecstasies do not give them any headache and do not leave them stupefied. In other words, it is not something in their heads, it is a sensory reality. It is a M'arifat with no loss of consciousness. And as we go into the language of the Sufis you will see how they describe a loss of consciousness which becomes another consciousness. They talk about fana' and then talk about the fana' of the fana'. In the Diwans the Shaykhs speak about going across deserts that do not have any end, that do not finish.

وَفَٰكِهَةٖ مِّمَّا يَتَخَيَّرُونَ ۝ وَلَحْمِ طَيْرٖ مِّمَّا يَشْتَهُونَ ۝
وَحُورٌ عِينٞ ۝ كَأَمْثَٰلِ ٱللُّؤْلُؤِ ٱلْمَكْنُونِ ۝

And any fruit they specify
and any bird-meat they desire.
And dark-eyed maidens like hidden pearls.

All this is the language of Ibn al-Farid. He is dismissed even by very knowledgeable people like Ibn Khaldun –

whom in many things we take with great respect and care – because they do not understand. Not only that but what they do not recognise is that all of this is from the Qur'an. The whole of the great song of Ibn al-Farid is in these lines. And all this He, subhanahu wa ta'ala, has been describing, "As recompense for what they did."

$$ جَزَآءَ بِمَا كَانُوا يَعْمَلُونَ ۝ $$

As recompense for what they did.

So the reward of this M'arifat after death is the recompense for what they did. Not the recompense for who they were but the recompense for what they did. The human being is an acting animal, so what he does is what defines his post-mortal destiny. This is the important thing.

$$ لَا يَسْمَعُونَ فِيهَا لَغْوًا وَلَا تَأْثِيمًا ۝ $$

They will hear no prattling in it,
nor any word of wrong.

They will hear no prattling in it, they will not hear superficial talk, and not any word of wrong. This means that they have come from a life that has liberated itself from the prattling, and liberated itself from words of wrong. So when people speak wrong words this means a denial of this experience, which is why the Sufis want to leave behind them a clean record. On the material side they want to follow Rasul, sallallahu 'alayhi wa sallam, they want to pay the debt. On the moral side they want to have forgiven the enemy, they want to have forgiven the ones who have done them wrong in order that they have this closeness to Rasul, sallallahu 'alayhi wa sallam.

$$\text{اِلَّا قِيلًا سَلَٰمًا سَلَٰمًا ﴿٢٦﴾}$$

All that is said is, 'Peace! Peace!'

This is a most tremendous Sura. All that is said is Salam, Salam, peace, peace. This saying of peace is the Ihsan of the Islam. This is why we find it very offensive when the kuffar start telling us Islam means peace. It does not mean peace, it means submission, and in fact it also means war. But for the muminun, in the Ghayb – and by the Ghayb we mean the heavenly Malakut – it means 'salam, salam'.

Salam brings us to the fact that as I said there was the Mulk and the Malakut, but the Mulk and the Malakut are not conjoined, they are separate/together. Like the "Kun fa yakun" what separates the unseen world and the seen world is what in the Qur'an is called Barzakh, which is that between the Mulk and the Malakut is Jabarut. Jabarut is not above, Jabarut is that which makes a separation, not in space or time, but in realities, between the Mulk and Malakut. Jabarut is light, 'Jabr' or the Power of Allah, subhanahu wa ta'ala, and lights of Allah. Therefore the Muqarrabun are the ones who pass into Jabarut, they vanish into Jabarut, into the lights of the Essence. They are disappearing, they are absorbed. And that is what is inside this Ayat. "All that is said is salam, salam."

$$ اِلَّا قِيلًا سَلَٰمًا سَلَٰمًا ۝ $$

All that is said is, 'Peace! Peace!'

In other words there is no Mulk, there is no Malakut, they are illuminated by Jabarut. Inshallah we will continue tomorrow.

II

وَأَصْحَبُ ٱلْيَمِينِ مَآ أَصْحَبُ ٱلْيَمِينِ ۝ فِي سِدْرٍ مَّخْضُودٍ ۝

وَطَلْحٍ مَّنضُودٍ ۝ وَظِلٍّ مَّمْدُودٍ ۝ وَمَآءٍ مَّسْكُوبٍ ۝

وَفَٰكِهَةٍ كَثِيرَةٍ ۝ لَّا مَقْطُوعَةٍ وَلَا مَمْنُوعَةٍ ۝ وَفُرُشٍ

مَّرْفُوعَةٍ ۝ إِنَّآ أَنشَأْنَٰهُنَّ إِنشَآءً ۝ فَجَعَلْنَٰهُنَّ أَبْكَارًا

عُرُبًا أَتْرَابًا ۝ لِّأَصْحَٰبِ ٱلْيَمِينِ ۝ ثُلَّةٌ مِّنَ ٱلْأَوَّلِينَ ۝

وَثُلَّةٌ مِّنَ ٱلْءَاخِرِينَ ۝ وَأَصْحَٰبُ ٱلشِّمَالِ مَآ أَصْحَٰبُ ٱلشِّمَالِ ۝

فِي سَمُومٍ وَحَمِيمٍ ۝ وَظِلٍّ مِّن يَحْمُومٍ ۝ لَّا بَارِدٍ وَلَا كَرِيمٍ ۝

إِنَّهُمْ كَانُوا۟ قَبْلَ ذَٰلِكَ مُتْرَفِينَ ۝ وَكَانُوا۟ يُصِرُّونَ

عَلَى ٱلْحِنثِ ٱلْعَظِيمِ ۝ وَكَانُوا۟ يَقُولُونَ أَئِذَا مِتْنَا وَكُنَّا تُرَابًا

وَعِظَٰمًا أَءِنَّا لَمَبْعُوثُونَ ۝ أَوَءَابَآؤُنَا ٱلْأَوَّلُونَ ۝ قُلْ إِنَّ

ٱلْأَوَّلِينَ وَٱلْءَاخِرِينَ ۝ لَمَجْمُوعُونَ إِلَىٰ مِيقَٰتِ يَوْمٍ مَّعْلُومٍ ۝

ثُمَّ إِنَّكُمْ أَيُّهَا ٱلضَّآلُّونَ ٱلْمُكَذِّبُونَ ۝ لَءَاكِلُونَ مِن شَجَرٍ مِّن زَقُّومٍ ۝

فَمَالِـُٔونَ مِنْهَا ٱلْبُطُونَ ۝ فَشَٰرِبُونَ عَلَيْهِ مِنَ ٱلْحَمِيمِ ۝

فَشَٰرِبُونَ شُرْبَ ٱلْهِيمِ ۝ هَٰذَا نُزُلُهُمْ يَوْمَ ٱلدِّينِ ۝

نَحْنُ خَلَقْنَٰكُمْ فَلَوْلَا تُصَدِّقُونَ ۝

And the Companions of the Right:
what of the Companions of the Right?
Amid thornless lote-trees and fruit-laden acacias
and wide-spreading shade and outpouring water
and fruits in abundance never failing, unrestricted.
And on elevated couches.

We have brought maidens into being
and made them purest virgins,
devoted, passionate, of like age,
for the Companions of the Right.
A large group of the earlier people
and a large group of the later ones.

And the Companions of the Left:
what of the Companions of the Left?
Amid searing blasts and scalding water
and the murk of thick black smoke,
providing no coolness and no pleasure.
Before that they were living in luxury,
persisting in immense wrongdoing
and saying, 'When we are dead
and turned to dust and bones,
shall we then be raised again,
or our forefathers, the earlier peoples?'

Say: 'The earlier and the later peoples
will certainly all be gathered
to the appointment of a specified Day.

Then you, you misguided, you deniers
will eat from the tree of Zaqqum,
filling your stomachs with it
and drink scalding water on top of it,
slurping like thirst-crazed camels.
This will be their hospitality
on the Day of Judgement!'

We created you so why do you not confirm the truth?

* * * * *

Allah, subhanahu wa taʻala, has explained about the first group. These are the ʻArifin, the Muqarrabun, the ones who have drawn near. Remember that one of the names of Allah, subhanahu wa taʻala, is Al-Qarib, He is the Near One, so to be Muqarrabun is to be under this name of Allah, subhanahu wa taʻala, which is the Qarib. Also He explains in the Qur'an that Allah, subhanahu wa taʻala, "is nearer to you than your jugular vein." That means it is a nearness which is nearer than nearness. It is not by distance, it does not have any distance in it, even miniscule distance. It is in fact presence, Hadhrat al-Rabbani – Presence of Lordship. Now Allah, subhanahu wa taʻala, has explained of the Forerunners, the Muqarrabun, "A lot of the earlier people and a few of the later people."

Next He explains about the Companions of the Right, then He goes on to the Companions of the Left. Now, about the Companions of the Right, Allah, subhanahu wa ta'ala, says, "A large group of the earlier people and a large group of the later ones." But of the Companions of the Left, Allah, subhanahu wa ta'ala, says, "The earlier and the later peoples will certainly all be gathered to the appointment of a specified Day." The distinction Allah, subhanahu wa ta'ala, makes about the Companions of the Left is that they have denied Allah, subhanahu wa ta'ala. He calls them "the deniers".

The evidence Allah, subhanahu wa ta'ala, puts down before them is, "We created you so why do you not confirm the truth?" In other words the Event of the creation, that is the 'Kun', is denied. In fact the denial is the denial of Existence itself. It means therefore that the confirmation of the truth is not based on an idea, that therefore Da'wa is not calling people to the rational argument of Islam. It has a rational argument, but it is not the rational argument but the experiential denial that makes the deniers deny. They deny in the face of the event of existence.

There is the famous meeting of Thomas Carlyle, who was very close to Islam and the first person in Western society to write in honour of Rasul, sallallahu 'alayhi wa sallam, and some grand lady in London. She said, "Mr. Carlyle, I accept the universe." And Carlyle is reported to have said, "By God madam, you had better!" That is really the voice of certainty, because there is in some way a rejection of existence involved in the act of kufr, which is why it is called kufr because it is covering up the evidentiary.

We are just about to come to the dimensions of how Allah, subhanahu wa ta'ala, explicates it.

أَفَرَءَيْتُم مَّا تُمْنُونَ ۝ ءَأَنتُمْ تَخْلُقُونَهُ ۖ أَمْ نَحْنُ
الْخَالِقُونَ ۝ نَحْنُ قَدَّرْنَا بَيْنَكُمُ الْمَوْتَ وَمَا نَحْنُ بِمَسْبُوقِينَ ۝
عَلَىٰ أَن نُّبَدِّلَ أَمْثَالَكُمْ وَنُنشِئَكُمْ فِى مَا لَا تَعْلَمُونَ ۝ وَلَقَدْ
عَلِمْتُمُ النَّشْأَةَ الْأُولَىٰ فَلَوْلَا تَذَكَّرُونَ ۝

Have you thought about the sperm you ejaculate?
Is it you who create it
or are We the Creator?

We have decreed death for you
and We will not be forestalled
in replacing you
with others the same as you
and re-forming you
in a way you know nothing about.
You have known the first formation,
So will you not pay heed?

So now this astonishing Sura has four questions that Allah, subhanahu wa ta'ala, puts to the human creatures. The first one is about the sperm. We touched on this earlier, the matter of the dynamic of life. When Allah, subhanahu wa ta'ala, asks about reflection about the sperm it is that people knew that it was this that created life, and activated life, this factor, this element, this dimension has in it something that activates a process from which the child emerges. So that is a creational event, it is an event in itself.

We can go back and look in the dictionary of the Qur'an which defines every important root in the Qur'an and explains it. The root of Waw-Qaf-'Ayn is given three aspects which are then backed up by Ayats of Qur'an. The three aspects are very significant. The first one is the passing of intellect, the intellect of man which passes, which dies. The second aspect of Waqi'a is towards the heavens because it refers to the Ayat where Allah, subhanahu wa ta'ala, tells about the death of Sayyiduna 'Isa and how he was raised up to Him. And the third dimension of the Waqi'a is the death of the Arwah, the time of the death when the Arwah are released and freed from the body. To this it gives two references in Surat an-Nahl, which speak of those who died with good angels, and then those wrongdoers who died with other angels. In other words there were specific angels to take the people Allah was pleased with into the Next World, and another set of angels to take those He was not pleased with.

So this division is an absolutely uncompromising division. But it puts together two completely distinct, opposite aspects of life, you could say life/death, and makes them the same from a point of view of spiritual unveiling. That is that the sperm contains this pulse, this dynamic from which unfolds what we now call the DNA and so on, that one part of this unfolding creates a liver and another part creates a kidney. It does not cross over, and if it does it is like an aborted foetus that has gone wrong in the sense that all the other foetuses have gone right. They obey this command. Now no-one nor any analysis can explain the process by which this happens. It is not a mystery, and we actually know the physical process, but that there should be such a process and the design of the process, and the nature of the design, are part of this astonishing reality, not in which we live but of which we are the product. And so Allah, subhanahu wa taʼala, is placing the coming-into-being of the creature together with the reality of the going-out-of-existence of the creature. It is that both of these two opposites are encounters with the Divine. So that Allah, subhanahu wa taʼala, says, "Is it you who created or are We the Creator?"

The illusion is that the parents created the child, but that is not the case, because this dynamic was in non-existence, came into existence, and a process took place from which this unfolding of the human creature happened. "Is it you who created or are We the Creator?" And then immediately having said that He says, "We have decreed death for you," – so He has decreed that this process should take place, and also this other process which He has decreed, which is your death. The bringing-into-being of you is a Divine event and the taking-out-of-existence is the same Divine event, because there is One: la ilaha illallah, wahdahu la sharikalah, nothing associated with Him. It is one Divine power in both these situations. "And We will not be forestalled in replacing you with others the same as you and re-forming you in a way you know nothing about. You have known the first formation so will you not pay heed?" You have recognised the bringing into being of yourself, now are you not going to recognise that you are also going to be brought into being a second time? Just to get the perspective of this there is a very beautiful Sufic narration where a poor woman began to cry, and her husband said, "What is the matter?" And she said, "Oh, it is so awful. We have no food and I do not know how I am going to feed the family." He replied, "Do not say such a thing, do not ever say such a thing!" He said, "Look here, when the child was in the womb did Allah not feed it? Was there not blood flowing to the child and the child was fed by your blood?" She said, "Yes." "When the child came out did not milk start to flow from your breast? And you fed the child with the milk?" She said, "Yes." And he said, "And when it reached a certain age, did not the teeth come out of its mouth and at that point you fed it solid food? Allah has been feeding the child all the time, is He going to stop now?" This is one continuous process. So when the peasants say, "You eat till you die," or "Live old horse and you'll get corn," all of these sayings are confirming the reality that Allah is the provider, He is the Razzaq, with no secondary cause. The child is not the child of the parents in the spiritual sense. They are the instruments of it, but the creative act is the Divine act of life coming into being and creating the new creation.

But what we are being told here is that this death and the decreed death are one phenomenon. This is the Waqi'a al-Waqi'a, it is the event of the Event, it is in fact post-mortem, the spiritual reality, in the sense that post-natal is the procedure from which the human creature acts what he acts in order that there is written for him what is written for him, which defines what will be waiting for him in the Next World. So the reality of this world is in fact that it is a reflective reality of what comes after it. This devastating opposite set of realities of the Companions of the Right and the Companions of the Left is the indication that that is what is being worked out in the human situation. The human situation has Companions of the Right and it has Companions of the Left. That is who we are, the humans. We are of these two groups.

Now we come to the second question Allah, subhanahu wa ta'ala, asks.

$$ \text{أَفَرَأَيْتُم مَّا تَحْرُثُونَ ۝} $$

$$ \text{ءَأَنتُمْ تَزْرَعُونَهُ أَمْ نَحْنُ ٱلزَّٰرِعُونَ ۝} $$

$$ \text{لَوْ نَشَآءُ لَجَعَلْنَٰهُ حُطَٰمًا فَظَلْتُمْ تَفَكَّهُونَ ۝} $$

$$ \text{إِنَّا لَمُغْرَمُونَ ۝ بَلْ نَحْنُ مَحْرُومُونَ ۝} $$

Have you thought about what you cultivate?
Is it you who make it germinate
or are We the Germinator?

II

If We wished We could have made it broken stubble.
You would then be left devoid of crops, distraught:
'We are ruined, in fact we are destitute!'

The first question is, "Have you thought of the sperm?" and the second question is, "Have you thought about what you cultivate?" So the reality of the creature is the reality of the creation, of the earth. The reality of the person is also the reality of the world. What you cultivate, again you do not do it, Allah does it. "Is it you who make it germinate?" This impulse, this pulse of life – this seed that looks dried, a husk, in your hand it looks absolutely dead – you put it in the earth, and the rain comes and the season comes. When the season is right and when the earth is right and the rain comes, when all of these things come together, suddenly there moves up this green shoot. This is the world in which we are standing, this is what Allah has put us on.

Allah says, "Did you make it germinate or are We the Germinator?" Once that is posited, that is the foundational reality upon which you must judge your own existence – you have to measure yourself at this level by this comprehension, which is why the People of the Right have a knowledge that the People of the Left do not have, because the latter have covered over the answer, and if they cover over the answer it is a licence for them to imagine that they are the masters of the universe and they can do what they like. But Allah says, "If We wished We could have made it broken stubble. You would then be left devoid of crops, distraught: 'We are ruined, in fact we are destitute!'"

أَفَرَءَيْتُمُ الْمَآءَ الَّذِى تَشْرَبُونَ ۝ ءَأَنتُمْ
أَنزَلْتُمُوهُ مِنَ الْمُزْنِ أَمْ نَحْنُ الْمُنزِلُونَ ۝
لَوْ نَشَآءُ جَعَلْنَهُ أُجَاجًا فَلَوْلَا تَشْكُرُونَ ۝

Have you thought about the water that you drink?
Is it you who sent it down from the clouds
or are We the Sender?
If We wished We could have made it bitter,
so will you not give thanks?

Then Allah, subhanahu wa taʼala, asks about your life
and asks about the earth, and then He asks about the
water. Again the same question, "Are we the Sender?"
This fecundating, life-giving water, is it yours or has is
come from Allah, subhanahu wa taʼala? This is what has
to be answered.

He then takes another dimension, which is why they
are the Companions of the Left, because they are not
giving thanks. You see, He then takes it a step further,
He says that if you think you have created the earth and
then it does not yield, you say, "We are destitute." So
your first condition is a complaint. And about the water
that brings it to life, He says, "We are the Sender," you
have not made this water come. Then He says, "So will
you not give thanks?" The thing that is demanded of the
Companions of the Left that would allow them to pass
over to be Companions of the Right is that they give

thanks. All through the Qur'an there is a repetition of two things, that the 'hamd' precedes the 'shukr'. In the words of the 'ulama, "Alhamdulillahi wa shukrulillah." Why? Because hamd belongs to Allah. "Alhamdulillahi rabbil 'alameen," Praise belongs to the Lord of all the Worlds. Shukr belongs to us to give to Allah.

First you have to recognise that you are a created event, and in a spiritual sense you are one created event, you are the created event of the 'Kun', and you have been enthroned with knowledge. "So will you not give thanks?" After the 'hamd' comes thanks. Now thanks is from the slave to the Lord. Rasul, sallallahu 'alayhi wa sallam, said, "The 'ibadah that Allah loves most is the du'a of the Mumin." Why? Because it is a recognition of helplessness and it is asking Allah for help, it is asking Allah to deal with, to solve, to take on, to encompass. Which is why these suicide people have insulted Allah and slandered Allah, because it is an abnegation of His solving the situation and thinking that there can be mercy. It is as if Allah had withheld his mercy to allow them to kill themselves. Allah says in the Qur'an, "Allah never puts on someone more than they can bear." Therefore there cannot be a reason to kill yourself, because you have to stay alive and have your victory.

Connected to shukr we put the du'a because thanks is thanking Allah for what you have received and really the du'a is asking for more. It is saying, "And this, and this," it is recognising the ongoing, continuing Rahma of Allah, subhanahu wa ta'ala.

أَفَرَءَيْتُمُ ٱلنَّارَ ٱلَّتِي تُورُونَ ۝ ءَأَنتُمْ
أَنشَأْتُمْ شَجَرَتَهَآ أَمْ نَحْنُ ٱلْمُنشِئُونَ ۝
نَحْنُ جَعَلْنَهَا تَذْكِرَةً وَمَتَعًا لِّلْمُقْوِينَ ۝

Have you thought about the fire you light?
Is it you who make the trees that fuel it grow
or are We the Grower?
We have made it to be a reminder
and a comfort for travellers in the wild.

So there we have the dimensions of the question from
the sperm to what is cultivated to the water that you
drink and then the fire that you light. In other words
the elements of existence: air, earth, fire and water, the
elements of existence are recognised as coming from
Allah, subhanahu wa taʻala. Not only that, but there is
another dimension here that Allah has indicated about
the fire that you light, that the fire is not something
that, as it were, just sparks into existence from nothing,
rather it has a fuel. Everything is prepared and is there
before. The fuel for the fire is there before you come
to light the fire, or make the fire. This is the same with
provision. "We have made it to be a reminder and a
comfort for travellers in the wild," and that is that when
you light the fire it has been prepared for you by Allah,
subhanahu wa taʻala, over years. The tree has grown
and has been growing for years. And then at a certain
point you light that fire, but it has been waiting for

you from when it was a seed, and it grew in the earth, and it became a tree, in order that you could come and break off the branch and gather it and set fire to it. The provision is a continuous process.

The same also with the food. As in the story I mentioned of the Sufi with his family, the matter of provision is not that the meal is put in front of you and you say this is provision from Allah, it is much more extraordinary. The food, as the Sufis say, has been coming to you for years. The farmer has his flock of sheep, the sheep have given birth to the lambs, the man has taken the lambs to the market, he has sold them in the market, and then the lamb has gone to the butcher, and the butcher has butchered it, and then you have bought the meat. So there is the whole process of the food, and then the food is taken to the kitchen and is prepared, and eventually it comes in front of you. All the vegetables have come from the garden, the sheep has come from the hill, and again in it is the lighting of the fire to cook it. All these processes have gone on over years to culminate in a moment of existence when you partake of all this that Allah has provided for you. So this giving thanks has not got any end.

فَسَبِّحْ بِاسْمِ رَبِّكَ ٱلْعَظِيمِ ۝

So glorify the name of your Lord, the Magnificent!

"Bismi-rabbika al-adheem," and again the reason this is the Wird of the Alawiya Tariqa is because the Ism of Allah is the 'Adheem, and the Ism al-'Adham as we know is the door of M'arifat, it is, "Allaaah." Shaykh al-Alawi would say, "And so you must recite the Supreme Name." That is the message of the Sufis. And so you must recite the Ism al-'Adham because this knowledge is so tremendous that to grasp it is to set you above all people.

فَلَا أُقْسِمُ بِمَوَاقِعِ النُّجُومِ ۝ وَإِنَّهُ لَقَسَمٌ لَّوْ تَعْلَمُونَ عَظِيمٌ ۝ إِنَّهُ لَقُرْءَانٌ كَرِيمٌ ۝ فِي كِتَابٍ مَّكْنُونٍ ۝ لَّا يَمَسُّهُ إِلَّا الْمُطَهَّرُونَ ۝

And I swear by the falling of the stars –
and that is a mighty oath if you only knew –
it truly is a Noble Qur'an in a well protected Book.
No-one may touch it except the purified.

Allah, subhanahu wa ta'ala, says, "And I swear by the falling of the stars – and that is a mighty oath if you only knew – and I swear by the falling of the stars it truly is a Noble Qur'an in a well protected Book." This is very significant because Allah puts Qur'an and Book together.

Allah says, "Fala, uqsimu bi mawaaqi'il nujum," so He uses the same word: "I swear by the Waqi'a of the stars." Allah says, "I swear by the Waqi'a of the stars," because the Waqi'a as we have said is death, death of the person, but, "I swear by the Waqi'a of the stars – and that is a mighty oath if you only knew – it truly is a noble Qur'an," it is a noble recitation, "in a well protected Book." So it is a recitation in a well protected Book. And that means it is in itself an event, it is in itself a reality encased in the phenomenon of descending on the heart of Rasul, sallallahu 'alayhi wa sallam. The "well protected Book" is Rasul, sallallahu 'alayhi wa sallam, and the Qur'an is what is in the heart of Rasul, sallallahu 'alayhi wa sallam, which is why the Laylat al-Qadr is the night in which it descended into his heart. The Night of Qadr: again, we have been talking about Mulk and Malakut, and He swears by the blacking-out of existence that this is this noble event of the revelation of Qur'an on Rasul, sallallahu 'alayhi wa sallam, and that is Qadr, that is Power, that is Majesty, that is neither Mulk nor Malakut but the Barzakh between the Mulk and the Malakut, because it comes from the Jabarut, and it emerges in the Malakut with Jibril and it descends from Malakut into the Mulk, into the heart of Rasul, sallallahu 'alayhi wa sallam. That is why Allah says, "It is a noble Qur'an in a well protected Book," and it is by a swearing, by an oath about the abolition of the stars.

Then He says, "No-one may touch it except the purified." On the face of it, it is telling us that it is the adab that you do not touch the Qur'an except when in wudu – no-one may touch it except the purified. But we can take two dimensions from this. That is that no-one can really approach Rasul, sallallahu 'alayhi wa sallam, unless they are purified, and if they are not, they get burned up. "Perish Abu Lahab!" because he did not recognise that this man was not just the son of his father, but was the Rasul of Allah. So he could not approach, he could not touch, he could not get near to Rasul, sallallahu 'alayhi wa sallam.

$$\text{نَنزِيلٌ مِّن رَّبِّ ٱلْعَٰلَمِينَ ۝}$$

Revelation sent down from the Lord of all the worlds.

So what was sent down on Rasul, sallallahu 'alayhi wa sallam, is from the Lord of all the Worlds. Now the modern kuffar are saying, "Well you know, you have got your god and we have got ours," as if the Muslim god is some other god from the christian god, and so on and so on. But it is the revelation from the Lord of all the Worlds. It is the Lord, the Creator of the universe who is that One Who has sent down the message on Rasul, sallallahu 'alayhi wa sallam.

$$\text{أَفَبِهَٰذَا ٱلْحَدِيثِ أَنتُم مُّدْهِنُونَ ۝ وَتَجْعَلُونَ}$$
$$\text{رِزْقَكُمْ أَنَّكُمْ تُكَذِّبُونَ ۝}$$

Do you nonetheless regard this discourse with scorn and think your provision depends on your denial of the truth?

Again this is the addressing of the Companions of the Left, "Do you, despite all this, look on this discourse with scorn and think your provision depends on your denial of the truth?" An amazing unveiling of the nature of the kafir. They deem it necessary to avoid the Divine phenomenon and the worship of the Divine in order to get on with the business of acquiring their stuff and their provision. They cannot do it unless they make this cover-up. And Allah, subhanahu wa ta'ala, exposes it and He says, "You look with scorn on this," in other words you are rejecting it. And then "You think your provision depends on your denial of the truth," not your provision depends on your scientific analysis of how the earth yields and how you increase the yield by genetically modifying the crops. No, no! It is dependent on you denying the truth, because you could not go through all of these procedures unless they had as a foundation a denial of the truth. The whole technological project, the whole atheist programme is based on the denial of the truth. It is not based on some ongoing surfing along the benefits of technical advance.

فَلَوْلَا إِذَا بَلَغَتِ الْحُلْقُومَ ۞ وَأَنتُمْ حِينَئِذٍ تَنظُرُونَ ۞ وَنَحْنُ أَقْرَبُ إِلَيْهِ مِنكُمْ وَلَكِن لَّا تُبْصِرُونَ ۞ فَلَوْلَا إِن كُنتُمْ غَيْرَ مَدِينِينَ ۞ تَرْجِعُونَهَا إِن كُنتُمْ صَادِقِينَ ۞

> Why then, when death reaches his throat
> and you are at that moment looking on –
> and We are nearer him than you but you cannot see –
> why then, if you are not subject to Our command,
> do you not send it back if you are telling the truth?

In other words it comes back to this certainty, this 'Yaqin'. Allah asks the question, "When death reaches the throat, and you are that moment looking on," when you are at the death bed and Allah says, "We," Allah, "are nearer him than you but you cannot see. Why then, if you are not subject to Our command, do you not send it back if you are telling the truth?" How is it that you then do not say, "Keep living! Keep living!" You cannot do it.

At that moment, there is a presence. There is the presence of the dying man, there is the presence of the kafir watching him, and there is Allah watching them, and watching them with a nearness to the dying man that is so near that the observer cannot see it. And the reality of that moment is hidden from them. Therefore, what Allah unveils for us from this is that death is not this terrible thing that is veiled, or this meaningless thing that the kuffar have to say in the end that it is. But it is the very secret of the Absolute Majesty of Allah, subhanahu wa taʼala. The non-existence of what we consider real is put in its non-place. Because what we are really coming to is an understanding about the nature of the individual death and the abolition of the stars, of the cosmos.

فَأَمَّآ إِن كَانَ مِنَ ٱلۡمُقَرَّبِينَ ۝

فَرَوۡحٌ وَرَيۡحَانٌ وَجَنَّتُ نَعِيمٍ ۝ وَأَمَّآ إِن كَانَ مِنۡ

أَصۡحَٰبِ ٱلۡيَمِينِ ۝ فَسَلَٰمٌ لَّكَ مِنۡ أَصۡحَٰبِ ٱلۡيَمِينِ ۝ وَأَمَّآ إِن كَانَ

مِنَ ٱلۡمُكَذِّبِينَ ٱلضَّآلِّينَ ۝ فَنُزُلٌ مِّنۡ حَمِيمٍ ۝ وَتَصۡلِيَةُ جَحِيمٍ ۝

But the truth is that if he is one of
Those Brought Near,
there is solace and sweetness and a Garden of Delight.
And if he is one of the Companions of the Right,
'Peace be upon you!'
from the Companions of the Right
And if he is one of the misguided deniers,
there is hospitality of scalding water
and roasting in the Blazing Fire.

This is the contract offered to the human creature. If he is one of the Muqarrabun there is solace and sweetness and a Garden of Delight. In other words the actions on this earth that have brought that person near to Allah, subhanahu wa ta'ala, transform into solace, sweetness and a Garden of Delight in the Unseen. If he is one of the Companions of the Right: peace be upon him, 'Salam', from the Companions of the Right. And if he is one of the misguided deniers then there is the fire and the terrible scalding water.

إِنَّ هَـٰذَا لَهُوَ حَقُّ ٱلْيَقِينِ ۝ فَسَبِّحْ بِٱسْمِ رَبِّكَ ٱلْعَظِيـمِ ۝

This is indeed the Truth of Certainty.
So glorify the Name of your Lord, the Magnificent!

So Allah, subhanahu wa ta'ala, says, "This is indeed the Haqq al-Yaqin." Now the 'Haqq al-Yaqin' becomes clear to us, while those people who cannot understand the Yawm al-Qiyama cannot even think about it, since it has not got any kind of meaning for them, such people even think in terms of how millions of people are going to rise up on the same day, what it is going to be like and so on.

What is interesting you see, what we now discover is that the thing is already predetermined to have meaning for us. And of course the physical recognition of it comes in the Hajj. The Hajj has not got any particular salat connected to it, like the stoning, or the Tawwaf. The thing that makes the Hajj is that, even if for an instant, you have to stand on 'Arafat. And when you stand on 'Arafat, what is the reality of standing on 'Arafat? It is wherever you look you see two or three million people all standing in their shrouds, in their burial robes. It is like a dress rehearsal for the real thing. So you see the possibility, you see the reality of it.

What we discover is because of the nature of this event that we have seen, the Waqi'a, which even in the definition of this term in the dictionary of the Qur'an is identified with Allah's, subhanahu wa ta'ala, raising

II

up Sayyidina 'Isa on his death, is that when the human creature dies, he passes from the in-time to the non-time. Therefore, in that sense everyone dies at the same time, from the beginning, from Sayyidina Adam until the end of the world. The dying of the people is at the same instant, because it is beyond 'instant'. The in-time of the Mulk stops before the non-time of the Malakut and the Barzakh of the Jabarut. There is no timeness in it, so if you pass from the in-time to the non-time then you all are there at the same time, or rather non-time. So the Yawm al-Qiyama is The Day. Rasul, sallallahu 'alayhi wa sallam, said, "Ya Abu Bakr, Yawm al-Yawm!" He meant that Day of this day, that Day is the day there is no day. That is why Abu Bakr nearly collapsed, and this is the Waqi'a, this is indeed the Haqq al-Yaqin. "So glorify the Name of your Lord, the Magnificent!" So recite the Ism al-'Adham to stay in this knowledge, to live in this knowledge and not to forget it in the business of the day, not to forget it in the enormous splendour of the creation that Allah has offered to us. So you must recite the Name of Allah, the Ism al-'Adham.

Fatiha.

* * * * *

www.ingramcontent.com/pod-product-compliance
Lightning Source LLC
Chambersburg PA
CBHW021841090426
42811CB00033B/2105/J